The
Colonial Schooner
1763-1775

Halifax entering Boston Harbor, 1769

The Colonial Schooner
1763-1775

Harold M Hahn

Naval Institute Press

© Harold M Hahn 1981
First published in Great Britain in 1981 by
Conway Maritime Press Ltd

Library of Congress Catalog Card No. 80-84052

ISBN 0-87021-927-8

Published and distributed in the United States
of America by the Naval Institute Press,
Annapolis, Maryland 21402

This edition is not authorized
for sale outside Canada, the United States
and its dependencies

Printed and bound in Great Britain

Contents

Introduction   7

Part I – The Historical Background

1   Ships and Politics in the New World   11
2   The First Six Schooners in the Royal Navy   21
3   Trials and Tribulations of the Navy's Schooners   29
4   *Chaleur* – First Schooner in the Navy List   37
5   Twin Schooners for Jamaica   43
6   *Sultana* – The Smallest of Them All   53
7   *Halifax* 1768-1775 – Prologue to a Revolution   61
8   George Washington's Navy – 1775   73

Part II – The Models

9   The Drawings   83
10   Framing *Hannah*'s Hull   105
11   Finishing *Hannah*'s Hull   113
12   *Hannah*'s Deck Furniture and Fittings   121
13   Tools and Equipment   129
14   Framing and Planking *Halifax*   135
15   Carving Ship Decoration and Figures   155
16   Finishing and Displaying *Halifax*   165
17   Masting and Rigging the Schooners   171

Introduction

Outside of my initiation into the ancient order of shellbacks by Father Neptune when our troopship crossed the equator, I have just one claim to a personal seafaring heritage. My mother's father was a sailor throughout the 1870s and 1880s and circled the globe on sailing ships several times during that period. We met just once, when I was about two years old. I was his first grandchild; and as it turned out, the only one he was ever to see, so my visit to his lonely shack in the Nevada desert was a special occasion. He must have sensed this because he went to the trouble of cobbling up a hobby horse out of wood crates in honor of my brief visit.

Fred Maxwell was born in Copenhagen, Denmark in 1861. His Danish mother died when he was born. His Scottish father was killed a few years later while serving with the Danish Army at the time when the provinces of Schleswig and Holstein broke away to join the German Confederation in 1864. His father had made financial provisions for him; but after several years of abuse, the little orphan ran away from the private institution where he had been placed. He was picked up on the waterfront at the tender age of seven by an English sea captain and his wife who took him on board to raise as a foster son. Apparently, Grandpa lived afloat until the late 1880s when he left the sea for good at San Francisco. Years later, while growing up in Montana, my mother would ask him to recall his life at sea for her. He answered her queries with 'It's too terrible to tell a young girl.' Still, she remembered the pride he took in his skill at knotting and splicing rope and his use of the sailor's palm for sewing which included seascapes embroided in silk.

While living in Great Falls, Montana, Grandpa became acquainted with Charles Russell, the famous painter of western scenes. This contact led him to take up the painting in oils which filled the lonely hours in the Nevada desert where he prospected for gold in later years. Since he had no formal training, his work would be classed as primitive. Six of his paintings somehow came into the possession of the Nevada Historical Society in Reno where they are now exhibited. Five are of landscapes remembered from his early wandering about the West when he would stop at intervals to live with various friendly Indian tribes. The sixth painting portrays sailing ships as they appeared off the island of Oahu.

Grandpa was caught out in a blizzard in 1933. He was hiking fifteen miles to the nearest town for supplies. His remains were not found in the desert until four years later. They were identified by the wrapped and addressed painting which he had planned to mail to my uncle in Oakland. I was an impressionable boy just entering his teens when my mother was first advised that her father was missing with the implication that he was presumed dead. We were living some two thousand miles distant, and the lack of personal contact precluded any serious emotional reaction to this news on my part. Yet Grandpa Maxwell occupied a niche in my concept of family which bordered on the legendary and influenced my self-image and aspirations for the future. This involvement was fostered and kept alive by the few indirect contacts that had been made in previous years.

After a lapse of fifty years, I can still conjure up the fragrance and flavor of the pine nuts that Grandpa garnered and sent to us in a small cardboard box as a Christmas gift. Then there was the box of rock samples, plastered with air mail stamps, that he sent to my father in the vain hope that an independent assay would reveal he had struck a rich vein of ore. We kept a few of his oil paintings in our attic. None was ever framed because my mother failed to appreciate the primitive mode of expression which had yet to be raised to respectability by Grandma Moses. However, to my unsophisticated eyes, they were marvels to behold whenever I was allowed to unroll the canvases which crackled from neglect and gave off a pungent, oleaginous odor.

This knowledge of a grandfather who had been a sailor and an artist held romantic connotations for me as a boy that shaped inclinations which already were directed toward drawing and craftwork. It was a combination that created a natural attraction to ship modeling. In some ways, I regard this as a true legacy from Grandpa which in the end has had a far greater effect on my life than might have been produced by any bequest in real property.

It was quite easy to become actively involved in ship modeling during the early 1930s. The occupation itself is as old as recorded history but until the 1920s, its pursuit was limited largely to men who had a personal acquaintance with the sea and sailing ships or to specially qualified professionals. Detailed information and good ship plans had not been readily available. Then following the First World War, those obstacles to participation by the general public were gradually eliminated; and ship modeling became a popular pastime. In the United States, two men can be singled out as having made the greatest contribution to this change. Their influence on the ship modeling fraternity is undiminished these many years later. The books written by Charles G Davis are still being reprinted as important reference works and the prolific production of Howard I Chapelle has been an inspiration to all model builders. His elegant draughtsmanship which derived from his training as a marine architect created high standards for ships' plans. The work of those two men was newly available to me when I was first drawn to ship modeling.

A third authority was the one who really started me off. I suspect that in his day he attracted more people to ship modeling than anyone before or since. It was a dull copy of the *Popular Science Monthly* magazine that failed to include an installment from the constant stream of articles written by E Armitage McCann. He performed a service that has never been duplicated. Those well-illustrated descriptions of building ship models were a lure that firmly established my interest in the work. My first model was constructed from the Baltimore Clipper design which McCann had named *Swallow*. While building that model, I acquired a copy of Chapelle's book *The History of American Sailing Ships* which introduced me to the subject of colonial schooners on which this book is based. The first chapter of Chapelle's book entitled 'The Colonial Period' presents the plans and a description of the schooners *Chaleur*, *Halifax* and *Sultana*. A later chapter, 'The American Schooner', details a plan for what Chapelle identified as the *Marble Head*. Those four designs held such a special appeal to me that when I learned reproductions of the drawings in the book were available, I purchased a copy of the *Marble Head* drawing scaled to $\frac{1}{4}$in per foot.

After setting model building aside in favor of other commitments for more than twenty years, I returned to it in 1960. It was like taking up a new hobby although the basic knowledge and books that I had acquired as a boy were still available and certain skills had been picked up over the intervening years. Remembering the *Popular Science Monthly* magazine as a primary source for model building information, I purchased a copy. Alas, the times had changed. The Captain McCann articles with offerings of plans and supplies were no more. The only recognition of ship modeler's needs appeared in a few advertisements which had to serve for my re-entry into the pleasures of ship modeling. The advertisement which caught my immediate attention pictured a model of the schooner *Sultana*. One of my old favorites had been replaced in kit form.

I have never built models from kits, preferring to work from scratch. The immediate subjects that I chose for modeling at that time were not schooners but the thought of tackling them stuck like a burr. Finally, the idea of using the available designs of eighteenth century schooners to create a diorama evolved. This endeavor was begun in 1969 and consumed more than four years of my spare time. The completed diorama

was acquired by the Mariner's Museum, Newport News, Virginia, where it is now on display.

In the course of producing the tiny plank-on-frame models needed for the diorama, I developed a construction procedure that I consider superior to any previously offered to model builders. The articles that were published to present this technique were well-received, and it was suggested that I should write a book on the subject. The small size and relative simplicity of the schooner designs makes them ideal for a first attempt in this advanced form of model building.

Serious model builders take a genuine interest in the history and background of the ships that they recreate in miniature. The very nature of the work promotes a climate which is conducive to intellectual curiosity. From the beginning, I felt that my book should incorporate some historical background along with the specific model building methods and plans. The outlook was not promising since there was very little information to be found on the subject in available literature. I did learn that original log books from the schooners were still preserved in the Public Records Office in London. In this country, the logical place to start my investigation seemed to be with Howard Chapelle. I doubt that to this day we would even know that plans for the colonial schooners existed if Chapelle had not brought them to our attention in his books. They have always been more or less available amongst the great quantity of draughts preserved by the British Admiralty. I understand that this large collection of plans, which is now in the care of the National Maritime Museum, Greenwich, has never been fully catalogued. The schooner plans would be of small interest to the British and could well have remained in obscurity.

In the late summer of 1973, I visited Mr Chapelle at his Maryland home, 'Tolland', on the east shore of Chesapeake Bay. It was with high hopes of being set on the right track for researching the schooner story and perhaps securing some pertinent information. I met with disappointment when Chapelle advised simply that very little was known about the subject and that he had put everything he knew about the schooners into his books. Subsequently, I was to discover that much of this published information was incorrect. I have since been advised that Chapelle depended to a great extent on others for his historical accounts while he followed up his primary interests in design theory and construction details of the ships under study. Since his books continue to appear as reprints without revision, it is necessary, as in the case of this book, to authenticate the correct story as revealed by contemporary documents.

The big break in locating historical documentation came when I contacted Commander W E May, RN (ret), in London. Commander May had been Deputy Director of the National Maritime Museum. Following his retirement from that position, he undertook work

The author's Colonial Shipyard diorama in the Mariner's Museum, Newport News.

as a professional researcher. He was well qualified for that work because of his intimate acquaintance with the various archives such as the Public Records Office in London. I enlisted his help in my project. As the investigation flowered, so did our enthusiasm. A whole new world of knowledge was opened up to me. It soon became evident that much significant yet hitherto unpublished historical information was preserved in the form of original contemporary documents by the London Public Records Office alone. The material was not conveniently indexed and had to be sifted out from the tremendous volume of papers. Still, it was there and offered rich rewards to the diligent searcher.

In this book, I shall commit what is perhaps the unpardonable literary sin of quoting many of those documents verbatim. They tell the schooner story so well that I am chary of transcribing them into my own words for fear of destroying their flavour and perhaps distorting their message. They come as close as we could hope to actually recreating in the mind's eye the events and conditions of their day. This process is difficult at best since we are predisposed to interpret ideas and events in the context of our own present day beliefs and experiences. An appreciation of history depends as much on an understanding of contributory influences as it does on a knowledge of facts and happenings.

We lose sight of the continuity of the dozen years which preceded the American Revolution by concentrating on a few well-publicized events such as the *Gaspee* affair, the Boston Massacre, and the Boston

Tea Party. People are surprised to learn that colonists were engaging in overt acts against the armed schooners of the Royal Navy as early as 1764. As the account progresses, it should become apparent how important a role the schooners inadvertently played in shaping the course of events. Frigates and Ships-of-the-Line like impregnable fortresses were a law unto themselves. As such, they presented an impersonal, heavy-handed deterrent while the small, lightly armed Navy schooners, given the responsibility of policing smuggling activity, were vulnerable to attack from irate colonists. This placed them in the forefront of the troubles that ensued. With all this in mind, I shall survey the overall picture to set the scene for the individual schooner histories that follow.

I hope that this acquaintance with colonial schooners and their significance in the history of our country will promote greater interest in building models of them. Although the book is particularly concerned with the stories of schooners in the Royal Navy, it should be recognized that all of the vessels mentioned were built in the colonies for civilian use as packets, or in fishing or trading ventures. They can therefore be regarded as typical colonial schooners as the title of the book implies. The only exceptions are the two schooners built at New York expressly for service on the Jamaica station. Actually, the whole book stems from the existence of Admiralty draughts which detail to various degrees the hull designs of five American schooners built in the 1760s and bought for service in the Royal Navy. This is a real treasure trove for the model builder. Authentic designs for small vessels of American origin from such an early period are rare indeed. American records of this sort are non-existent. It is only by courtesy of the British Admiralty that we know what those schooners looked like. Photostats of the original Admiralty draughts are reproduced in this book by permission of the National Maritime Museum. Thus, the reader will be able to study the original source material which initiated the research into this story of colonial schooners.

The second half of the book describes the construction of two schooner models with complete plans supplemented by in-progress photographs of the processes involved. The model of *Hannah* is my reconstruction of what the first armed vessel in George Washington's Navy might have looked like. The second model presents *Halifax* as she appeared after being refitted for service in the Royal Navy. The book has not been written to serve as a basic manual on ship modeling for which purpose there are a number of excellent examples available. Rather, it is a personal account of my experiences in building the two models. I hope that the ideas offered in the text will prove useful to the novice as well as the experienced craftsman who may never have tackled the problem of building a plank-on frame model.

The two models were built to the 1/48 or ¼in per foot scale. Because of space limitations, the plans in the book have been reduced. In general, advanced model builders doing plank-on-frame work have been thrown on their own resources when it came to preparing the necessary drawings. Many experienced model builders do not feel themselves capable of doing this drafting work or perhaps are simply unwilling to tackle it. While presenting the two sets of plans, I would like to suggest by example that the drawings required are not beyond the capabilities of most persons possessed of the skill to build such models.

My model of *Hannah* was built expressly to serve as an illustrative example in this book. It is now on loan to the Navy Memorial Museum at the Washington Navy Yard. The model of *Halifax* was built as a commission for a patron who thoughtfully suggested that I select a subject which could be used for the book that he knew I was contemplating writing. These two relatively simple designs afford a good starting point for ship modelers aspiring to build plank-on-frame models. Once embarked on such a course, they are unlikely to return to the less satisfying method of carving hulls from the solid.

The book itself is unusual in that so much of it is devoted to the historical background of the schooners. As I accumulated contemporary documentation uncovered by Commander May and began to piece it together into a logical sequence, I came to realize that here was an important story that had never been told before. It certainly deserved preservation for the benefit of marine historians as well as interested ship modellers. In addition to Commander May's essential contribution, I should like to acknowledge the valuable help and advice furnished by Merritt A Edson, Jr, Secretary and Editor for the Nautical Research Guild. Dana McCalip of Chicago kindly shared his copy of David Bruce's journal which affords added dimensions to the story of *Sultana's* first six months of service in the Royal Navy. I hope that my book will make a useful and enjoyable addition to the literature published for my fellow ship modelers.

The author's plans of *Hannah* and *Halifax* reproduced in this book are available separately at ¹⁄₄₈ (¼in per foot) scale, from 1212 Gordon Road, Lyndhurst, Ohio 44124, USA. Each ship is represented by a set of six 20in x 30in sheets at a cost of $28.00 per set. This includes packaging in mailing tubes and postage within the continental United States. British and European customers should add $5.00 for airmail shipments. A list of other plans suitable for plank-on-frame models is available on request.

NOTE ON TRANSCRIPTIONS

Quotations from eighteenth century documents follow the originals in spelling and punctuation, however arbitrary and inconsistent. A frequent occurrence in the manuscripts of the period are scribal contractions, where the final letter was raised 'in the air' – a practice which survived until recently in odd cases, like 'Mʳ'. The more esoteric contractions have been expanded inside square brackets, but most have been printed as written, except that the final letter is set in a smaller type-size instead of being raised up (for example: empd employed).

CHAPTER ONE

Ships and Politics in the New World

For the first 300 years after Columbus discovered the West Indies, the New World developed almost exclusively as a maritime civilization. Ships and the building of ships and smaller vessels were of primary importance. In the early years of exploration and colonization, ships were the lifeline to Europe. The ability or inability thereof to construct a vessel often spelled the difference between life and death – between success or failure of an expedition. The very first voyage of discovery made by Columbus provides an example.

On Christmas Eve 1492 the *Santa Maria* ran onto a coral reef off the island of Hispaniola. Desperate efforts to save the ship were in vain. The stores were salvaged as were the timbers and planks of the ship, the wood being used to build a small fort which Columbus named La Navidad. He was left with just the tiny *Niña*, the commander of the *Pinta* having deserted the small fleet some time earlier to seek his own fortune. Columbus was faced with the problem of providing for more crew men than the *Niña* could accommodate. When *Niña* sailed home, thirty-nine not too unwilling volunteers were left behind in La Navidad with supplies. One year later on his second voyage to the New World, Columbus returned to Hispaniola to relieve the men he had left there. He found that they had been killed by the natives and La Navidad had been burnt to the ground.

On 9 April 1576 John Oxenham sailed from Plymouth with fifty-nine men in two ships, the larger of which was 100 tons; the purpose of the Elizabethan foray was to raid Spanish treasure. The supplies included two pinnaces carried in pieces. Seven of the crew died before the expedition reached the Isthmus of Panama; there the pinnaces were assembled and the freebooters met with some initial successes before the Spaniards mounted a counter attack and managed to capture one of the lightly guarded ships. Oxenham salvaged the iron work and cordage from the second ship so that another ship could be constructed at a later date; he and his men then built a 45ft 12-oar pinnace beside a river which flowed to the Pacific Ocean. Their marauding continued until they were betrayed by their over-confidence and eventually hanged by their Spanish captors. A few members of the original company who were not caught managed to build a small boat, seize a coasting vessel, and return to England.

On his famous voyage in the *Golden Hinde*, Sir Francis Drake carried along the ready-shaped frames and planks for a pinnace, which he had set up in Salada Bay on the coast of Chile in January 1579. During this period, the Spaniards believed they were in sole possession of the waters on the Pacific side of South America and their unarmed vessels were easy prey for small, oared boats.

Early colonization of the North American Continent also met with failure when the link to the home country was broken. In 1590, tardy supply ships found no trace of the Colonists on Roanoke Island. The enigmatic word 'Croatoan' carved on a tree was all that remained of Sir Walter Raleigh's endeavors. A few years later, the hard-pressed colony at Jamestown found that the best way of becoming acquainted with the uncharted wilderness and what it had to offer was in small boats that could traverse the rivers and creeks. To the north in 1614, the Dutch trader Adriaen Block lost his vessel *Tiger* when it burned in the Hudson River near the present site of Albany. He was fortunate in being able to build a replacement which he named *Onrust.*

When the *Mayflower* anchored off Cape Cod in 1620, the most urgent task was to assemble the large shallop which had been transported in sections. This work was vital to enable an expedition to explore the shore line for a suitable site before winter closed in. The story of the landing at Plymouth Rock is an honored episode in American History.

The settlers at Plymouth were bound by debt to the English merchants who had sponsored them, reports of Spanish treasure having fostered dreams of riches to be gained in the New World. The English colonists were faced with the hard fact that they needed all the food they could grow for their own consumption. Furs, wood products, and fish were the only riches that they could convert to payment of their debts. This led to construction of boats and small vessels for the fisheries which were to dominate the New England economy for many years to come and to shape the very character of the people.

The period of weak dependence on England passed quickly for the infant colonies. Expansion along the coastline with a steady influx of immigrants to swell the population soon turned them into sturdy, self-reliant children. The apron strings of the sometimes indulgent or abusive and oft-times negligent mother country stretched tenuously across the vast, turbulent Atlantic Ocean. Skilled men of low birth attracted by the need for their services to a land which promised a freedom of action not open to them in England made the journey – amongst them were trained ship's carpenters.

Fishing boats from Europe had been spending the summer season off the coast of Newfoundland for more than one hundred years before the Pilgrims arrived at Cape Cod and so it was only natural that the newcomers should turn to fishing as a livelihood. The abundance of excellent timber close to hand and the presence of ship's carpenters soon produced a native fleet of fishing boats. By 1634, one merchant at Marblehead was reported to have 8 fishing boats active. Soon after this, Portsmouth was employing 6 great shallops, 5 fishing boats with sails and anchors, and 13 skiffs. By 1642, the London publication *Plain Dealing; or, News from New England* stated that the people of the colony 'were building of ships, and had a good store of barks, catches, lighters, shallops, and other vessels.' In 1665, it was recorded that Massachusetts had in service about 80 vessels of 20 to 40 tons, 40 from 40 to 100 tons, and a dozen larger ships. During this time, the growth of shipbuilding was also progressing in accordance with demand in the other colonies.

Much of the development took place during the period when Cromwell was Lord Protector. When Charles II came to the throne, the ruling class became concerned that the colonies were beginning to threaten England's position in maritime commerce. In 1668, Sir Josiah Child who had been chairman of the East India Company stated 'Of all the American plantations His Majesty has none so apt for the building of

An engraving by the American patriot, Paul Revere, showing British ships of war landing their troops at Boston, 1768. From the *Picture History of the US Navy* by Theodore Roscoe and Fred Freeman (Scribner's, 1956)

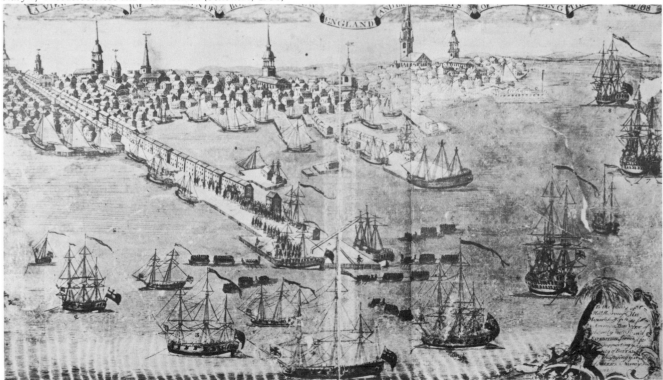

ships as New England, nor none comparably so qualified for the breeding of seamen, not only by reason of the natural industry of the people, but principally by reason of their cod and mackerel fisheries, and in my opinion there is nothing more prejudicial and in prospect more dangerous to any mother kingdom than the increase of shipping in her colonies, plantations or provinces.' This was typical of England's colonial-mercantile policy. Throughout the colonial period, England's leaders looked upon the North American settlements primarily as a means to improve their own economic status. This attitude was not always detrimental to the welfare of the colonies, but it did keep them in a subservient position which was alien to the spirit of freedom and independence which was bound to develop in their unique situation.

The reaction to the threat of New England's shipping to the prosperity of England's maritime commerce was drastic. In 1670, the lords of trade and plantations ordered that the boat fisheries of New England should be broken up and destroyed; the boats in particular were to be captured and burned. This edict had some appreciable effect but did not stop the colonists from building more boats. They also expanded their operations into the hunting of whales and seals and this increased activity resulted in a search for new markets. Thus further employment was offered to their vessels and they were able to build larger ships as they grew more prosperous. This readily developed shipbuilding potential also enabled the colonists to satisfy as time went by a large percentage of the demand for ships from merchants in England and the West Indies.

Unfortunately, there is no accurate graphic record of merchant ships and smaller vessels of the seventeenth century though there are distorted or inadequate artist's versions. There are also written records which offer verbal descriptions and give names to the various types of vessels. There is enough information to make their prospect tantalizing to the model builder but insufficient for reconstruction of a truly satisfying, authentic replica. In contrast, the schooner designs with which this book is concerned are established by detailed draughts made from the actual vessels. This makes it possible to create a model which duplicates the original schooner in miniature. Still, it is well worth the effort to study and appreciate the role that seventeenth century boats played in the evolution of sailing craft.

William A Baker has made a definitive investigation in his two books, *Colonial Vessels* and *Sloops and Shallops*. These books with their reconstructed plans give as close an approach to the subject matter as is likely to be found. Shallops, pinnaces, sloops, catches, and barks were names that identified very loosely defined classifications of vessels. It would appear that the terms were often used interchangeably in contemporary records either through carelessness or possibly ignorance. With the present day demand for precise definitions,

Mr Baker's presentation was made difficult by the vagaries that he found in source material.

Shallops were open boats propelled by oars and could carry a mast and sails. They were primarily ship's boats but came to be used independently for fishing and transportation by the colonists. They were built either as double-enders or with a transom stern. Their size ranged to more than a forty foot length. The term 'great shallop' was used for the larger ones. The shallop was too large to be carried on the deck of a ship like the *Mayflower*, so we find the one used by the Pilgrims being assembled from fitted sections carried below decks during the voyage. There is no specific information detailing the construction of those parts or provisions for putting them together. The work must have required some degree of skill since assembly of the Pilgrims' shallop delayed the expedition for a number of days that could be ill-afforded at the time. The work required of the *Mayflower* crew was further complicated by the fact that mistreatment received in the crowded space during the trip had caused the seams in the planking to open up. Contemporary references to shallops continued throughout most of the eighteenth century before usage of the term began to die out.

A definition of the term 'pinnace' can be even more confusing than the one for a shallop. In general, the pinnace was at least partially decked over as compared to the open shallop. The pinnace was a longer, narrower boat although Baker notes recorded dimensions in which examples of the two types were almost identical. Like the shallop, the pinnace was normally subordinate to a ship to which it belonged although they are known to have operated independently. They were built with either carvel or clinker planking and were designed with a square stern. Baker mentions, as an extreme example, the pinnace *Providence* of 1637 as having a 90ft length of keel, 26ft breadth, and 300 tons burden. Depending on the size of the vessel, sails were rigged on as many as three masts. The term 'pinnace' survived as the name for a class of small boat carried on a man of war.

Sloop sounds like a type of vessel which could easily be defined. By modern definition, she would be a relatively small boat with a single mast and fore-and-aft sails. This was not so in the seventeenth and eighteenth centuries; the oft-repeated definition for a sloop in mid-eighteenth century advised that sloops 'Are Sailed and Masted As Men fancys leads them sometimes with One Mast, with Two, and with Three, with Burmudoes, Shoulder of Mutton, Square Lug & Smack Sails, they are in Figure either Square or Round Stern'd.' This definition could as well be applied to the pinnace described above except for reference to the possibility of a round stern. The image of a single masted vessel does persist however. It may be well to hold to that in order to reduce the confusion despite the exceptions that may be cited.

The 'catch' or ketch is another variety of vessel

which was commonly recognized and the term survived to the present day as identification for a type of rig. We visualize a ketch as having a main mast at about the midsection of the boat and a mizzen set well aft, a rig used by bomb ketches to provide an open field of fire for their large mortars. However, colonial 'catches' did not fit into the straightjacket of rules. One positive difference between the catch and the types of vessels described above appears to have been in the hull construction. This is thought to have been sturdier and more akin to the fabric of a ship than to the lighter 'boat' construction. In this sense, the ketch might be thought of as being related to the schooner designs which are the subject of this book.

The bark is still another type of vessel which might be considered as a predecessor leading to the schooner class which evolved in the eighteenth century. She was built for fishing and coastal trading as were the schooners of a later day. The identification of vessels as barks continued throughout the eighteenth century in contemporary record books. Today, the term 'bark' denotes a type of rig which is not related to the design of a colonial bark.

While the first schooner was on the stocks, one wonders how the builder or the future owner was planning to register her. He did not know that she was a 'schooner' – it was posterity's responsibility to tell him that. Was he thinking in terms of a ketch, a bark, or perhaps a small brigantine? Was the hull a radical new design or just another modification of local shipbuilding practices? To this day, there is no origin for the word 'schooner' which is acceptable to the authorities. There is just one story to account for the name, but it has been discredited and much maligned. To me, it has the ring of truth in spite of the way it has been mutilated in the telling.

The tenth census of the United States which was published in 1880 included a history of fishing vessels and the shipbuilding industry in the country. It offers the following story:

> In 1745 Andrew Robinson, of Gloucester, built a vessel with square stern, which was fitted with two masts, bearing a sloop sail on each and a bowsprit with jib. She was sharp on the bottom and fast, and, on being launched, sped over the water so fast from the impetus gained by descending from the ways as to elicit from a bystander the remark, 'See how she scoons.' 'Scoon' was a word used by plain people to express the skipping of a flat stone over the surface of the water when skillfully thrown, and the builder of the vessel, having been somewhat at a loss for a name for the new rig seized upon the trifling incident referred to and replied 'a scooner let her be'.

In his book, *The Fore and Aft Rig in America* , E P Morris quotes another version of the same story taken from a book which had been published in 1860.

Although the account was quite similar, it indicated that the great event had transpired in 1713. It was related that the story had been derived from earlier correspondence concerning information which had been handed down from an original witness. The difference in dates is rather startling, but the origin of the word 'scooner' is described in a fairly consistent fashion. Both accounts make much of the fact that the 'scooner' had a new rig which typified the schooners of later years.

Mr Morris proceeds to discount the whole story on the basis of the fact that the fore-and-aft rig was known to have existed before 1713. He sums up his argument by saying 'Here then is positive evidence that the Gloucester tradition was in error; Captain Robinson was not the first contriver of schooners.' This criticism is not valid if one omits the dependence of the term 'scooner' on the association with the rig which raconteurs a hundred years later used to embellish their story. In the seventeenth and early eighteenth centuries, it has been pointed out that a type of vessel was generally known by the hull design. The character of the rigging and the types of sails used varied considerably depending on how the vessel was employed. It is only in more modern times that such a strong emphasis has been placed on identification by rig.

In a way Mr Morris acknowledges this argument and then goes on to attack the credibility of the word 'scoon' itself. He then advises that research by the best literary authorities has failed to uncover the existence of such a word. He covers the whole subject thoroughly and it would seem with no stone unturned. Finally, he consigns the whole subject to oblivion as a sort of Parson Weems fable intended to enhance Robinson's memory and in any case of negligible value. He has built a very strong case, but I remain unconvinced.

'Scoon', if the word did exist, was undoubtedly a slang expression. It would not necessarily have been a commonly used word or universal in nature and could easily have disappeared with the passage of time. One might consider the emergence and disappearance of slang terms in our own time. It is only in recent years that colloquial slang has been accorded extensive recognition in the dictionaries. Finally when writing a book about colonial schooners, I would be remiss in my duty if I failed to mention the only story purported to account for the origin of the word 'schooner'. Morris points out that there are other nautical words which cannot be traced to their source and wishes to place 'schooner' in the same limbo. The reader can make his own choice; and whatever that choice may be, certainly no harm has been done.

If the 'scoon' story is to be discredited along with Captain Robinson's claim to fame, it would seem that we are indeed left with no apparent source for the word 'schooner.' However in his endeavor to debunk the traditional story, Morris may have missed a very plausible explanation. Merritt Edson has brought to our

Schooners on the stocks. From the diorama in the Mariner's Museum.

attention a Dutch map published in 1657 which details the New England coast as known at that time. There is a body of water labeled on that map as 'Schoone Haven'. These words have been interpreted as 'fair' or 'beautiful harbour'. Subject to proper application, this fact could actually reinforce a corrected version of the Captain Robinson story.

Schoone Haven on the map is the bay just north of Cape Ann on the Massachusetts coast. This places it in very close proximity to the Gloucester site of the traditional account. 'Schoone' could be converted very easily and logically to the word 'schooner.' We may well question the form in which the established version of the story came to be passed down from one generation to another with its obvious resort to dramatic embellishment and possibly incorrect conversion of the term 'scoon' to suit the purpose. Still, there now can be no question that a true, contemporary origin for the word 'schooner' has been established. The variety of spellings used in the eighteenth century can be accounted for readily when we consider the loose practices of that period.

The schooner was a milepost along the road which led in the evolution of ship design to the extreme Baltimore Clipper type and culminated in the magnificent clipper ships of the nineteenth century. Such evolutions paralleled the increase in scientific knowledge and engineering technology which grew very slowly in the eighteenth century, and accelerated tremendously in the present century when the sailing ship could no longer compete economically. When the schooner evolved, men were gradually becoming aware of a potential for progress, but lacked the technology to realize rapid advances. They should be credited with having an earnest desire to make improvements but not with a prescience for profound changes.

The life of William Hutchinson spanned the period of the eighteenth century with which this book is concerned. A *Treatise on Naval Architecture* which he wrote provided some insight into the status of ship design during the last quarter of the century. In the introduction to his book, he says 'It must be allowed, that the best way to do right, is to observe and see what we think wrong, which in the course of this work, I have endeavored to make my rule. Although the drafters and builders of ships should be the best judges, how to make them answer best, the different trades they may be designed for, yet, as a seaman, I hope to be excused pointing out what I have thought great defects in practice.' This statement is consonant with the idea that ship design of those days was based on empirical data gained from experience and tempered by custom and perhaps some degree of intuition.

Benjamin Franklin made some pertinent observations on this subject in his autobiography. Always a keen observer and analyst of his environment, he had

15

occasion to remark on the imperfect state of ship design and usage. In 1757, the Pennsylvania Assembly appointed him as its representative to present a petition to the king. Franklin's packet sailed from New York in June with a fleet on its way to a proposed seige of Louisburg. It parted company for its destination, London, when five days out. Franklin relates 'Our captain of the paquet has boasted much, before we sailed, of the swiftness of his ship; unfortunately, when we came to sea, she proved the dullest of ninety-six sail, to his no small mortification.' The captain solved his problem by asking all persons aboard to gather at the stern of the ship. This shift of weight corrected the packet's poor performance; and after the water casks stowed in the bow had been moved aft, 'the ship recover'd her character and proved the best sailer in the fleet.'

This experience prompted Franklin to make further observations and to draw conclusions from them. 'It has been remark'd, as an imperfection in the art of ship-building, that it can never be known, till she is tried, whether a new ship will or will not be a good sailer; for that the model of a good-sailing ship has been exactly follow'd in a new one, which has prov'd, on the contrary, remarkably dull. I apprehend that this may partly be occasion'd by the different opinions of seamen respecting the modes of lading, rigging, and sailing of a ship; each has his system; and the same vessel, laden by the judgement and orders of one captain, shall sail better or worse than when by the orders of another. Besides, it scarce ever happens that a ship is form'd, fitted for the sea, and sail'd by the same person. One man builds the hull, another rigs her, a third lades and sails her. No one of these has the advantage of knowing all the ideas and experience of the others, and, therefore, cannot draw just conclusions from a combination of the whole.'

Converting logs of timber. From the Colonial Shipyard diorama.

He goes on to propose that 'a set of experiments might be instituted; first, to determine the most proper form of the hull for swift sailing; next, the best dimensions and properest place for the masts; then the form and quantity of sails, and their position, as the wind may be; and, lastly, the disposition of the lading. This is an age of experiments, and I think a set accurately made and combin'd would be of great use. I am persuaded, therefore, that ere long some ingenious philosopher will undertake it, to whom I wish success.' The use of the term 'philosopher' in the latter statement where we would now use 'scientist' or 'engineer' is further indication of the status of such inquiries in those days.

Franklin's mission in 1757 was in essence an attempt to persuade the 'True and Absolute Proprietarics of the Province of Pennsylvania' that their colonial estates should be taxed in common with those of the colonists. The proprietors had been benefitting without contributing to the welfare or defense of the colony that they controlled as absentee landlords. This again was typical of the British attitude which viewed the colonies as a source of income while disclaiming responsibilities. Such an attitude was self-defeating since forcing the colonists to shoulder their own problems fostered the sense of independence which brought about the inevitable separation of 1776.

The difference between the colonial policies followed by England in comparison with those of the other European Powers helps to explain why the American Revolunion came to be. All of the colonial powers looked to benefit economically from their overseas possessions. France and Spain, however, kept a tight rein on their colonies so that they became, quite simply, extensions of the mother country. Frenchmen were still Frenchmen and Spaniards still Spaniards whether at home or abroad. On the other hand, the

English colonists under a more liberal if negligent rule began to think of themselves as Americans as one generation succeeded another. They retained a loyalty to England; but when that loyalty conflicted with their own interests, those interests took precedence. Fundamentally, British colonial policies were tailored to suit the merchant class of England; William Penn expressed the opinion in 1701 that it was 'trade which must make America valuable to England'. In general, those policies did not work to the detriment of the colonial entrepreneur. Often the restrictions actually provided them with a sort of protected monopoly without exacting too great a toll. Where the restrictions were unreasonable, England, showing a benevolent negligence, allowed the colonists to circumvent them.

The Molasses Act of 1733 was designed to help the British colonies in the West Indies. By means of prohibitive duties levied on molasses and sugar bought from foreign held islands, it was meant to give a monopoly to their own planters. This was a very short-sighted move since the entire production of the British possessions could provide but a small percentage of the demand in the New England Colonies where molasses and rum formed a cornerstone of their trade. If the Molasses Act had been strictly enforced the New England economy would have been severely impaired, but in fact the end result of the act was to make smuggling a respectable activity. One contemporary observer wrote 'There is no error in a commercial nation so fruitful of mischief as making acts and regulations oppressive to trade' and then not enforcing them. The Molasses Act was not enforced. Some of the most highly regarded families in New England became wealthy and influential by engaging in smuggling.

This *laissez-faire* situation prevailed until the advent of the French and Indian War. With a concern for personal gain at the expense of patriotic duty, the colonial smugglers rode a wave of prosperity by actually supplying the French enemy with provisions. This help from the opposing side is said to have enabled the French forces to prolong the war. With the intention of suppressing the smuggling activity while at the same time securing revenue to help prosecute the war, the British initiated strict enforcement of the Molasses Act. While the revenues from this source were increased, smuggling increased even more and prospered with the incentive of war-time demand.

The aura of respectability afforded to smuggling by lax enforcement of the law for over twenty-five years was a great hindrance to making the new policy effective. Americans were able to influence or control the Vice-Admiralty courts in their favor: Governors were known to have been bribed by the smuggling elite, prominent lawyers labored on their behalf. In Rhode Island, a leading lawyer claimed that courts of Vice-Admiralty were 'subject to mercantile influence; and the king's revenue sacrificed to the venality and perfidiousness of courts and officers.' Nevertheless, the British policy of enforcement began to have a telling effect on that part of the colonial economy which was fueled by smuggling activity. In 1760 and 1761, vigorous efforts by the Royal Navy in the West Indies threw those smuggling centers into confusion. Still in 1762, New York's Lieutenant Governor Colden stated that enforcement of the law was difficult because it depended largely on people who had connections with the smugglers or feared reprisal from them.

From the colonist's viewpoint which has been perpetuated as the official account of American history, the custom house collector became a villainous person. The 'writs of assistance' which enabled him to search with considerable success for contraband goods were labeled an improper invasion of privacy. It soon became evident at the conclusion of the Seven Years War that stricter enforcement of the law and collection of taxes was to become a permanent policy, not just a war-time measure. The end of the war also signaled the end of the artificial prosperity that had been created; the combination of a depressed economy with strictly enforced taxation was a crushing blow to the colonial merchant class.

The year 1763 with its Treaty of Paris marked the emergence of the First British Empire. Paradoxically, it also marked the beginning of the end for that empire because of the British policies instituted at the same time led directly to the American Revolution. Parliament authorized use of the navy against smuggling in the colonies. Absentee custom officials living in England were required to earn their stipends by repairing to their posts in the colonies. Illicit trade including that which was carried on with continental Europe was to be suppressed. Warships arrived in colonial ports early in 1764 to increase the number of seizures. The years that followed saw a series of poorly handled measures for taxation of the colonies. In themselves, they were not so unreasonable, but the poor timing and the callous indifference of the British ruling class escalated their significance.

When the Treaty of Paris was signed on 10 February 1763 the French dream of an empire in North America was ended. England acquired Canada, Nova Scotia, and Cape Breton along with the surrounding islands; she obtained the right to navigate the Mississippi; in the West Indies, she took possession of Grenada, St Vincent, Dominica, and Tobago; Spain surrendered the Floridas to her. With these and other gains made during the Seven Years War, the first British Empire was established only to disintegrate some twelve years later. William Pitt was credited with creating this new Empire, although as one writer noted, he scarcely stirred from London, could hardly have controlled or guided the decisions of commanders in the distant fields of action, and actually had been forced out of office before hostilities were concluded and the Peace of Paris drawn up.

Halifax, Nova Scotia, 1764.

Sawyers at work. From the Colonial Shipyard diorama.

Lord Bute, who succeeded Pitt, was concerned, while arrangements for the treaty were being made, about causing long term enmity in the vanquished French and Spanish. In an attempt to be concilatory, he returned to them conquered territory which later proved to be a thorn in England's side. France was allowed to keep rich sugar islands in the West Indies which provided an excellent base for her still powerful navy. She also retained the islands of St Pierre and Miquelon in the Gulf of St Lawrence along with the right to fish on the coast of Newfoundland. These little islands offered sites for naval bases, and, more important to the schooner story of this book, centers for the smuggling of French goods into Canada.

On 11 November 1763 from St James's, the Earl of Halifax wrote to the Lords of the Admiralty 'I transmit to Your Lordships by the King's Command, an Extract of a letter from the Honble James Murray, Governor of Quebec . . . And I am to signify to your Lordships His Majesty's Pleasure, that you do forthwith give the necessary orders for carrying into immediate Execution the Measures proposed in the said Extract, in such Manner as your Lordships shall judge to be, at the same Time, Most effectual for the intended Purpose, & most consistent with the Good of His Majesty's Sea Service' [PRO ADM 1/4126].

James Murray, the newly appointed Governor of Quebec, had written a long letter from Canada on 27 September 1763 to the Earl of Egremont. The extract from that letter to which King George, attached special significance reads:

The Knowledge I have of this continent, and the Experience I have had of the many Abuses committed in the different Custom Houses in America – several of which have been reported to the Commissioners of His Majesty's Customs – have long convinced me, that smuggling was to be prevented by His Majesty's Ships of War only.

The distribution of the Frigates appears to me admirable; but as Your Lordship desires I should offer any Hints, which I may think conducive to this Salutory End, I take the Liberty to observe, that without Cutters and stout Shallops, to cruize within the River St Lawrence from the Isle aux Coudres to the island Anticosti, it will be impossible to prevent a very great Contraband Trade from the Islands of Miquelon and St Pierre. That These Islands are already filled with French Merchandise, is most certain; that Said Merchandise may be pour'd into Canada by Shallops which will hug the Shore, and take refuge in the Shallow Bays, where no Frigates, nor even Cutters dare approach them, is most Evident. It is not in the Power of Man in such an Extensive River as this, to prevent smuggling on Shore; It must, and may, be done afloat by Vessels drawing as little Water, as those made use of by the Smugglers; but these Vessels must be under the Direction of His Majesty's Sea Officers, and should be manned from the Crews of the King's Ships; if manned by the Inhabitants of the Province, and under the direction of any Residenter of this Country, it is easy to foresee the Consequences.

In my former Reports I have had the Honour to make the above Observation in part, and I now beg leave to add that it will be very necessary, His Majesty's Sea Officers should be empowered to examine, when they please, all the fishing Posts in the Lower parts of this River, many of which, it is fear'd, will become Magazines of French Goods, and a Law prohibiting the Use of every French Commodity in this colony is much to be wished for [PRO ADM 1/4126].

The Admiralty Board had already sent instructions to Admiral Colville in Halifax. In a letter dated 23 August 1763, they advised that 'Their Lordships will send you two Cutters, as soon as they can be got ready, commanded by Lieutenants, who will have powers to seize Smugglers, and may also answer the purpose of carrying your Dispatches to the several Provinces within the Limits of your Command; In the meantime their Lordships permit you to hire a Sloop or Schooner for that purpose, to be manned from the Ships of your Squadron if you find that necessary' [PRO ADM 2/536]. However, further orders to Colville under the same date specified that he should '. . . never purchase or cause to be purchased for His Majesty, any Ship or Vessel whatsoever, nor to cause any Wharfs, Storehouses, Magazines, Fortifications or other Buildings of any kind to be erected, without first representing the want thereof to us, and sending home Plans thereof with Estimates of the Expence, and receiving our directions thereon' [PRO ADM 2/91 pp14, 15].

Having been prompted by the King's order as transmitted by Halifax's letter of 11 November, the Lords of the Admiralty advised the Navy Board:

Gentn   7th Jany 1764

Whereas in pursuance of the King's Pleasure signified by the Earl of Halifax one of His Majesty's Principal Secretaries of State, by his Letter of the 11th of last Month, We have ordered Rear Admiral Lord Colvill, Commander in Chief of His Majesty's Ships and Vessels in North America, to cause Six Marblehead Schooners or Sloops to be purchased for His Majesty upon the best and cheapest terms that may be, to be employed under his Lordship's Command directing the Naval Officer at Halifax to draw Bills upon you for the Expence attending the same; we do hereby and direct you to accept and pay such Bills as shall be drawn upon you for that purpose and to cause the said Vessels to be registered on the List of the Royal Navy by the following names Vizt

> *Chaleur*
> *Gaspee*
> *Magdalen*
> *Hope*
> *St John*
> *St Lawrence*

and their Complements to be established at thirty Men each agreeable to the enclosed scheme; we having directed Lord Colvill to cause them to be named accordingly, and to be fitted Stored, and Victualled, and delivered into the Charge of the Lieutenants whom we have appointed to Command them, and who are also to take Charge of, and Indent for the Provisions Stores and Ordnance, that may be supplied them, and to Account for the same according to the Rules of the Navy.

Navy Board   Egmont   G Hay   Pitt
[PRO ADM 2/433 pp459-60]

CHAPTER TWO

The First Six Schooners in the Royal Navy

In 1763, Alexander, Lord Colville, Rear Admiral of the White, was Commander-in Chief of the British Naval Forces attached to the North Atlantic Station. Ten years earlier, he had been appointed with rank of Captain to command the *Northumberland* of 70 guns. He had held this command for nine years. During that time, he had taken part in expeditions to Louisburg in 1757 and then, in 1758 when he became a commodore, was given the command of the North Atlantic. In 1759, he served under Saunders at the seige of Quebec which marked the defeat of French forces in Canada. Following that, he returned to his North Atlantic post. After a brief sojourn in England, he returned to Halifax in 1763 in the *Romney* to resume the command with the rank of rear admiral. It became his responsibility to purchase, outfit, man, and supervise the activities of the first six schooners which were entered on the list of the Royal Navy. The Lords of the Admiralty in London selected names for the schooners and appointed lieutenants to serve as their commanders while making out Colville's instructions. They chose the term 'Marblehead schooner' to identify the new class of navy vessel.

Admiral Colville wrote a long report to Philip Stephens, Secretary of the Admiralty, to detail subsequent events:

> *Romney* in Halifax Harbour 19 May 1764
> Sir
>
> Upon my arrival here I hired a stout sloop to serve as a Tender to carry my Dispatches to the different Provinces within the extent of my Command, agreeable to the authority given me by their Lordships. In the winter I received intelligence that there was a Contraband Trade carrying on at the Island of Cape Breton and as the Season would not admit of sending any of the Men of War I forthwith armed the Tender and sent her to put a stop to that business, and although she did not take any Vessels yet I am persuaded that the appearance of an armed Vessel upon the Coast at that time of the Year had a very good effect, and prevented many smuggling attempts which would otherways have been made. Upon her return she made a small Seizure at Canceau of Eleven Hogs heads of French Wines which have been condemned in the Court of Vice Admiralty here; since that she has been employed in examining the Harbours upon the Western Coast of this Province, and as Lieutenant Desbarres is now arrived to make surveys of the Coast and Harbours of Nova Scotia, she shall be appropriated to his convenience for that Service.

[paragraph omitted]

> The *Juno* arrived at New York on the 28 March and Captain O'Bryen sent me their Lordships order of the 4 Janry directing the Purchase and fitting out of six Marblehead Schooners or Sloops, which I received by a Sloop that came from New York on the 19 April; and on the 27 Directions were sent to Boston, by the Naval Officer, for purchasing three of the best Marblehead Schooners or Sloops, from Seventy to ninety Tons that could be procured, to be delivered at this Place with all possible Dispatch, and one of them is

already arrived. Besides these, two Schooners were purchased at this Place which are now fitting out, at the Yard, in the manner directed by their Lordships: They are very fine Vessels between Ninety and a hundred Tons each; one of them was built last Fall at a new Settlement of this Province called Chester, twelve Leagues to the Westward of Halifax, and in less than a fortnight I expect another Schooner that is ready to be launched at the same Place which will compleat the number of six. I wish I could have procured all the Vessels at this Place, because much time together with the expence of Commission at Boston and bringing them from thence, would have been saved; but this is the worst time of the year for buying such Vessels, as most of them are fitted out for the Summer's Fishing when that Season is over they become plenty and cheap. There is no small ordnance in Store at this Place, fit for Sea Service: I therefore directed the Captains of the Frigates to deliver their three Pounders and part of their Swivels, with all their appurtenances, into the charge of the Ordnance Storekeeper, in order to their being supplied by him to the schooners. The Contractor for victualling will supply them with Provisions. All the necessary alterations and Improvements to render them fit for His Majesty's service, will be made at the careening Yard, and a proper assortment of sea stores supplied from thence. – Thus far their Lordships orders will be punctually obeyed, but it gives me great concern to be under the Necessity of acquainting you, that inferior Officers and Seamen to man these Vessels cannot be raised in this Part of the World. The Lieutenants after waiting a Month at New York took their passage in a Sloop which arrived at this Place on the 11th Instant, and shall be put in possesssion of the Vessels as fast as they can be got ready: the whole number of People brought with them including Themselves, six Clerks, six Servts, & two Surgeon's Mates amounts to thirty, and they have represented to me that they were at considerable Expence in maintaining and paying for the Passage of themselves and these People, and beg that their Lordships will order them some allowance on this account.

[remainder of paragraph omitted]

The Sloop from New York is now about to return to that Place, and I embrace the opportunity of writing to you; but cannot as yet determine upon any method of procuring seamen and petty Officers for the Schooners. I once thought of taking a few from each Ship, but the proportion of Marines, makes the number of Seamen so low, that considering their present Complements, their Sick and Short, I think the Ships cannot be fit for Service if any further Reduction is made: and yet I am so desirous of obeying my orders, that if no alternative occurs, I will lay up the *Alborough* for a Season, and distribute her men as far as they will go, to enable some of the Schooners to proceed into the

River S Lawrence. But whether I am reduced to this necessity or not their Lordships may be assured that no Endeavours shall be wanting in me to forward the Service expected from these Vessels.

[three paragraphs omitted]

I am
  Sir
  Your most obedient and most humble Servant
    Colville

[PRO ADM 482 pp356-8]

The *Juno* brought to New York thirty men to form the nucleus of crews for the schooners along with the orders to Colville from the Lords of the Admiralty. Lieutenant Candler who had been assigned to command the *Hope* brought his servant and a clerk; Robert Dugdale for the *Magdalen* brought a clerk and two able seamen; Ralph Dundas for the *St Lawrence* had with him a clerk, his servant, and two able seamen; Thomas Allen, directed to command the *Gaspee*, included a clerk, a surgeon's mate, a master's mate, his servant, and two able seamen; Thomas Laugharne, given command of *Chaleur*, had a clerk, servant, and one able seaman. Thomas Hill of the *St John* completed the entourage with a clerk, surgeon's mate, gunner's mate, servant, and two able seamen, [PRO ADM 1/482 p359]. These men arrived at Halifax from New York on 11 May 1764.

Admiral Colville was indeed diligent in following the orders to procure and fit out the six navy schooners. In a letter dated 10 June 1764 he was able to report: 'the three Vessels that were commisioned from Boston have arrived, and I bought a Sloop here which compleated the number of six: The enclosed Table will shew their Lordships the Dimensions of the Vessels, their Age and first cost, and I shall give the Navy Board a particular account of whatever may be necessary to acquaint them with on this Subject. They are very fine Vessels and I hope will answer the purpose extremely well. I have some reason to expect that the prospect of Gain or Novelty may tempt seamen to enter for these Vessels that would not for any of the King's Ships, I have therefore dispatched four of them to spread themselves in the principal Ports between Casco Bay and Cape Henlopen, in order to raise as many men as they can and to return here about the first of August [PRO ADM 1/482 p361]

The tabulated schooner statistics that Colville mentioned were as follows:

Name	Type	Where Purchased	King's Tonnage	Age	Cost
Hope	Schooner	Halifax	105-40/94	9 months	545-9-3
S Lawrence	Schooner	Halifax	114-65/94	2 years	445-0-0
Gaspey	Sloop	Halifax	102-44/94	1yr, 7mo	420-0-0
Magdalen	Schooner	Boston	90-3/94	3 years	432-15-0
Chaleur	Sloop	Boston	116-91/94	9 months	500-0-0
S John	Schooner	Boston	unknown	2 years	500-0-0

From this and preceding information, it can be seen that the term 'Marblehead schooner' should not be taken literally. Because of its great involvement with the fishing trade and consequent employment of a large fleet of schooners, Marblehead, Massachusetts, apparently had become synonymous to the Lords of the Admiralty with the schooner size of vessel. Certainly, Admiral Colville did not feel restricted to buying schooners at Marblehead or those which had their origin there, nor is there evidence of any unique or superior design inherent in schooners built at Marblehead. The term 'Marblehead schooner' as used to identify the class of vessel in the Royal Navy was common for some five years after its inception and then began to disappear

On 26 July, Admiral Colville wrote a report which closed with:

> In my Letter of the 10 June I informed their Lordships that I had dispatched four of the Armed Vessels to spread themselves in the principal Harbours between Casco Bay and Cape Henlopen in order to raise men. Lieutenant Hill in the *St John*, who went first upon this Service, returned last night with very little success, the Merchants having to all appearance entered into a Combination to distress us as far as they are able, and by threats and promises to prevent Seamen from entering for these Vessels. The behaviour of the People at Rhode Island to Lieutenant Hill in an affair of his Duty as a Customhouse Officer was so extremely insolent and unprecedented that I think it my Duty to lay before their Lordships an account thereof under his own hand, at same time to observe that from his conversation I have reason to think there are many aggravating Circumstances omitted in this Account which would appear upon a strict inquiry into the affair. [PRO ADM 1/482 p370]

Lieutenant Hill and his men on the *St John* had indeed been through a harrowing experience at Rhode Island. His report [PRO ADM 1/482 pp372-3] to Admiral Colville told the story from his viewpoint and that of his men who were left in charge of the schooner during his absence. On 30 June while at Newport, Rhode Island, Hill was advised of a brig unloading in a creek near Howland's Ferry. When the *St John* arrived at the scene, it was discovered that the brig had finished unloading and sailed. He seized the 93 hogsheads of sugar which had made up the cargo and sent a boat to apprehend the brig. That vessel, *Hasto* of Newport, Wingate, Master, from Monto Christo, was taken at daybreak. Lieutenant Hill had the hogsheads of sugar reloaded. The owner, fearing that the Lieutenant intended to send the brig with its cargo to Halifax, had Hill arrested and arranged that the case should be tried at Newport. On 4 July the Collector of Customs there took the brig from Lieutenant Hill's custody on the grounds that he was not qualified by oath of office

to make the seizure. At this point, the Lieutenant set out for Boston to consult the Surveyor General on the extent of his authority.

While he was gone, the crew that he left in charge of the schooner found itself in a dangerous situation in which serious consequences failed to materialize only because the *Squirrel,* a 20 gun 6th rater, was present at the same anchorage. On Monday 9 July at 2pm, a man who had deserted from the *St John* was seen on the wharf, and an armed boat was sent to seize him. A large mob assembled to rescue the deserter and when the boat attempted to return to the schooner, the mob took Mr Doyle, the Officer of the boat, and hailed stones on the boat which injured most of its crew. The mob further threatened to 'sacrifice' Doyle and to haul the schooner on shore to burn her. At 5pm, the schooner sent to the *Squirrel* for assistance; meanwhile the mob had commandeered a sloop and moved out to board the schooner, but seeing that the schooner's crew was about to make a determined defense, had sheered off and returned to shore. *Squirrel* signaled the *St John* to move out for protection under the frigate's stern. On seeing this, members of the mob went out to the battery on nearby Goat Island and had the cannon fire on the schooner.

A more complete knowledge of this amazing event which took place almost eleven years before the start of the American Revolution can be gained by reading the account rendered to Admiral Colville by the officers of the *Squirrel.* Captain Smith reported:

> On Monday last I was on shore and on my return received the inclosed Account from my Lieutenant of a most insolent and ignorant abuse of Power in the Government of this Place; on which I immediately sent onshore for the Gunner of the Fort to know his authority for firing on the Kings Colours; He produced an order for stopping that Vessel signed by two of the Council, The Deputy Governour being absent at that time. – I, in company with my Lieutenant waited on the Governour and Council to demand a proper acknowledgement of the Insult they had committed; in order to inform your Lordship of it, I found them a sett of very Ignorant Council. They agreed that the Gunner had acted by authority and that they would answer for it when they thought it necessary. It appears to me that they were guided by the Mob whose intentions were to murder the Pilot and destroy the Vessel, I am very sorry they ceased firing before we had convinced them of their Error. But I hope it will by your Lordships representation be the means of a change of Government in this licentious Republic. [PRO ADM 1/482 pp379-80]

Lieutenant Hugh Backie, who was in charge during Captain Smith's absence from the *Squirrel,* gave this description of the event:

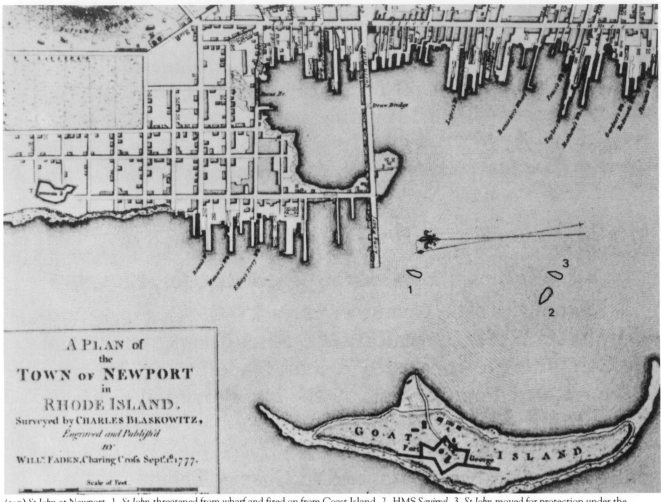

(top) *St John* at Newport. 1. *St John* threatened from wharf and fired on from Coast Island. 2. HMS *Squirrel*. 3. *St John* moved for protection under the storm of the 20 gun *Squirrel*.
(bottom) A detail from Paul Revere's engraving, showing two armed schooners.

Beaver	5 Mermaid
Senegal	6 Romney
Martin	7 Launceston
Glasgow	8 Bonetta

On friday Sept: 30th 1768. the Ships of WAR, armed Schooners, Transports, &c Came up the H[arbour] a Spring on their Cables, as for a regular Siege. At noon on Saturday October the 1st the [troops] and Train of Artillery, with two peices of Cannon, landed on the Long Wharf: then Form[ed] playing, and Colours flying, up KING STREET Each Soldier having received 16 rounds of.

In the afternoon as I was walking the Deck I saw a Gun fired from the *St John,* soon after her Boat with a Petty Officer came onboard and told me that the Master had pursued a Deserter on shore, that the Mob had rescued the Deserter, detained the Master and wounded all the Boats Crew, and that the Gun fired was for the Boat to return onboard, that the People from the Town hailed the Schooner and desired them to send the Pilot onshore or they would sacrifice the Master, and had manned several Boats to board them: I then ordered him to return onboard and to make a signal if they attempted anything further, likewise to bring the Schooner out and anchor near us. Soon after several Gentlemen came onboard and said they came to represent the occasion of this disturbance least the Officer of the Schooner should have made a misrepresentation of the affair. They said there was a Theft committed by three of the Schooners People, that they had one in possession and wanted the other two who were onboard the Schooner, that a Peace Officer had went off and they had refused him admittance, and they now imagined he would return with an armed force to gain admittance. I told the Gentlemen the offenders should be sent onshore. The signal was then made by the Schooner pursuant to my former directions, I immediately sent a Boat and a Petty Officer to order her out of the Harbour; on which the Gentlemen told me they would fire on her from the Fort. I then told the Officer if they fired from the Fort to go on shore to the Fort and let them know it was my orders for her to move and anchor near us, and that the Men should be delivered to Justice, and if he fired again I should be obliged to return it They still continued their Fire, I then ordered a Spring on our Cable and went onshore to the Fort to let them know the consequence of their behaviour. I found no other Officer than the Gunner governed by a tumultous Mob who said they had orders to fire and they would Fire. They used me with very great insolence and knocked me down and would have detained me. I then returned to the Boat ordered the Ship to prepare for action, and proceed on board the Schooner and brought her to Anchor near the Ship they then ceased firing. I then went onshore to demand Justice of the Deputy Governour for the treatment I had received at the Fort, he replied I must pursue the Law; I told him I would redress myself if they were to be found as he seemed not active to do me Justice. I then returned to take the People off who had insulted me but could not find them. [PRO ADM 1/482 pp379-80]

As the schooners which had been sent out to recruit crews returned to Halifax one by one, it became clear that Admiral Colville's hopes had been in vain. When the Lords of the Admiralty established the schooner class on the Navy List, they had assigned a complement of thirty men to them and had set down the composition of the crew [PRO ADM 2/433 p460]. A lieutenant was to command with pay of five shillings per day; the remainder of the crew was to be paid according to status at the same rates as the men in a 6th rate ship. There was to be a Master's Mate, a Midshipman, a Boatswain's Mate, Gunner's Mate, Carpenter's Mate, Surgeon's Mate, a man to act as clerk and steward, and a servant to the Lieutenant; the remaining 21 men rounded out the crew of 30 as seamen. In a letter dated 22 September 1764 Colville related some of the problems he was having in securing qualified men for the schooner crews.

In my letter of the 9 of Septr I pointed out the different Services on which the six new purchased Vessels are employed, and I think it my Duty to inform their Lordship's that notwithstanding all imaginable Care has been taken to make these Vessels as compleat as possible, yet the want of a Master or some trusty officer to assist the Commander in the general Tenour of his Duty, but more particularly in the Care of Stores, is but too obvious from the manner they have been conducted. Two are to winter at Quebec: if in one of these or any other that may be detached to a distant Station the Lieutenant should die, there would be no one aboard properly qualified to succeed in the Command. I got the best Men I could for Pilots which in some measure supply the want of Masters; but good Mates or Midshipmen are not to be had: the Establishment of Wages does not appear to be any Inducement for such to enter in these Parts, and the unexpected Decisions of the Judges of the Admiralty, with the Prejudice raised by the smuggling Merchants of New York and New England against these Vessels increases the Discouragement. Only two Surgeon's Mates came out of England for the six Vessels; and I have not been able to procure but one more, a very young green Lad from New York; so that there are three of these Vessels now at Sea without the least assistance for any of their People that may be sick or hurt. We have but one Surgeon's Mate in the *Romney* neither the Navy Board nor my own Enquiry could procure a second when fitting out. In twenty six sail under my command there are only thirteen Surgeon's Mates. It would give me great Pain to be deemed a Relator of Grievances; but I flatter myself their Lordships will look upon what I have now wrote, as proceeding only from a Sense of my Duty to lay before them, the true State and Condition of the Ships and Vessels under my command. And I beg leave to add, that I would not trouble their Lordships with the recital of such matters if it was in my power to apply Remedies to them. [PRO AM 1/482 pp404-5]

Other letters from Admiral Colville to the Admiralty in London throughout the fall months of 1764 and on into the following winter advise the locations and activities of the six schooners [All in PRO ADM 1/482]. *Chaleur* had returned in August without enlisting any seamen. Lieutenant Laugharne reported having had an unpleasant experience with a mob in New York at about the same time as Lieutenant Hill's troubles at Newport. Hill in the *St John* was sent to cruise in the St Lawrence to suppress smuggling activity. He was instructed to winter at Quebec. When *Chaleur* returned, Laugharne was ordered to follow the *St John* with the same instructions. Lieutenant Dugdale came into Halifax in the *Magdalen* to report a similar lack of success in recruiting. Early in September, *St Lawrence* and *Hope* were sent to Newfoundland in another attempt to raise men. Following that, their orders were 'to cruise between Cape Raye, St Paul Island, & Louisbourg, against illicit traders.' They were to return to Halifax by December if crowded with men. *St Lawrence* did reappear in November after having raised thirty-nine men in Newfoundland. Lieutenant Dundas reported that he had called at St Peters on 20 October with a letter. He had discussed the peace treaty with the French Governor and been well treated.

Early in November, Colville reported that the schooners mustered the following numbers of men in their crews: *St John* – 25, *St Lawrence* – 13, *Hope* – 10, *Gaspee* – 27, *Chaleur* – 22, and *Magdalen* – 26. In the middle of December, he advised the dispositions of the schooners: *St John* and *Chaleur* were in the St Lawrence as previously noted and expected to winter at Quebec; *St Lawrence* was at Louisburg off the coast of Cape Breton Island; *Magdalen* was in New England waters to prevent smuggling; *Gaspee* was being employed against smuggling off Nova Scotia but Colville intended to send her to the New York area; *Hope* was something of a mystery – she had not returned from her mission to Newfoundland. There was no explanation for her prolonged absence, but it appears that she may have remained there on detached service for a couple of years. Before *Magdalen* was sent to patrol the New England Coast, her original commander, Robert Dugdale, was subjected to an unpleasant experience as indicated by the following document:

> By the Right Honble the Lord Colville Rear Adml of the White & Commander in Chief of his Majy Ships and Vessels employed and to be employed in the River S Lawrence and along the Coasts of Nova Scotia the Islands of St John & Cape Breton thence to Cape Florida and the Bahama Islands
>
> Whereas I have been acquainted by the Collector of his Majesty's Customs at this Port, that Lieutenant Robert Dugdale Commander of his Majesty's armed Schooner the *Magdelen*, being at Louisbourg in the Month of August last, did take, or suffered to be taken aboard, on freight, a certain Quantity of Provisions, as Beef, Pork and Butter; and that the same was landed at this Place according to agreement with the Merchant or Owner. And as such Conduct is contrary to the established Rules of the Navy, you are hereby required and directed to assemble a Courtmartial with all convenient Speed, and to try the said Lieutenant Robert

A reconstruction of an eighteenth century fishing schooner used in the Colonial Shipyard diorama.

Dugdale for the same. Dated onboard his Majesty's Ship the *Romney* in Halifax Harbour the 12th of November 1764.

To

Captain Joseph Deane	Colville
Commander of his Majesty's	
Ship the *Mermaid*	

[PRO ADM 1/482 p431]

On 17 November 1764, a court-martial was convened on board the *Romney* at Halifax to try Lieutenant Robert Dugdale of the *Magdalen* [PRO ADM 1/5302]. The presiding officers were: Captain Joseph Deane, President; Captain William Harris; Captain Richard Smith; Captain James Ferguson and Commander Thomas Bishop. The evidence which was presented claimed that while the *Magdalen* was at Louisburg in August Dugdale was approached by a merchant named Gethins who asked if he could have a passage to Halifax in the schooner, for which he offered to pay. Dugdale said it would cost him nothing unless he cared to give the clerk something. Gethins then asked if he could ship some provisions. Dugdale claimed that he had refused permission for this. Unfortunately when the Lieutenant told his officers that Gethins could sail with them, he failed to mention his refusal to ship the provisions.

While Dugdale was ashore, Gethins appeared on board with a friend, George Sherlock. They brought with them a boatload of provisions from a brig anchored about a half mile away. They told Midshipman John Ramsey that they had Dugdale's permission to load them on the schooner; Ramsey, knowing of the passenger arrangement, assumed that the merchant was telling the truth. 85 casks of beef and pork and 50 firkins of butter were stowed away. The clerk, William Gill, who supervised the work, received £6 5s 0d for his pains. When it had become too late to get rid of the cargo at Louisburg, Dugdale discovered its presence aboard. He was extremely angry and told Gethins that he must get rid of the provisions as soon as possible.

The *Magdalen* arrived at Halifax on 9th September. That night Dugdale slept ashore, something that he did very occasionally. Henry Newton, the Collector of Customs, was informed in the evening that an illicit landing was to be made. Since there was no merchant vessel in the harbor to make such a landing, he discounted the information. However when the warning was repeated in the morning, he went to the wharf just as Sherlock was unloading the provisions. After making enquiries, he decided to let the stuff through. However in order to keep himself in the clear, he informed Admiral Colville of the affair. Colville was distressed that one of his schooners specially employed against smuggling should be compromised in such a fashion and so convened the court-martial.

In its findings, the court did not believe that Dugdale had been innocent of any part in the transaction and found him guilty. He was cashiered and declared incapable of ever serving the Crown again in any capacity. As the story has been told, the penalty sounds rather harsh. It certainly is to be wondered what happened to Robert Dugdale after he had been cast out of the service in the New World where he had arrived so recently.

Lieutenant Harvey, formerly an officer in the *Mermaid*, was sent to Boston to take command of the *Magdalen* which continued to patrol the New England coast on the lookout for smugglers. The schooner returned to Halifax on 15 February, and thirteen men promptly deserted. Word was received that *Chaleur* and *St John* had arrived at Quebec on 28 October of the previous year. In April, orders were sent to them that they should refit as necessary at Quebec and continue to cruise in the St Lawrence. *Magdalen* in company with the *Senegal* sailed 27 March 1765 to cruise off St Peter Island. *Gaspee* arrived at Halifax in April from New York with two new Surgeon's Mates; one was appointed to the *Gaspee* and the other to the *St Lawrence* which had recently returned to Halifax after wintering at Louisburg.

In June, Admiral Colville received instructions from the Lords of the Admiralty that he should try to enlist a 2nd Master and Pilot instead of a Master's Mate for each schooner. Colville replied that he doubted that he could get anyone for £3 10s 0d a month. Throughout the year he reported the same dispositions for the schooners: *St John* and *Chaleur* remained in the St Lawrence River; *Magdalen* cruised in the Gulf of St Lawrence; the *St Lawrence* patrolled between the islands of Cape Breton and St Pierre, and *Gaspee* maintained its station off the coasts of New England and New York. Lieutenant Dundas of the *St Lawrence* reported in a letter dated 25 June that on a visit to the island of St Pierre he found a small vessel from Boston trying rather unsuccessfully to get £10,000 from the French for supplies furnished to them. Correspondence received from Captain Leslie of the *Cygnet* in August related that a mob in Rhode Island had threatened to burn his ship. In a letter dated 7 June 1766, the Admiral reported:

I have again appointed Captain Deane to command the King's Ships & Vessels employed for the Summer in the Gulph & River St Lawrence, and he will sail the first opportunity with the *Mermaid* and *Senegal* for his station; I have likewise directed him to draw the *St John* schooner from the River & to employ her in cruising about the Bays of Chaleur and Mirmichier where I am informed that the French from St Peters are attempting to carry on an illicit Commerce with the Indians. Lieut Laugharne in the *Chaleur* Sloop is to continue in the River St Lawrence, the *Mermaid* and *Senegal* with the *St John* Schooner are to return to Halifax when the season, or want of Provisions should make it necessary. . . The *St Lawrence* & *Magdalen* Schooners are at present on the Coast of Cape Breton but I expect the *Magdalen* to return here daily. [PRO ADM 1/482 p509]

There are a couple of paragraphs having particular significance to be gleaned from a letter dated *Romney*, Halifax, 31 July 1766:

The *Jamaica* Sloop arrived here from New England the 12th of June & after being cleaned & refitted she returned to her Station. The *Magdalen* schooner has likewise been careened & fitted and I have sent her to relieve the *Chaleur* Sloop in the River S Lawrence because I think it necessary that the Vessels which have been two Winters at Quebec should have a thorough Examination & Refitment in the King's Yard.

[paragraph omitted]

I am sorry to acquaint you that His Majesty's Schooner the *St Lawrence* had the Misfortune to be blown up at Niginish in the Island of Cape Breton about 3 O'Clock in the Afternoon of the 26th of last month; by This Accident four Men lost their Lives, the same number were dangerously hurt and the Vessel sunk instantly in six Fathom Water; Lieutenant

Dundas with the rest of his people arrived here this Day in a Sloop which he hired for the purpose, and as there is no prospect of having a sufficient number of Captains to hold a Court martial at this Place, I have ordered him and his Officers to be carried to England in the *Viper* Sloop, which Vessel put in here the 22d Instant for a supply of Provisions, there being none to be had at North Carolina, and she has been detained some Days by contrary Winds since she was ready to sail. [PRO ADM 1/482 p514]

The *St Lawrence* was first of the schooners to be lost. Lieutenant Dundas and his officers were transported to England, and on 6 September 1766, a court-martial was convened on board the *Bellona* at Portsmouth [PRO ADM 1/5303]. The panel of judges included: Captain Michael Everitt, President; Captain Henry March; Captain John Bentinck; Captain Robert Hathorn; Captain William Bennett; Captain John Luttrell and Captain John Maccartney.

By the Admiralty order of 3 September, the court was to try the following officers and crew of the schooner *St Lawrence* for her loss: Lieutenant Dundas; John Holcombe, Master; David Gregg, Midshipman; George Maxwell, Clerk; and Joshua Cox, Able.

On 26 June 1766, the *St Lawrence* was lying at anchor at Niginish, Cape Breton Island, about twenty leagues north of Louisburg. A thunder storm started about noon and increased in intensity until about 3pm when the ship was struck by lighting. The magazine immediately blew up; and in less than a minute, the ship sank. There were two boats alongside at the time. One went down with the ship; the survivors got into the Moses boat and rowed ashore. It was discovered that three men had been lost and that six were injured. There had been 26 men on board at the time with a few other men on shore.

The midshipman had been in his cabin when the magazine exploded, and he was blown up through the deck planking. The clerk, who had also been below, had no recollection of what had happened to him.

A message was sent to the *Canceau* which arrived a few days later. Of the injured taken aboard her, one subsequently died. Fishing vessels were hired and with the assistance of the *Canceau* an attempt was made to raise the schooner. They did in fact raise her a couple of feet off the bottom, but then the slings broke; it was thought that she was made too heavy by sand which had infiltrated. All that was recovered were some anchors, damaged sails, and the bodies of the three men. The court acquitted the officers and men of all blame.

On 12 August 1766, Admiral Colville advised 'in my letter of the 7 June by the *Hind* I acquainted you that I had send Lieutenant Allen in the *Gaspee* Sloop to the Westward with my despatches to the Governors of His Majestys Provinces, and to the Captains of the Kings Ships stationed on their Coasts. Mr Allen having performed that Service returned here two Days ago. *Gaspee* is refitting. When ready she is to take the S *Lawrence*'s men and a cable to the *Cygnet* at New London and then join the *Guarland* on the coast of New England' [PRO ADM 1/482 p520].

Meanwhile, Vice Admiral Philip Durrell had left England to relieve Colville as Commander of the North Atlantic Station. He arrived at Halifax on 22 August, very ill and he died on the 26th. Colville had spent many bleak years on the North Atlantic Station. Durrell's arrival had brought orders for his return to England and in spite of his relief's untimely death, Admiral Colville was determined to take advantage of those orders. Wasting no time, he turned command of the station over to the senior officer at Halifax, Captain Deane of the *Mermaid,* and sailed for England in the *Romney* on 5 September.

CHAPTER THREE

Trials and Tribulations of the Navy's Schooners

The story of schooner service in the Royal Navy does not paint a pretty picture. The reasons are fairly obvious but could stand amplification to forestall any charge of bias in the presentation. Any command in the peace time Navy might have been considered a plum to be sought after. As many ships were laid up in ordinary, so were many officers left 'on the beach' at half pay with reduced opportunities for their employment. However, it is questionable, as the service developed, that command of a schooner could have been considered an unqualified blessing. From a study of the records, it would appear that as many men suffered Robert Dugdale's fate of being dismissed from the service as were able to survive and continue the climb up the promotion ladder. As Colville had pointed out, the position of schooner command was singularly lacking in support. It was one of considerable responsibility with small promise of reward or recognition. It is interesting to note that while some few schooners such as *Chaleur*, *St Lawrence*, and *Sultana* retained the same commander throughout their useful life in the Navy, others had many changes of command.

If anything, service in a schooner was even more unpalatable to the ordinary seaman. Human life was held cheap in the mid-eighteenth century; shipboard records are well punctuated with notations of deaths. A small schooner crowded with thirty men and sailing in the rough North Atlantic must have furnished very insalubrious living conditions. Of course, sailors were accustomed to the physical vicissitudes which could

make their life miserable, but schooner service demanded that they should endure more than the elemental discomforts. People ashore and seamen in private service were egged on by the merchants, smugglers, and corrupt customs officials who feared the threat to their activities which was posed by the navy schooners. They made life miserable and frustrating for the crew members. The wonder is not that the schooners experienced so many desertions but that they were able to remain active at all. Admiral Colville gave a vivid description of these conditions and their effect on a schooner's crew in a letter dated 12 January 1765.

By the Account of the Disposition of the Ships & Vessels under my Command which I sent you the 14th of last month it will appear that the *Gaspee* armed Sloop was then employed in looking after Smugglers on the Coast of Nova Scotia, last night she returned from that Service and Lieut Allen informs me that having examined the Harbours between this & Cape Sable he was forced into Casco Bay by contrary Winds and a strong Current. Upon his arrival there he found the Business of the Custom House in the greatest confusion, Vessels arriving and sailing daily without paying any Regard to the Regulations lately established, or without so much as taking the least notice of the Customhouse, he therefore stopped two or three of them and applied to the Collector of the Customs at Falmouth for his advice & Assistance in order to prosecute them agreeable to his Instructions from the Commissioners of the Customs, but that Gentleman

29

declined being anyways concerned therein. It would seem that the *Gaspee*'s people now, finding they had no prospect of reaping an advantage from their Seizures, resolved to leave the Vessel as soon as possible for a Midshipman with three Seamen, who had the Watch, in the night Time took the Boat & went onshore and have not since been heard of. – A few Days after Mr Allen sent his Boat with another Midshipman, his Clerk, the Boatswain's Mate and three Seamen to board a Sloop which was turning into the Harbour, but no sooner had the Boat got alongside the Vessel & the Midshipman & Clerk steped into her, than the Boatswains Mate and the Seamen put off the Boat & rowed right ashore. The Midshipman & Clerk, with the Sloop's Boat & some of her People gave Chase to them but they got clear off. – Mr Allen not having a sufficient number of Hands left to navigate the Vessel, impressed four Men out of some Vessels that were coming in, but upon his going onshore the Mob seized his Boat & dragged her into the middle of the Town and insisted upon the four Men's being set to liberty before they would restore his Boat or suffer him to go onboard the Vessel in any other. In this situation he was under the necessity of complying with their Request and finding it would be to no manner of purpose for him to remain longer there, he waited on the Collector & delivered two Vessels, which he had detained, into his Charge – Another Seaman left the Boat whilst he was upon this duty, so that having lost nine of his best Men it was with the utmost difficulty that he got the Vessel here.

I have acquainted Captain Antrobus with Lieut Allen's account of the state of affairs at Casco Bay, & recommended it to him to send one of the Vessels under his command, to that Place, as soon as he can spare one. [PRO ADM 1/482 p432-3]

Admiral Colville followed circumspect policy of reassigning the schooners to new patrol areas after they had encountered prejudicial problems. In the summer of 1764, *St John* and *Chaleur* had experienced rough treatment from mobs in New York and Newport, Rhode Island. Those two schooners were then assigned to service in the St Lawrence River and wintered at Quebec for a couple of years, far from the scenes of their humiliation. Colville apparently reasoned that once a schooner had gained such notoriety in a particular locale her effectiveness would be seriously impaired. In March of 1768, *St John* did have occasion to visit Rhode Island once again. On her return to Halifax, she reported the loss of six men by desertion. After being careened and refitted, she was once again stationed in the St Lawrence River. *Gaspee*, under Lieutenant Allen, had been mistreated at Casco Bay while assigned to patrol the waters off Nova Scotia. She was then sent to the New York–New England area. Ironically enough, this reassignment eventually led to her destruction in 1772.

From the time Admiral Colville turned over the command to Captain Deane and departed for England in September 1766 until Commodore Samuel Hood arrived 5 July 1767, the records are rather sparse. Deane was not the senior officer stationed in the area designated as the North Atlantic Station. It can be surmised that he was glad to pass the responsibility to Captain Arthur Kennedy, who commanded the 28 gun frigate *Coventry*, and was stationed at New York. He rather reluctantly became the focal point for orders emanating from England. This transitory authority which made him responsible for naval affairs in general as well as the handling of his ship in particular placed him in an awkward position, but it did afford him a special role in the schooner story which will be detailed later.

Commodore Hood arrived at Halifax to take command in the *Romney* which had been Admiral Colville's flagship. As one of his first actions, Hood reported in a letter dated 28 July 1767 'I have purchased a vessel to be named *St Lawrence*, in obedience to their Lordships Commands, which is now fitting' [PRO ADM 1/483 p8]. Thus, the schooner blown up off Cape Breton Island had a successor to carry on her name. A letter dated 5 September advised that 'The *Magdalen* Schooner is arrived here. and will proceed to Virginia agreeable to their Lordships Command as soon as she is refitted, and new sails can be made for her, of which she is in great want. His Majesty's Sloop *Gaspee* is just arrived from New York; leaky and without Gripe having been ashore near Rhode Island and is preparing to Careen' [PRO ADM 1/485 p8]. The next time *Gaspee* ran aground off Rhode Island was to prove fatal. On 30 November, it was noted that the 'missing' schooner *Hope* under a Lieutenant Dawson had arrived from Newfoundland: 'She was much out of repair by wintering at Newfoundland Her Decks have been wholly New, and as soon as she is in all respects ready for sea I shall send her to winter in the neighborhood of Boston' [PRO ADM 1/483 p42].

In the summer of 1768, disorders in Boston began to loom large amongst Commodore Hood's problems. In May, he had transferred himself into the *Launceston* at Halifax and sent the *Romney* and *St Lawrence* to join the *Hope* at Boston. In June he augmented this show of force with the *Beaver*. Finally in November, Hood, himself, sailed to Boston in the *Viper*. Re-employing the *Romney* as his flagship, Hood decided to winter at Boston in company with the *Mermaid*, two sloops, and three schooners. Richard Murray had taken command of *St John* and William Dudingston was the lieutenant in *Gaspee*. Commodore Hood remained at Boston in the *Romney* until the end of July 1769. In May, he had reported that 'The Commissioners of his Majesty's Customs – have expressed their opinions, that if a sloop of war was stationed in the River Delaware near the town of Philadelphia, and a King's Schooner in the

Bay, it would greatly contribute to the prevention of smuggling, and the Improvement of the Revenue, which it is imagined, may be encreased at the Port above twenty thousand pounds a year – I … had stationed the *Gaspee* Schooner in the River before I received the Commissioners Letter' [PRO ADM 1/483 p212].

In August 1769, Hood returned in the *Romney* to his command post in Halifax. In November, he sent the schooner *Hope* to England. 'The repairs which His Majesty's Schooner the *Hope* stands in need of, being too great to be done here, I now send her home, agreeable to my Instructions, and I transmit by her an account of the state and condition of His Majesty's Ships and Vessels under my command'[PRO ADM 1/483 p236]. The schooner *Magdalen* had been sent to England back in May with despatches from Lord Botetourt Governor of Virginia [PRO ADM 1/483 p235]. While at Portsmouth, the crew of the *Magdalen* petitioned to be paid off. The Admiralty approved the requests of only three men, George Cuzens, Ferdinand Roach, and John Payton, that they be discharged from the service. They had been with the schooner since 1764. Lieutenant Henry Collins was appointed to be her new commander, and she sailed for Virginia on 9 September 1769. After *Magdalen*'s return to Virginia, events took place which resulted in a court-martial the following year.

On 19 June 1770, a court martial was convened on board the *Romney* at Halifax [PRO ADM 1/5304]. The officers of the court were: Captain Mark Robinson of *Fowey*, president; Captain Hyde Parker; Captain Robert Linzee; Commander Thomas Hayward; and Commander James Wallace. Lawrence Ross, Carpenter's Mate of the *Magdalen*, was accused of most daring insolence and contempt to his superior officer, of being quarrelsome and of embezzling stores.

Evidence was given by Lane, the Master, Benoit, the surgeon, and Nicholas Truscott, a midshipman, among others. Ross had appeared to be perfectly normal during the voyage from England to Virginia, but afterwards he became very quarrelsome. On one occasion, the Master sent him to return a Gondola that had brought off stores but then noticed that Ross was quite drunk. He became violent and refused to come back on board. As a result it was necessary to bring him on board forcibly and confine him. On another occasion, he threatened Truscott with an axe. He was extremely quarrelsome with other members of the ship's company. The surgeon was of the opinion that Ross's behavior was due not so much to drink as to his being lunatic, possibly brought on by drink. The court found the charge proved and sentenced Ross to be dismissed.

Ross was then given a hearing in which he charged the Midshipman with having assulted him. The same court proceeded to hear this case. Truscott was accused of having come on board drunk in the middle of the night, of cutting down the hammocks of Ross and other men, and of having chased Ross and hit him. After hearing the evidence, the court dismissed the charge as being 'litigious and frivolous'. Truscott was acquitted. Whether justice was done or not, this account certainly breathes life into the characters and conditions on board a schooner.

On 12 June 1770, the Admiralty wrote to Hood that having served for three years as commander of the North Atlantic Station he was due to be relieved [PRO ADM 1/483 p301]. On 25 September, he reported that *Sultana* had brought Admiralty instructions to him which ordered him to move the squadron headquarters from Halifax to Boston [PRO ADM 1/483 p303]. He did so leaving for Boston on 2 October [PRO ADM 1/483 p308]. On the 10th of that month, he was relieved as commander of the North Atlantic Station by Commodore James Gambier and sailed for England on the 14th. Commodore Hood had completed an active tour of duty during which there had been numerous changes affecting the roster of schooners in his squadron: he had purchased the second *St Lawrence*; *Sultana* had joined him in 1768; *Halifax* had been acquired in 1768 and made her appearance at Boston the following year. It had been necessary for him to send the seriously deteriorated *Chaleur* to England where she was condemned and sold out of the service. As the original schooners suffered from advancing age, maintaining their fitness for active duty became a serious responsibility which the Halifax Yard could no longer handle.

James Gambier did not serve for long as commander on the station. However, during that time he was much concerned with smuggling activities along the coast of the thirteen colonies. He wrote a long letter which detailed the problems he was encountering and the need for more schooners.

Salisbury in Boston Harbour 6 Novr. 1770

Philip Stephens Esqr

Sir

Their Lordships will permit me respectfully to represent to them the apparent utility of more small Vessels to check, if not prevent, the very great illicit trade which is being carried on all along the coast of North America, the district of which is extremely extensive, being six hundred leagues in length, and only seven schooners for the whole coast, one of which is constantly employed on the Bahama Island Station, and the others obliged frequently to be detached away on occasional services, more especially at this time when the late disturbances and present situation of affairs in this province has caused administration to order Boston to be the port of rendezvous, and the most particular attention to paid to what shall pass there. I beg leave to represent to their Lordships that six schooners, in addition to those already on the Station, would be extremely serviceable in seizing the numerous smuggling ships and vessels with which this station swarms, and are so injurious to the King's Revenue:– they will be able, by drawing little water, to lay in the numberless small harbours and Creeks that are along the coast, and be also qualified to follow the Smuggling Vessels into shoal water.

The said six Schooners at thirty men each, will, in point of numbers, only equal the complement of a Frigate of 180 men, and be no greater expence to Government in cleaning and refitting; and, upon enquiry, I am informed such Vessels are to be hired, or purchased, at a moderate price, and cheaper than if built by the King's Shipwrights.

With such Vessels I would respectfully propose varying their stations, and when any of them shall have been successful on any particular one, in making Seizures and thereby incur the resentment of those concerned in carrying on the said illicit trade, which is commonly the consequence of seizures, such Vessel, to obviate any riots or disturbances, should be detached to a different Station, replacing her by some other. My predecessor Mr Hood will, I am persuaded, if their Lordships please, represent to the Board the utility of such a Measure.

Last Post I received a Letter from Lieutenant Dudingston commanding the *Gaspee* Schooner at Philadelphia acquainting me that he had deferr'd sailing until he should receive my further orders, having just made seizure of a large Ship from Ireland with India Muslins and other Comodities onboard, the Collector of His Majesty's Customs at that port representing to him that, as the seizure was valuable, He did not think it safe unless he remained there until after condemnation, keeping a strong guard on board the Ship until then, and that he could not himself put men onboard to take charge of her, as there were but few Custom house Officers belonging to the Port, and those generally employed onboard Vessels that were landing goods which paid Duty, and onboard the Custom house Boat. The Commander of the Schooner at the same time acquaints me of his having received information that five other Ships of the same sort were expected at that place, as a further reason for his remaining until he should receive my directions in view of endeavouring to intercept them, the *Gaspee* being the only King's vessel there. In this case I am apprehensive I shant find it expedient to send the *St John* Schooner home to refit, agreeable to my Intentions in my last letter to the Board, having no small Vessel but her with me, should I find it necessary to reinforce the *Gaspee*, or the affairs of this Province, or other duty, require sending her on any immediate service, the *Halifax* having sailed some days ago with despatches for Administration, the *St Lawrence* being on the Bahama Island Station, the *Magdalen* at Virginia being the only King's Vessel to attend that place and the same with regard to the *Sultana* at Rhode

Island, the *Hope* at Halifax where she is very necessary for the protection of the King's Yard and Port.
I am
Sir
Your most obedient
humble Servant etc.
J Gambier
[PRO ADM 1/483 p330-1]

Samuel Hood and James Gambier commanded the North Atlantic Station in the rank of commodore. It would appear that, as the problems in the American Colonies multiplied, the Lords of the Admiralty concluded that men of higher rank should shoulder the responsibility. In any case, Gambier's tour of duty was cut short when Rear Admiral John Montagu arrived at Boston on 13 August 1771 to supersede him in the command. The orders that Montagu carried with him called for Gambier to return to England in the *Salisbury*. This he did, sailing on 30 August. *Gaspee* had arrived at Boston on the 15th, and the new commander sent her on to Halifax to be cleaned and refitted. She was back at Boston by January, 1772 ready for sea duty. With the end of the winter season, *Gaspee* sailed to resume patrolling for smugglers. Lieutenant Dudingston had experienced some success at Philadelphia and had full intentions of extending that performance to the New York, Rhode Island station to which he was newly assigned. He arrived at Rhode Island on 22 March; here he found a letter from Admiral Montagu and in his reply, he described the unhelpful attitude of the Governor and of the Commissioners of Customs.

It can be very difficult to arrive at the truth of an historical event where passions had run high. Accounts that have been handed down are commonly colored dramatically to favor the original sources and the country in which they have been published. The story of the *Gaspee*'s destruction as found in American history books terms Dudingston 'arrogant' and the *Gaspee* 'obnoxious.' The Rhode Islanders had threatened to burn Royal Navy vessels before, and they repeated this threat against the *Gaspee*. Dudingston could hardly be faulted for trying to follow his orders in the apprehension of smugglers. Whether he was unduly arrogant or overbearing in his conduct of those duties would be difficult to determine at this late date. That he did make things uncomfortable for illicit traders in Rhode Island is obvious. The merchants of Providence pretended they did not know that *Gaspee* was a Navy vessel directed and empowered to suppress smuggling. They went to the local courts with a demand that Dudingston should be arrested and made to show his authority for stopping and searching vessels. This legal maneuver failed. However, the populace had been inflamed and the Lieutenant and his schooner were threatened with dire consequences. A quirk of Fate stepped in that brought this threat to fruition.

Gaspee shared the Rhode Island Station with the sloop of war *Beaver* which could not work as close inshore as the smaller vessel. At noon on 9 June 1772, *Gaspee* left the company of *Beaver* to sail up Narragansett Bay toward Providence. Dudingston, sighting the small packet *Hannah*, ordered her to heave to for an examination. According to the American version, the 'wily' Captain Benjamin Lindsay refused to comply and during a chase up the bay lured *Gaspee* into shoal waters some seven miles south of Providence. There *Gaspee* went aground and was expected to remain so until she could float free with the high tide at 3am the following morning.

The news spread through Providence like wildfire. Eight long boats were collected and had their oars and oarlocks muffled. A drummer paraded through the streets calling for volunteers to man the boats. By 10pm the force was organized with a sea captain at the tiller of each boat. Captain Abraham Whipple was in command of the operation. The flotilla approached in the dark and was not discovered until it was too late to train a cannon on the boats. Dudingston, rudely aroused by the ensuing commotion, came on deck wearing only his shirt. While attempting to defend his command, he was wounded by a ball which broke his left arm and lodged in his groin. The attacking force swarmed on deck and overpowered the crew. Two surgeons who were part of the mob bandaged the Lieutenant's wounds; then, he and his men were tied up and rowed ashore to Pawtuxent, some two miles away. There they watched as their schooner was destroyed by fire which reportedly ended with an explosion when it reached the magazine. This event has been hailed as an early stroke for freedom by the colonists, and Abraham Whipple became a folk hero when he challenged the British to catch him for punishment.

Captain Linzee brought the *Beaver* up the following afternoon when he learned from the Collector of Customs what had happened. He found that local authorities had already secured the guns and a few stores from the destroyed schooner. These were recovered and later sent to Halifax. On the 12th, the sheriff attempted to arrest the sorely wounded Dudingston for the theft of goods belonging to a Jacob Green. The Lieutenant was too ill to be moved and this charge was lost in the shuffle of inquiries and court appearances that followed. Admiral Montagu did not have enough ships on hand to furnish officers for a court-martial, so Dudingston, his master, midshipman, and five seamen were sent home in *Beaver*. Lieutenant Dudingston was tried on board the *Centaur* at Portsmouth on 17 October 1772. He was honorably acquitted.

A Commission of Enquiry was set up in Rhode Island to investigate the *Gaspee* affair with a view to determining and bringing to justice the responsible ring leaders. The commission which assembled at Newport in January 1773 was composed of Joseph Wanton, the Governor of Rhode Island and Providence, Daniel Horsmander, Fredrick Smythe, and Peter Oliver who were Chief Justices for the provinces of New York, New Jersey, and Massachusetts Bay, and Robert Auchmuty, Judge of the Vice-Admiralty Court of Boston. Admiral Montagu represented the Navy. After being in attendance for several months, he substituted his senior captain so he could leave to attend to the urgencies of his command. The proceedings of this Commission were confused by what appeared to be false testimony from both sides and evasive tactics on the part of the Americans in particular. It was requested that Dudingston be returned from England. The Admiralty Minutes for Tuesday 16 February 1773 indicate the response to this request:

> Rear Admiral Montagu having requested that Capt Dudingston, late Commander of the *Gaspee* Schooner may be sent out to Boston, as he would be able to point out to the Commissr some of the persons concerned in burning the Schooner the Board made enquiry into the state of Mr Dudingston's health, but find him incapable of proceeding thither without manifest danger of his life; but there being on board the *Marlborough* a Midshipman & a Seaman who were present while Capt Dudingston's wounds were dressing, & are consequently as likely to know the persons of the Rioters as well as the Captain himself; Resolved that the Earl of Dartmouth be acquainted therewith, & desired to receive & signify His Majesty's pleasure touching the sending out of the said Persons.
> [PRO ADM 3/79]

Midshipman Dickenson and Able Seaman Chivers arrived at Newport on 29 April in the brig *William Charles Ackworth*.

The judges on the commission delayed in taking action because some of them were up for election that summer and they did not want to offend their constituents. As the Commission sat on through May and June, it became evident that a whitewash was in progress. Evidence which might have led to identification of the ring leaders was discarded as false or insufficient and the investigation died out. While the Commission apparently wanted to make Lieutenant Dudingston the scapegoat, the Royal Navy took the opposite view. Finally recovering from his wounds, Dudingston lived on until 1816 and rose to the rank of rear admiral.

The traditional story that *Hannah* had drawn *Gaspee* into shallow water and her eventual destruction is seriously questioned by Commander May who made a detailed study of the records. He says that there is no mention of this chase in any of the British reports. Actually if *Gaspee* had gone aground while engaged in such a pursuit, there would have been some excuse for the misadventure. As the records present the case, Dudingston could well have been castigated for picking a poor anchorage where as the tide fell the schooner came to rest on the bottom. At low tide, the crew was actually able to walk around the *Gaspee*. One explanation for the error in anchoring the schooner is that the master was away in Boston with four seamen at the time. There were just eighteen men onboard; of those, six never reappeared and were assumed to have taken the opportunity to desert.

Gaspee was the second of the original six 'schooners and Sloops' to meet destruction, and the third to be lost to the service. Only the Hope, Magdalen and St John were left. St Lawrence had been replaced by a vessel given the same name, and Halifax and Sultana had been added to the little squadron. Hood had received instructions to send one schooner to England each year for refitting; Hope and Magdalen had made the trip in 1769. Gambier had planned to send St John to England for an overhaul next but was prevented by the exigency of the situation at Boston. On 25 October 1771, Admiral Montagu wrote: 'I have sent home the Saint John as she is most in want of repair, and her Company has received no Wages these seven years. I shall be glad to have her out again as soon as the season of the year will permit, as she will be much wanted to look after the smugglers that swarm upon this coast'[PRO ADM /484 p57].

The St John returned to Boston on 10 June 1772 under the command of Lieutenant William Grant. She brought letters from the Admiralty which included instructions that settled one bone of contention. Montagu had been trying to charge the Commissioners of Customs for the cost of schooner pilotage which was usually incurred when they were working on behalf of the Customs. The Commissioners had demurred at this and the question was referred to England. The Admiralty advised the decision that the pilotage of schooners should be charged to the Commissioners of Customs.

The St Lawrence under Lieutenant Ralph Dundas had been assigned to patrol the waters between East Florida and the Bahamas at the southern extremity of the North Atlantic Station. In August 1771, Admiral Montagu sent orders to New Providence that she should come to Boston. She sailed to comply with those orders on 14 November. When the St Lawrence had not appeared by April of 1772, Montagu wrote of his fears for her safety. When she did finally arrive at Boston on 16 May, Lieutenant Dundas explained that the schooner had been driven off the coast and forced to winter in the West Indies. After taking on provisions, she sailed for New Providence on 22 May. She continued on at this station until June of 1774 when she was ordered home. St Lawrence was last noted as being at Portsmouth, England, in January 1775 after which she was apparently sold out of the service.

In the spring of 1772, Montagu had chartered the schooner Sally at Halifax for £25 0s 0d per month. The 13 August minutes of the Admiralty Board read 'Resolved that Rear Admiral Montagu be order'd to purchase a Vessel to supply the place of the Gaspee Schooner, lately burned at Rhode Island, & to cause her to be manned, armed, victualled & stored in the same man-

ner as the former was' [PRO ADM 3/79]. Montagu wrote in a letter dated 16 December 1772 that he had sent the Sally to Halifax to be surveyed as a possible replacement for the Gaspee. The new Gaspee was commissioned 9 January 1773 with Lieutenant William Hunter in command. She was termed a 'brig' on the Navy List.

This second Gaspee had an eventful career to match that of the original schooner. Her initial cruise put her off Rhode Island during the winter of 1773-74. From there, she was sent to the Gulf of St Lawrence where she was the only vessel on that station in July according to a letter from Admiral Graves who had replaced Montagu at Boston. In December 1774, Graves wrote that he had ordered the Gaspee, 'lately returned from protecting the Fisheries in the Bay of Chaleur and Gaspee,' to patrol between Casco Bay and Passamaquody Harbor as a means of discouraging the smuggling of arms and ammunition into the colonies. On 4 March 1775, Admiral Graves wrote to Philip Stephens, 'Last Saturday Sen Night the 19th February Lieutenant Hunter in the Gaspee returned suddenly from his Station to Boston and acquainted me that on the 13th lying at Falmouth in Casco Bay, four Seamen belonging to the Brig took the Boat from alongside and rowed towards the Shore, and that upon the Master and himself firing at the Boat to make them return having in vain called to them for that purpose and received very abusive answers, one Man was wounded, the other three rowed the Boat ashore and deserted at Falmouth where the wounded man died.' On 27 of February, Lieutenant Hunter and Maltis Lucullus Ryall, his master, were tried by a court-martial convened on board the Somerset at Boston. They were exonerated in the death of John Lutey, seaman, whom they had shot in the act of desertion. It will be recalled that the original Gaspee had encountered similar problems in Casco Bay some ten years earlier. With the start of the American Revolution and repeated attacks on Royal Navy vessels along the New England Coast, Admiral Graves decided to chastise Falmouth. The following winter, a small squadron under Captain Mowatt bombarded and destroyed the town, an act which gained much notoriety.

After a cleaning at Halifax, Gaspee returned to the St Lawrence River. The advent of war had changed priorities. At Quebec on 6 August 1775, Sir Guy Carleton instructed Lieutenant Hunter 'you will, with as much dispatch as practicable proceed with the Armed Brigantine Gaspee under your Command to Montreal, or as high up the River, as you can with safety to your Vessel, and there Cooperate with His Majesty's Land Forces in the Defence of the Province' [PRO ADM 1/485]. Gaspee did reach Montreal, and when, during the early stages of the fighting, Colonel Ethan Allen and other Americans were captured, they were confined aboard the vessel in irons. When Montreal fell to the Americans in November, Gaspee

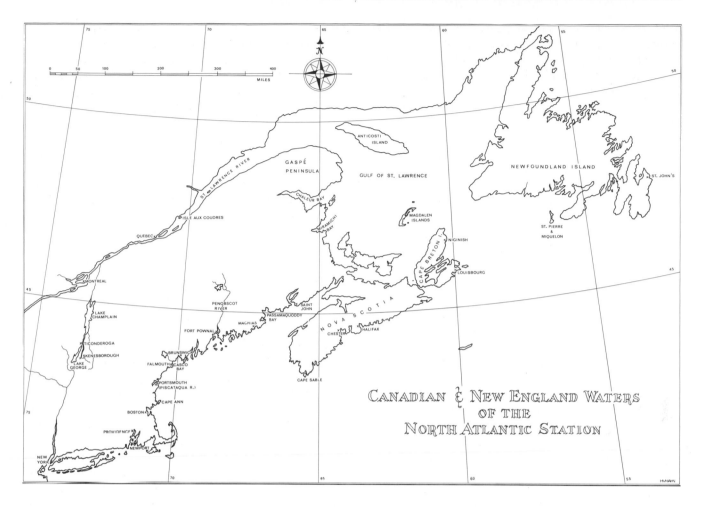

CANADIAN & NEW ENGLAND WATERS
OF THE
NORTH ATLANTIC STATION

along with seven sloops and schooners was taken. Governor Carleton had planned to make his retreat to Quebec aboard *Gaspee* but was forced instead to take an overland route in disguise.

The American forces moved on to beseige Quebec. There, they tried unsuccessfully for five months to capture the town. On 6 May, a British relief force led by Captain Robert Linzee in the frigate *Surprise* arrived off Quebec with a large detachment of marines. The Americans were forced to abandon their invasion of Canada and, in the process, they had 'scuttled and sunk his Majesty's armed vessel the *Gaspee*, which fell into their hands last Winter, but we hope soon to weigh her.' It turned out 'that the Rebels had only cutt two small holes in her bottom, which might easily be Stop't at low Water.' With *Gaspee* once again afloat, Lieutenant George Scott was named to command her. As the year progressed and preparations were made for Burgoyne's invasion of the colonies, Lieutenant Scott and some of his men in *Gaspee* were transferred to Lake Champlain to man the radeau *Thunderer*. *Gaspee* was subsequently sold out of the service.

Rear Admiral John Montagu's three year tour of duty was completed in 1774. Vice Admiral Samuel Graves arrived at Boston on 30 June to replace him. For some time, the situation in the colonies had grown so critical that it was felt necessary for some high ranking officer

to superintend the northern regions while the Commander in Chief of the North Atlantic Station concentrated on the more rebellious colonies. Commodore Molineux Shuldham had been stationed in Newfoundland since 1772 to serve that purpose. Before leaving England, while still at Plymouth, Graves had received instructions from the Admiralty that he should send home the schooners *Hope* and *St Lawrence* at the end of the cruising season. After he had arrived at Boston and had time to assess the situation, he noted that *Hope* would be sorely missed after she went home.

Hope was at Philadelphia covering the Delaware River during the summer. She sailed up to Boston in the fall, arriving there on 7 November. She was in bad condition after ten years of service and needed sheathing before it would be safe to make the voyage across the Atlantic. On 15 December, Graves wrote to the Admiralty that *Hope* had been sheathed though with great difficulty because sheathing board was in short supply. She was not being sent to England but would be retained on the station for the time being. *Hope* sailed for Rhode Island on 25 December. The tender which accompanied her lost touch near shoal water in a snow storm two days later and feared that she had been lost with all hands but *Hope* reappeared at Boston 28 February 1775. She had been blown off the coast in December and forced to make for Bermuda, and having

35

no pilot, she struck a rock on the way in but got off and managed to repair the damage. She left Bermuda on 18 February. Remaining in the Boston area thereafter, *Hope* was finally declared too rotten to salvage. Graves ordered her put out of commission on 14 December 1775. The brig *Sea Nymph*, built at Philadelphia to serve as a packet, had been taken from the Americans; she was renamed *Hope* and manned by Lieutenant George Dawson and the crew from the decommissioned schooner. This left only *Magdalen* and *St John* out of the original six schooners.

Magdalen was quite active in the Delaware River and on the Virginia station. During the summer of 1775 in company with the *Fowey* she remained in the York River to lend support and protection to Governor Dunmore in his contest with the Virginians. Dunmore wanted to send *Magdalen* to England with dispatches but was dissuaded because of her poor condition. That fall she did return to England, was refitted at Portsmouth, and sailed for Boston at the end of September under the command of Lieutenant Joseph Nunn. The summer of 1776 found her in the St Lawrence. She was finally sold out of the service in 1777 at Quebec. During the same period, the *St John* had been stationed in the Bahamas to replace the ailing *St Lawrence*; she was finally condemned in February 1777. A letter from Lieutenant Grant to Admiral Graves later that year advised that the schooner had sunk several times before being condemned. Thus, the last of the original six schooners on the Navy List had disappeared. The schooner class of vessel remained on the List for many more years but without the original 'Marblehead' term of identification.

With the second *St Lawrence* condemned in England in January and *Halifax* lost on the rocks near Machias in February, the Admiralty ordered Admiral Graves to buy two schooners as replacements. On 13 May 1775, Graves advised that 'In obedience to their Lordships Order I have purchased two Schooners, and established them as armed Schooners, One by the name of *St Lawrence*, the other of *Halifax*, meaning by the latter name to continue that of the late *Halifax* lost near Machias. I have given an order to Lieut John Graves to command the *St Lawrence* and Mr John De La Touche I have ordered to command the *Halifax*' [PRO ADM 1/485]. The two new schooners were sent to Halifax for refitting. After seeing some convoy duty from Halifax, the two vessels returned to Boston in Sep-

tember. The *St Lawrence* was sent south to the Bahamas where the *St John* was nearing the end of her usefulness. In 1776, with the British forces concentrating at New York after abandoning their position at Boston, Lieutenant Graves in the *St Lawrence* was ordered north. In September, the third *St Lawrence* was witness to an event which ends this schooner story with a serio-comic touch.

A court-martial was convened on board the *Bristol* at New York on 16 December 1776 to try Lieutenant John Graves and Acting Surgeon Thomas Page Christian of the *St Lawrence* [PRO ADM 1/5307]. The officers serving as judges were: Vice Admiral Lord Shuldham; Captain Hyde Parker; Captain John Raynor; Captain Thomas Symons and Captain Henry Duncan.

The *St Lawrence* had been guarding transports off Staten Island, and was at anchor in Newark Bay. On the evening of 24 September, the surgeon put his dog into the steerage to chase the Lieutenant's cat. The dog bit the cat so severely that it died during the night. Next morning the captain, rather upset, came up carrying his dead cat by the tail. He had some discussion with the surgeon which did not seem to have been very heated. Then the surgeon asked the master for two of the ship's pistols. This request was refused until Lieutenant Graves gave orders that they should be given to him. The Master, Samuel Bignall, tried to pacify Graves, but it was no use. The two officers got into the boat and were rowed ashore to an uninhabited island. After they had landed, the boat was ordered to lay offshore. The Lieutenant but not the surgeon was wearing a sword. The boat's crew heard two shots with about a second between them and were of the opinion that the Lieutenant had fired first. The surgeon then called for aid, and it was found that Graves had been wounded in the arm. They were back on board the *St Lawrence* after an absence of about a quarter of an hour. The Master sent a boat for the surgeons of other ships; but by the time they had arrived, Christian had dressed his Captain's wound. The Master then went to report to the Admiral. The wound was serious enough to make it necessary to relieve Lieutenant Graves of his command. At the trial, neither officer offered any defense. It was the finding of the court that Graves should be dismissed the ship. Christian, who was also found guilty of insulting behaviour to his captain, was dismissed the service and found incapable of serving the King in any capacity.

CHAPTER FOUR

Chaleur-First Schooner in the Navy List

Chaleur may not have been the first of the schooners actually to have been commissioned and serve actively in the Royal Navy, but the Navy List Book definitely does put her first on its list of schooners [PRO ADM 8/40]. This list appeared before any vessels had been purchased; and in fact, before Admiral Colville had even received his instructions to acquire 'six Marblehead schooners.' In addition, six lieutenants had been assigned to command those schooners. In the margin opposite the list of schooners was entered the note: 'Lord Colville is to purchase these vessels, which are to be commanded by the Lieutenants whose names are against each expressed – 4 to be stationed in the River St Lawrence & the other two where his Lordship shall think proper.'

In his book *The History of American Sailing Ships*, Howard Chapelle wrote: 'The *Chaleur* is said to have been an American-built schooner that had been captured from the French by the British frigate *Favorite* on the American coast and condemned at New York. Here she was finally purchased, in 1764, for the Royal Navy'. This information does not fit well with that which can be determined from contemporary documents. It should be recognized that when Chapelle wrote his book in the early 1930s, little or no research had been done on the subject, and he was pioneering in the field. It was natural to assume that a vessel named 'Chaleur' had French antecedents. However as has been pointed out, the names for the first six schooners were selected by the Lords of the Admiralty without any knowledge of the particular vessels which would

bear them. It is easy to surmise how the names were chosen. Initially, the schooners were intended for service in the River and Gulf of St Lawrence to suppress the smuggling of French merchandise from the islands of St Pierre and Miquelon. Their Lordships must have decided to use place names chosen from a map of the region to identify the new schooners. 'Hope' is the only name that does not readily fit this theory: there is a Chaleur Bay; the Gaspe Peninsula was Anglicized to 'Gaspee'; the Magdalen Islands are situated in the middle of the Gulf; and the names 'St John' and 'St Lawrence' were used to identify various towns and bodies of water.

In June 1764 when Colville accounted to the Admiralty for the six vessels he had purchased, he tabulated specific information about each one. He advised that for *Chaleur* he had arbitrarily selected a sloop purchased at Boston. According to his information she was only nine months old. He had authorized payment of £500 0s 0d for her. Her 'tonage as reported by the Owners' was 90. With a 51ft 6in 'Length of Keel for Tonage', he rated her 'King's Tonage' at 116-91/94. Her extreme breadth measured 20ft with a 'Depth in the Hold' of 8ft. Of the six vessels, *Chaleur* and *Gaspee* were listed as 'sloop built' while the other four were classed as schooners. The specifications do not offer any inkling as to the reason for this differentation.

The Muster-Table for *Chaleur* offers some pertinent information. It is headed with the notes: *Chaleur* Sloop Complement 30 Men per Order of the Right Honble the Lord Colville Rear Admiral of the White Dated

37

June 8th 1764. Began Wages 28 December 1763 and Sea Victualling the 11 June 1764 in Halifax Harbour Nova Scotia' [PRO ADM 36/7102]. Wages started on 28 December 1763 for Thomas Laugharne, Commander, Thomas Grant, his servant, and Samuel Barnes, clerk & steward, in England. Two able seamen were added on 2 January. Six more seamen were added to the list in early February. Presumably, this was still in England since the *Juno* did not arrive at New York until 28 March. Three of those six men are noted as having 'run' at New York on 22 April. Lieutenant Laugharne arrived at Halifax on 11 May. Following his arrival, seven more men were enlisted to serve in *Chaleur*. James Frisbee was noted as the Master's Mate; and on 11 June John Pearce was appointed midshipman. By 19 June, *Chaleur* was ready for sea, but her crew was far short of the specified complement of 30 men. In the next few days, 13 seamen were 'Prest' for service on the schooner. John Stewart volunteered and was made Boatswain's Mate, while Joshua Randell became the Gunner's Mate.

Chaleur put to sea on 22 June with Admiral Colville's orders to find seamen for the other schooners. The results of this cruise are best learnt from the report that Lieutenant Laugharne made to Colville on his return to Halifax:

My Lord,
The Fourth of July I arrived at New York with his Majesty's Armed Sloop under my Command and after remaining there a Few Days and having no prospect of answering the Intended Service of raising men agreeable to your Lordships Orders I sailed for Sandy Hook Judging it a more Convenient Place to procure men and after lying there Three days and meeting no Success and being the utmost extent of my Cruize to the Westward I judged it best for the Service to Proceed to the Eastward therefore returning by New York on the Eleventh in the Evening I perceived Five Vessels schooners and Sloops at anchor in a small Bay under Long Island and suspecting they were Carrying on an Illicit Trade I sent the Boat to Examine them with the masters mate at the same time gave him directions if he found them well manned to take what seamen he might reasonably Imagine could be spared without endangering the Navigation and safety of the Vessel and further on no Consideration to Impress but One out of Five Exclusive of the Master, upon the mates return he Informed me he had taken one out of Each Vessel which they very well could spare, we anchored the same Evening in the east river of New York So the ensuing Morning the twelth at seven in the morning I went on shore in the moses Boat on the Sloops service and on my Landing the Mob Immediately Seized the Boat, all my Endeavors was to no Purpose to prevent their getting her out of the Water I asked the first Person who laid hands on the Boat their Reasons for acting in such an unprecedented manner their reply

was that the Evening before there was some Seamen Impressed by our Sloop who they called Fishermen I assured them if they were acording to their Information Fishermen that I would Immediately give them an Order to get them on shore assuring them that it was my most distant thoughts either to Impress Fishermen or out of market Boats that the Persons Impressed never mentioned wether they were Fishermen or not, I sent off a Note by a Person from the Shore upon condition Nothing should happen to his Majesty's Boat but after the men were delivered up at their request the mob drawed the Boat before the City Hall and there Burnt her and it being recommended to me by a Note from Capt O'Brian of his Majesty's Ship *Juno* not to appear Publickly as my Life and people would be in great danger & seeing no Person in Quality of a Magistrate endeavouring to Disperse the Mob I sent to the Mayor of the City, as I was Informed the Lieutenant Governor was not in the City, to acquaint him of the proceedings of the Mob, he with several other civil Officers went to the place where the King's Boat had been Dragged to but before they reached it the Boat was Burned and the Mob dispersed I afterwards gave him Information against three of the ring leaders in this Riot two of which he Caused to be apprehended and agreeable to his desire I sent him the four persons belonging to the *Chaleur* who were with me in the Boat when she was Seized to give Evidence against the Delinquents but he thought proper only to admit the Petty Officer, I delivered the Charge against the Offenders to his Majesty's Attorney General to be put in Execution. I thought it necessary to purchase a Boat for the Heavey Service of the Sloop in Lieu of the One Destroyed by the mob. Judging it not Proper to make use of the Whale Boat only in the Intended service. I have Drawn Bills on the Navy Board for the same amounting to Eleven Pounds Thirteen Shillings and Four Pence Sterling.
I am my Lord
with the Greatest Respect
Your Lordships most Obedient Humble Servent
Thomas Laugharne
Chaleur Halifax
August 11th 1764
[PRO ADM 1/482]

It is interesting to note once again that *Chaleur* was exposed to the wrath of the New York mob at the same time that the *St John* was having difficulties at Newport, Rhode Island. At the time when schooners were first employed in the Royal Navy, these experiences made it quite evident how very vulnerable they were. Being small vessels to start with, they looked just like any number of merchant or fishing schooners on the coast. They could not hope to strike fear into the hearts of rambunctious colonists looking to vent their spleen on the King's representatives. With a maximum of thirty men in the crew, a few small, three pounder cannon, and some swivel guns mounted along the rails, they were fair game for men determined to take their measure. Commanding such a vessel could not have been a very enviable position.

With both *St John* and *Chaleur* returned, Admiral Colville's optimistic hopes were dashed for recruiting seamen not only for the schooners but for the larger ships in his squadron as well. Seaman John Fryer had deserted from *Chaleur* at New York. However, Lieutenant Laugharne had managed to enlist a surgeon's mate named Andrew De Normandie while there. *Chaleur* remained at Halifax for the rest of August preparing to assume the new duties that Admiral Colville was delegating both to her and to *St John*. They were to be stationed in the St Lawrence River, the area that Governor Murray had been most concerned about in his original request for help. This station was far from Colville's post at Halifax. Because the two schooners would be unable to communicate readily with him for extended periods of time, Colville drew up a detailed set of instructions to govern their activities:

Whereas I have appointed his Majesty's [vessel] under your Command to Cruize in the River St Lawrence between Quebec and Anticosti for the effectual prevention of Contraband Trade; you are hereby required and directed forthwith to repair to the said Station where you are to employ yourself diligently in the execution of the following Instructions.

1st

You are to take care to prevent all illegal Trade during your continuing on the said Station, also, so far as it may be in your power, to secure the Fishery and Coasts from Piratical Ships and Vessels, and if there shall be any such you are to use your utmost endeavours to take or destroy them wherever you can meet with them.

2d

His Majesty having by the 5th Article of the Peace concluded at Paris 10 Febry 1763 consented to leave to the Subjects of the most Christian King the liberty of Fishing in the Gulph of S Lawrence upon condition that they do not exercise the said Fishery but at the distance of three Leags from all the Coasts belonging to Great Britain as well those of the Continent as those of the Islands situated in the said Gulph, you are therefore when in the Gulph, to permit the Subjects of his most Christian Majesty quietly and peaceably to enjoy the privilege of Fishing agreeable thereto, and to use your best endeavors to prevent his Majesty's Subjects from giving them any disturbance therein by Acts of Violence or Injustice, or by any evasion contrary to the Spirit and Intention of the said Article, taking care to prevent the French from catching their Fish excepting at the aforementioned distance from the Coasts belonging to Great Britain; you are also very carefully to settle and guard the Fisherys of his

Majesty's Subjects, and to prevent the Subjects of France, from giving them any disturbance by acts of Violence or Injustice, or by any evasion contrary to the Spirit and Intention of the Said Article.

3d

And whereas by the aforementioned Treaty of Peace, Possession of the Islands of St Pierre and Miquelon, on the Coast of Newfoundland, are given up to France, In case any Endeavors shall be used to carry on an illicit Trade from them with any part of his Majesty's Dominions in North America, you are to be particularly attentive to the same and to prevent/if possible/all communication whatever between the said Islands of St Pierre & Miquelon and any part of his Majesty's Dominions within the extent of your Station. – And you will herewith receive the Copy of a Clause of an Act of Parliament to commence the 29th of next month, for your guidance in this Duty.

4th

You are not to land any of your Vessel's Company to any of the Fishing Vessels, neither are you to suffer to be taken onboard her any sort of Fish, either by way of Merchandize, Freight, or otherwise excepting what shall be necessary for the use and spending of the Vessels Company.

5th

When the Season will not permit your continuing longer in the lower parts of the River, you are to repair with his Majesty's Vessel under your Command to Quebec, where you are to lye up for the Winter, applying to the Contractor for Victualling the King's Ships, for such Provisions as you may from time to time be in want of.

6th

Upon your arrival in Quebec you are to communicate these orders to his Excellency the Governour of Canada, and occasionally to consult with him concerning your future operations, taking care to proceed upon the vigorous execution of your Duty as early as possible in the Spring, and to Cruize in such parts of your Station as may be most proper for the prevention of illicit Trade.

7th

Should the Governour at any time, from his Intelligence or acquaintance with the Country, point out a particular Place in the River or Gulph of S Lawrence as suspected of carrying illicit Trade at, you are to pay due regard to his opinion and advice.

8th

You are frequently to send me an account of your proceedings with State and Condition of your Vessels; and you are to continue on the Station hereby assigned you until further orders.
Dated onbd the *Romney* in Halifax
Harbour the 7 August 1764
Colville
[PRO ADM 1/482 pp391-2]

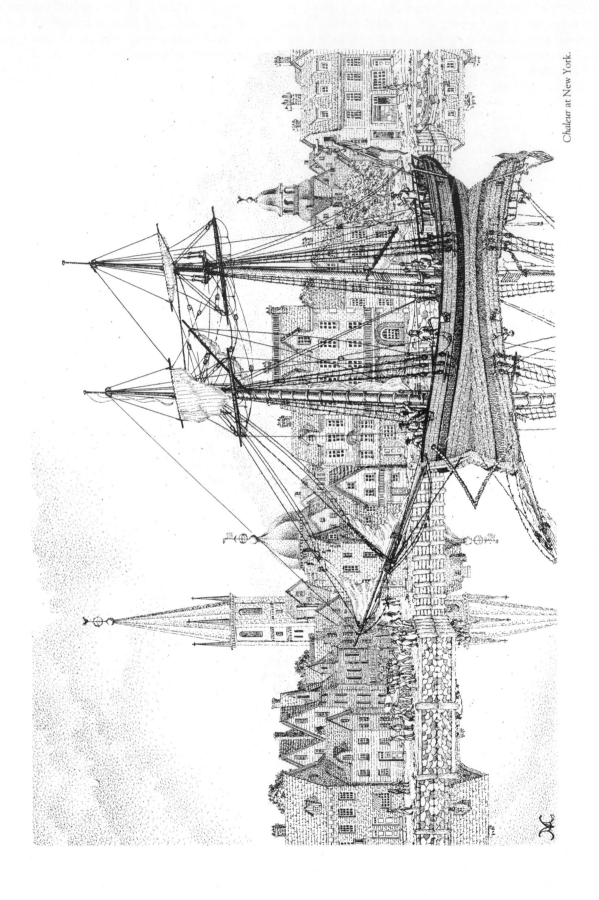

Chaleur at New York.

Chaleur's Muster Book indicates that she remained at Halifax until 29 August. On 7 September, she is noted as being at Gaspee. Then for the rest of that month and most of October, she was on her station in the St Lawrence River. From 29 October until 20 April 1765, *Chaleur* wintered at Quebec. After patrolling her station in the river until November, she once again spent the winter months at Quebec from 18 November until 5 May 1766. During the active season that followed, her location was noted alternately in the river and at Quebec. Finally in August, she was apparently recalled by orders from Admiral Colville who was expecting to be relieved in his command by Durrell. On 7 September, she called at Gaspee; and by 18 September 1766, *Chaleur* was back at Halifax. Durrell had died, and Colville was on his way home leaving Captain Deane in command at Halifax. By October, it was decided that *Chaleur* should be reassigned to the Bahamas Station. She sailed on the 19th after receiving a new mainsail and standing and flying jibs.

Chaleur arrived at Charlestown, South Carolina on 1 November and remained there for a week. After another week and a half on the coast, she sailed for the Bahamas, arriving at New Providence on 27 November 1766. There she remained through the winter months and until May of the following year. The month of March was spent careening and repairing the hull. Second Master George Hay noted in his log on 11 March, that they 'found 60 feet of the false Keele off.' On the following day, he recorded that they had 'found the Bottom full of Worm holes the People employed spilling them up.'

In May 1767, *Chaleur* sailed for Charlestown, arriving on the 19th. She stayed there until 7 June. On 30 May, Lieutenant Laugharne ordered a special observance: 'At 1pm fired 6 three pounders & 7 swivels, it being the anniversary of the Restoration of King Charles the Second.' After a brief sojourn in Rebellion Road, *Chaleur* returned to Charlestown and on 5 June 'Fired 12 three pounders and 9 swivels it being the anniversary of his Majesty's birth.' She then returned to New Providence where she remained from 16 June until 7 July. The period from 7 to 15 July was spent in 'Great Berray Island Harbour'. There Laugharne had 'the Boats employed sounding the Bay which we found to be Shallow and unfit for any vessel drawing above 9 or 11 feet water.' Returning to New Providence they stayed there until 22 December. Much time was spent careening and repairing *Chaleur*. On 16 August, 'Thomas Carbine was accidently shot through the leg owing to the discharge of a musket in a boat while boarding a vessel.'

During the first half of 1768, *Chaleur* joined forces with the sloop *Bonetta* and was almost constantly in her company. Except for a period in March and April when she returned to New Providence, *Chaleur* patrolled along the coast of Northern Florida, Georgia, and South Carolina. In May, the bars at the entrance to the St Johns and Nassau Rivers were sounded. At the Nassau River, they 'Found at low water on the Bar 8 feet at high water 15 & 16 But the passage very narrow.' At the beginning of June while she was at Charlestown, instructions were received for *Chaleur* to return to Halifax. Commodore Hood was becoming seriously involved in the troubles at Boston. He wanted to bring his squadron together to help in handling the difficult situation. *Chaleur* reached Halifax on 18 June 1768 after almost two years on the Bahamas Station.

On 1 July, the master's log notes 'Carpenter empd Converting the Sloop into a Schooner pr order of Commodore Hood.' It soon became obvious that *Chaleur* was in poor condition. The log entry for 19 July reads, 'The Schooner was Survd pr Order of Commodore Hood & the greatest part of the Treenails & plank in her Bottom was found worm eaten & Rotten & was found so bad in Sundry places that they were of Opinion She was not in a Condition to proceede for England with out Being Sheathed etc.' Commodore Hood wrote to Philip Stephens:

Launceston Halifax Harbour Augt 5th 1768
Sir

I am to desire you will be pleased to acquaint my Lords Commisioners of the Admiralty, that on examination into the defects of his Majesty's Armed Schooner the *Chaleur*, they appear too great to be repaired in this yard. Her bottom is entirely destroyed by the worm, and so rotten (being of red oak) that the acting master shipwright reported to me, that it was not safe in his opinion, to send her to sea, without being sheathed and desired I would order a survey upon her, which I did, and have sent the Report to the Navy board; In consequence of it, she has been sheathed & patched up for going to England agreeable to my Instructions from their Lordships. As soon as I came to a resolution of ordering her home, I sent notice of it, to Governor Bernard who was happy in so favourable an opportunity for his Dispatches; which were yesterday brought me. [PRO ADM 1/483 p 122]

The log book entry for 10 August, reads 'Came on Board 9 Soldiers belonging to the 14th regiment of foot & Eight Invalids Belonging to diffnt Ships of the Squadron.' The patched up *Chaleur* sailed for England that day and reached Plymouth on 9 September. She remained at Plymouth for a month. On the 15th, the Navy Board wrote to Philip Stephens:

In answer to your letter of the 13th instant signifying to us the directions of the Rt Honble the Lords Commrs of the Admiralty to propose whether the *Chaleur* Schooner, arrived from Halifax at Plymouth should be repaired at that yard or brought to any other for that purpose; We desire you will propose to their Lordships as the Dock at Plymouth are all engaged that she may be ordered to Woolwich to be repaired. [PRO ADM 106/2199 p127]

Chaleur left Plymouth on 9 October and arrived at Galleons Reach in the River Thames on the 13th. The Lords of the Admiralty ordered 'His Majesty's Schooner the *Chaleur* to be refitted at Woolwich for a voyage to North America' [PRO ADM 2/238 p193]. They gave instructions that her cannon and gunner's stores should be taken on shore at Gallions Reach for temporary storage and returned after the schooner had been made ready for sea. On 16 October, she was moved to Woolwich. On 9 November, the Lords of the Admiralty gave the following instructions to the Navy Board:

Gentn

Whereas you have represented to us, by your Letter of the 4th Instant, that the Officers of Woolwich Yard have acquainted you that from the defects already discovered in His Majesty's Schooner the *Chaleur*, they are of Opinion it will be more for the advantage of the Service to sell, than to repair her; We do therefore hereby desire and direct you to Sollicit the Lords Commissioners of His Majesty's treasury for Money to enable you to pay off the said schooner and to cause her to be paid off at Woolwich as soon as conveniently may be; And when the said Schooner shall be paid off, you are to cause her to be sold and the Money arising from the Sale paid into the Hands of the Treasurer of His Majesty's Navy, taking care she be inserted in the next Privy Seal that shall be obtained for the Sale of Old Stores as usual. [PRO ADM 2/238 p209]

The master's log ends on 19 November, 1768. This marks the end of *Chaleur's* career in the Royal Navy. When *Chaleur* was surveyed at Woolwich, her lines were taken off and a drawing was made in November 1768. (This drawing is identified among the collection of Admiralty Draughts as Regd No 4518/Box 64.) For most of her time in the navy service, *Chaleur* had been called a 'sloop.' If indeed, as the log book entry suggests, she had been somehow altered to conform to schooner design before leaving Halifax for England, then, the Woolwich drawing is a true representation of a colonial schooner. The drawing is well-detailed except for the lack of a stern view. A very important feature on the drawing is the record of dimensions for the masts and spars. Those dimensions furnish a basis for duplicating the naval rig used for other schooners of the same period. Without them, masting and sparring of those vessels would be sheer guesswork.

The schooner *Chaleur* as a physical presence in the Royal Navy had come to an end. However, the reconciliation of the Navy records had to be completed. Since 1763, there had been a regulation that 'Widow's Men' should be carried in the complement of each ship. A Widow's Man was a non-existant person included in the muster book whose wages and victuals were credited to a special fund from which pensions

Chaleur on the stocks. From the Colonial Shipyard diorama.

were paid to the widows of officers. The records reveal a number of instances where schooner commanders were reprimanded for failing to make such entries. The first muster book list for *Chaleur* did include a Widow's Man which appeared to have been added as an afterthought. However, Lieutenant Laugharne had apparently lapsed from this attention to detail and had to answer to the Lords of the Admiralty for it. They requested the Navy Board to investigate the case and received the following reply by way of their secretary Philip Stephens.

Sir   27th Jany 1769

In obedience to the Commands of the Right Honble the Lords Commrs of the Admiralty signifyed to us by your letter of the 24th instant to state the Case and report our Opinion what may be proper to be done on an application from Lieutenant Laugharne, that the omission of his not bearing a Widows Man on the books of the *Chaleur* Schooner may be dispensed with; We desire you will acquaint their Lordships that he has omitted to enter a Widows Man, but one has been inserted in the Muster book of the Schooner on passing his Victualling Account agreeable to their Lordships Order of the 20th Feby 1765, by which means his Complement is over borne, But we are of Opinion if the Lieutenant never received the Order for bearing a Widows Man the failure should be dispensed with, and beg leave to submit to their Lordships whether the same may not in future when any Captain or Lieutenant is under the like circumstances, we return the Letter as desired and are etc.

Philip Stephens   GC JW FM
[PRO ADM 106/2199 p194]

CHAPTER FIVE

Twin Schooners for Jamaica

The North Atlantic Station extended southward to include the Bahama Islands and the east coast of Florida. Beyond that line of demarcation, England held widely spaced possessions from the Sugar Islands in the Lesser Antilles to Honduras in Central America, some 1800 miles to the westward, and north to the even more distant coast of West Florida which reached to the mouth of the Mississippi River. In 1765, there was a Commander in Chief of Naval Forces posted in this area. Correspondence with the Lords of the Admiralty gave as the title of this position 'Commander in Chief etc at & about Jamaica etc.' Jamaica had been seized from the Spanish in the previous century, and Port Royal, on the south coast, had achieved notoriety as the base from which English freebooters, as epitomized by the famous Henry Morgan, preyed on the flow of New World treasures directed to Spain. Port Royal was destroyed by an earthquake in 1692 and eventually replaced by Kingston as the principal port of call on the island.

Sir William Burnaby was Commander in Chief on the Jamaica Station at Kingston in 1765. It can be imagined that maintaining control of the far-flung territories within his jurisdiction was a difficult task. One responsibility entailed charting the coastlines of possessions newly acquired from Spain. A Mr George Gauld had been sent out from England to conduct this work, and Sir William had been instructed by their Lordships to provide whatever assistance might be required. On 21 September, Burnaby wrote a report to the Admiralty in which he related some of the problems he faced and made suggestions which hold great significance in the telling of this story [PRO ADM 1/238]. He advised that 'The Harbors between the Mississippi & the Coast of Florida are only fit for small Vessels.' The sloop of war *Nautilus* had been ordered 'up the River Mississippi as far as the Iberville, 34 Leagues above New Orleans, to assist the Troops at that Post.' Burnaby was upset because it had been necessary for Captain Locker to venture so far up a river of which he had little knowledge. *Nautilus* had gone aground 'over a hundred times.' In order even to enter the mouth of the river, it had been necessary to unload the ship so that she would float clear of the bar and then to reload her stores. *Nautilus* had lost three anchors and their cables as a result of these difficulties. Calling in at Pensacola, Sir William learned that the sloop was in considerable distress and was forced to hire a vessel for £250 0s 0d to carry stores and provisions to her.

This experience led Sir William Burnaby to make some concrete suggestions:

These Considerations have determined me not to send any other Sloops as it is attended with so much expence to the Government and so great a Risk to the Vessels. I would therefore humbly recommend it to their Lordships, as a thing absolutely necessary, to have two Schooners built of 100 Tons each, to carry ten 4 pounders, and to draw 10 feet water for the River Mississippi and the parts adjacent; and two others of a less Construction of 50 Tons and eight 4 pounders, and to draw 8 feet Water, for the Bay of Honduras to survey that Coast between the entrance of the Bay and the Northern Triangles, which is the most dangerous Navigation I ever saw. . . . If their Lordships approve of these Vessels for the Services I have mentioned, I would propose their being built at New York, or New England.

He believed that the schooners could be built much cheaper and more expeditiously in the colonies than in England. The cost of a new schooner would be hardly more than the expense of hiring one to unload a sloop of war so that she might pass over the bar into the Mississippi River.

In a letter dated 16 November 1765, Burnaby reiterated his opinion concerning the need for schooners on the Jamaica Station:

> The *Alarm* is just arrived from Pensacola having finished the Plan of the Bay of Espirito Santo, which I shall send their Lordships by the *Essex*. Mr Gauld who is employed by their Lordships orders to take Plans & Draughts of the Coast of Florida, informs me, he could not have taken the Plan of that Bay in twice the time he did, had it not been for the Assistance of the Schooner, which I was obliged to hire for that purpose; I therefore hope their Lordships are sensible of the necessity of the Vessels being built, which I took the liberty to recommend for that Coast, and the Bay of Honduras, in my letter of the 21st September last by His Majy Ship *Africa*; and hope they will be pleased to give directions accordingly, (as the smallest of our Sloops on many occasions draw too much Water) by which means we shall soon be able to obtain compleat Plans of that Coast, and the Bay of Honduras. [PRO ADM 1/238]

Sir William Burnaby did well to repeat his suggestion that schooners should be built for the Jamaica Station. It was not until the following summer that their Lordships acted upon his recommendations. On 19 August 1766, they addressed instructions to the Navy Board:

> We directed Captain Kennedy of his Majesty's Ship the *Coventry*, which is stationed at New York, to contract for the building two Schooners of the burthen above mentioned, upon the best and cheapest terms for his Majesty, and to get them properly Rigged and equipped in all respects fit for Service, and to draw Bills upon your Board for the costs and charges thereof, taking care to transmit to you proper Bills of Sale and Vouchers for the same; We do hereby desire and direct you upon receiving such Bills of Sale and Vouchers, to accept and pay the Bills that Capt Kennedy may draw upon you for the Costs and charges of building the said Schooners and properly equipping them for Sea. [PRO ADM 2/236 p336]

Captain Arthur Kennedy did not actually take command of the 28 gun *Coventry* at New York until 25 September 1766. On doing so, he discovered that, with the death of Admiral Durrell, he had become the senior Captain 'then Employed in No America.' This signified that for the time being he was responsible as Commander in Chief of the North Atlantic Station.

Along with problems of tending the *Coventry* and supervising the construction of two schooners, this added up to complications greater than he was prepared to cope with. It appears that he gave priority to the two schooners. The Admiralty had decided to proceed with the smaller sized, 50-ton, vessels that Burnaby had requested. Sir William's optimistic hopes for rapid construction and quick delivery of the schooners to Jamaica were not to be realized.

Captain Kennedy reported to Philip Stephens the following spring:

> *Coventry* at New York 26th May 1767
> Sir
> I have received your letter dated the 4th March acquainting me that you had communicated to their Lordships mine of the 16th of January last. Be pleased to acquaint their Lordships that the Schooners are now launched having been detained upwards of three weeks for want of Masts for them, I am now fitting them for the Sea and hope they will sail by this day fortnight and dont doubt but they will be quite agreeable to their Lordships directions. Their Lordships will please to observe from the enclosed State and Condition of the Ships that I have not yet been able to get the *Coventry*'s Complement of Men compleated notwithstanding that I have employed a Vessel down at the Hook to raise Men out of Vessels bound in here, now upwards of two months such difficultys we meet with here in getting Men for His Majesty's Service, however as Ships are daily expected to arrive from Europe and the West Indies hope soon to be able to compleat the Complement, I am
> Sir
> Your most Obedient
> humble Servant
> Arth Kennedy
>
> To Philip Stephens Esqre
> [PRO ADM 1/2012]

Then on 6 July, Kennedy sent the bill for the schooners to the Navy Board. He had drawn upon the Board a set of Bills of Exchange at Thirty days sight payable to Henry White Esq [PRO ADM 106/1156]. The total came to £1386 10s 0d. In a postscript to this letter, he added the note 'I hope Admiral Parry will give the Character which are justly due these two Vessls being by every bodys Opinion that has seen them the Compleatest things that have ever been built here.' Kennedy made his final report on the schooners to Philip Stephens in August:

> *Coventry* at New York 24 Augt 1767
> Sir
> I have received your Letter dated the 11th June last acknowledging the receipt of mine of the 6 April. Please to acquaint Their Lordships that Commodr

Hood arrived at Halifax the 6th Ulto since which I have received His orders for puting myself under his Command etc. The two Schooners built here agreeable to Their Lordships directions sailed hence for Jamaica the 12 Ulto having been detained so long for want of Masts there being no Spars to be got fit for that use, they are reckoned to be two of the compleatest Vessels of the kind ever built and I hope they will give intire satisfaction for the purpose they are intended. Herewith is enclosed *a plan of their Hulls* and the State & Condition of his Majesty's Ship *Coventry* under my Command I am
Sir
Your most Obedient
Humble Servant
Arth Kennedy

Philip Stephens Esqr
[PRO ADM 1/2012]

On the margin of this letter is a note added at a later date in reference to the schooner hull plan. It reads, 'delivered to Sir Thos Slade to be copied – 31, Mar 1768'. Drawing Regd No 4520, Box 64 in the collec-

tion of Admiralty Draughts preserved by the National Maritime Museum is most likely the copy that was made from the plan Captain Kennedy sent to the Lords of the Admiralty. The drawing is the least complete of the schooner plans with which this book is concerned. The only identification on it is the sentence 'Marble Head Scooner Built at New York in July 1767.' It is quite evident that this drawing puzzled Howard Chapelle when he reconstructed the schooner design for his book *The History of American Sailing Ships.* With no historical background available on the subject, he decided that 'Marble Head' as it appeared on the drawing was the name of the schooner. It was only in later years that Chapelle was able to identify the plan with the two schooners named *Sir Edward Hawke* and *Earl of Egmont.*

On 10 December 1767, Captain Kennedy sailed for England in the *Coventry.* He ran into a snag when he offered his journal of the ship for certification and passing of his accounts by the Admiralty. The captain of a ship was expected to put to sea and cruise on his appointed station periodically. *Coventry* had not been to sea from the time Kennedy took command in September 1766 until he sailed for home. On 30 April

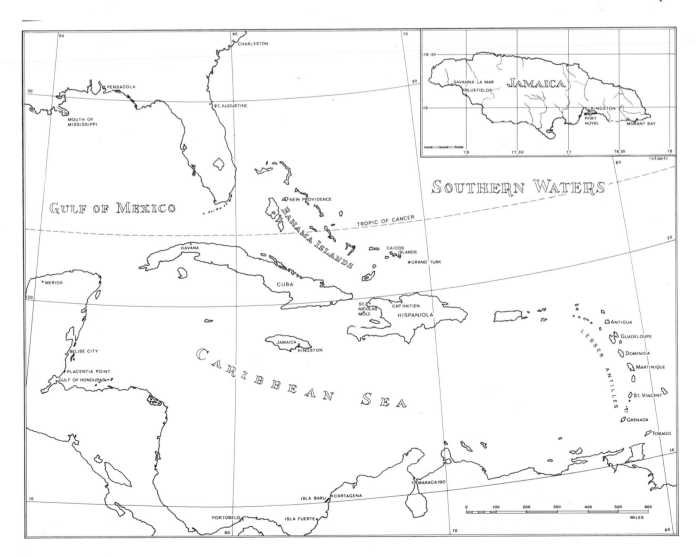

1768, Captain Kennedy wrote a letter while in London to explain this dereliction from duty and ask for consideration. His position had been very difficult with responsibilities as Commander in Chief keeping him in port and aggravated by the necessity of completing and manning the two schooners for Jamaica '– which was done wholly by the *Coventry*'s people & when they sailed, being manned intirely from the *Coventry*'s Complement agreeable to Their Lordsps Orders, there went in them the First Lieutenants, the Gunner, one of the Masters Mates, three of the (four) Midshipmen, & a number of the best of the Seamen; all of them Old hands, men who had come out of England in the Ship, as I could not trust the new raised Men in them.' [PRO ADM 1/2012]. When he received orders to return to England, his men had not yet returned from Jamaica, and he found it necessary to replace them before he could sail.

Sir William Burnaby did not remain on the Jamaica Station long enough to see the fulfillment of his request for schooners. He was replaced in the command by Admiral Parry early in 1767. In a letter dated 21 March, the Admiral noted some of the efforts made to provide small vessels to assist George Gauld in his surveying projects. 'The Vessel that had been purchased by Captain Carkett at Pensacola in consequence of Sir William Burnaby's Directions for that purpose, turned out so extremely crazey & rotten; that after repeated attempts they were obliged to run for the Harbour to save their Lives' [PRO ADM 1/238]. Some survey work was continued with the use of the sloop *Ferret* but attended by considerable difficulty. In an attempt to alleviate the situation, Parry 'therefore, as the Summer season was advancing, came to a resolution of purchasing a large Deal Cutter, thirty five feet in length, and eight in breadth – almost new; she sails & rows extremely well, and is well fitted in every respect, with Oars, Masts, Sails, etc., which I am told, by those who have been on that Coast, will answer very well in fine Weather, and will keep Mr Gauld employed 'till I can send him down a proper Vessel; which I shall be able to do, when the Schooners arrive here from New York.'

On 20 November 1767, Admiral Parry reported:

> On the first of September arrived here the two Armed Schooners built at New York, under the direction of Captain Kennedy; they had only one suit of Sails each, and were greatly in want of additional Stores before they could possibly proceed to sea – I ordered the Storekeeper to take an Inventory of their apparel, and Furniture, on board each, and give a receipt for them to the Officers whom Captain Kennedy had appointed to Navigate them hither – The Master Shipwright having examined them agreeable to my directions, reports them to be two very fine compleat Vessels of about seventy two Tons burthen, or upwards, drawing ten feet water, being two feet more than the original

plan specified – they must both soon be sheathed – I ordered them to be furnished with those Stores only as were absolutely wanted; – and as their Lordships directed that they were to be Officered & manned from the King's Ships, I complied strictly therewith, except with that of appointing a Lieutenant to each, which appears to me to be a very essential order and beg leave to point a few reasons why I have made an appointment; – One of these Vessels distinguished by the name of *Earl of Egmont*, to whom I have appointed Mr John Botham Her Lieutenant, and Commander, is gone down to the Bay of Honduras to establish regularity and enforce military discipline amongst the Baymen, who are a set of turbulent fellows, and who are in a state of anarchy and confusion in the absence of a man of war; – as this service must be managed with great prudence and circumspection, for the King's Officer must be obliged to hear and determine all disputes that are perpetually arising amongst them, and, not only that, but under the necessity of corresponding with the Governour of Merida, and the Commandant of Baccalan; for the Spaniards frequently exert their power beyond the limits of the late Treaty of Peace, and the Officer of a Vessel of War being on the spot is ready to support the British Subjects in this considerable branch of commerce, for upwards of one hundred and eighty sail of Merchant Ships and Vessels load from thence yearly.

The other armed Schooner which I have named the *Sir Edward Hawke* and appointed Mr William Moulden Her Lieutenant and Commander, sailed sometime since for Pensacola to be employed in assisting Mr George Gauld in the completion of the Survey carried on by him on the Coasts of Florida; – and as these Vessels are employed on such remote Services that I could not expect seeing them above once in six months, and as the *Preston*'s books must have been confused by having seldom an opportunity to regulate and settle them, – I therefore, to prevent such confusion, gave orders to the *Preston* to lend such men and Checque them on her Books as lent to the Schooners, and to the Officers of each to take up the Provisions allowed for their respective Complements of Men, keeping a strict account thereof, and sending them to the Navy and victualling in order that each may be enabled to pass their accounts, with each Board respectively. [PRO ADM 1/238]

Admiral Parry went on to point out that by this procedure he was limiting the expense of manning the two new schooners to the cost of the two Lieutenants and their servants. He had received no specific instructions to guide him in this matter and hoped that their Lordships would approve of his actions. At the time that Admiral Parry gave names to the two schooners from New York, both Sir Edward Hawke and the Earl of Egmont were members of the Admiralty Board. It is to be wondered if they were flattered to have their

Sir Edward Hawke. From the Colonial Shipyard diorama.

names used in this way. The absence of positive instructions regarding the new vessels continued for some time. Finally, the Lords of the Admiralty ordered the Navy Board on 25 May 1769 'Whereas we think proper that the two Schooners which were built at New York by our Orders under the direction of Capt Kennedy, and which are now employed at Jamaica under the Command of Rear Admiral Parry, shall be registered on the list of the Navy by the names of the *Earl of Egmont,* and *Sir Edward Hawke;* we do hereby desire and direct you to cause them to be registered on the List of the Navy by those names accordingly, and to cause them to be established with a complement of Thirty Men each, agreeable to the scheme on the other side hereof' [PRO ADM 2/238 p422]. The 'scheme' mentioned duplicated the complements adopted for the original six schooners that had been purchased for service on the North Atlantic Station.

Lieutenant Botham in the *Earl of Egmont* remained at Port Royal across the harbor from Kingston from 13 September, until 23 November 1767 while the Schooner was being manned and provisioned as Admiral Parry deemed necessary. On 23 November, she set sail for the Gulf of Honduras on her first cruise. During this cruise, Lieutenant Botham familiarized himself with such anchorages as Truxilla Bay, St Georges Cay, and Placentia Point along the coast of British Honduras or Belize as it was known at that time. British log cutters had arrived in the area as early as 1636 and were followed by more permanent settlers, although the Spaniards had tried unsuccessfully to drive them out. With the Treaty of Paris, they had

achieved some degree of recognition and promise of protection from the homeland. *Earl of Egmont* returned to Port Royal from this initial cruise on 22 February 1768.

Leaving Jamaica on 12 April, Botham sailed for the Gulf of Honduras a second time. On this cruise, he spent some time surveying around Banaqua and called in at St Georges Cay. After returning to Port Royal in July, *Earl of Egmont* cruised that fall to Forti Island and then on south to call at Porto Bello on the Isthmus of Panama. The winter months were spent at Port Royal until 7 February 1769 when the schooner sailed northeast through the Windward Passage to visit Turks and Caicos Islands at the easternmost reaches of the Bahamas. While returning to Port Royal, she stopped in at St Nicholas Mole on Hispanola. That spring, *Earl of Egmont* cruised around Jamaica. She landed the governor, Sir William Trelawney, at various places, saluting him with seventeen guns on each occasion. In the summer months, she once again sailed to the Bahamas, stopping at Cap Francois where the Commandant paid an official call. By September, she was back at Port Royal.

On 27 September while sailing to Savanna la Mar near the western end of Jamaica, Lieutenant Botham ran into some trouble which can best be described by means of the log book entries:

27 Sept 1769.

Light breezes and Cloudy, latter p[ar]t fresh breezes and Cloudy. 6 AM weighed and came to sail, worked out of the road. Empd turning up to Blewfields Bay 11 AM the Tavern at Blewfields NEbE. the breeze freshening took the T[op] sails in. The Forem[as]t went away 4 feet below the Hounds, & carried the M[ain]- topmast away 3 Feet from the Heel; got the rack in, Bore up for Savannah Le Mar at Noon standing into Ship Channel.

28 Sept 1769

do wr ½ pt came too in Savannah Le Mar road wth the S[mal]l B[owe]r in 3 fms water Veer'd to 1/3 of a Cable, the fort WNW Blewfields pt SEBE the Wtmost pt W½S Emp unriggᵈ and clearing the Rack of the Foremt & got it down upon Deck, AM the Carpenters empᵈ cutting new Hounds on the Stump of the Foremast Seamen empᵈ clearing the rigging and reefing the Foreshrouds got the F:topmast up for a M:topmt and rigged it, took the Bonnets off the Jibb, and foresl and SquareSl Reefed the flying Jibb, & Forestaysl to fit them to the hoist of the Jury foremast.

29 Sept 1769

First pt Squally wh heavy Rain Thunder and Lightening remainder light Winds and fair. PM Empᵈ reefing and Seizing the Forerigging 5 do got the Foremt in the Carpenter having cut new Hounds on it AM rigged the foremt and bent the Foresl and fore stays sent a Craft to Blewfields for Water.

30 Sept 1769.

Light winds and fair Wr PM Empᵈ Reeving the Rigging setting the lower Rigging up, and Ratling the Fore shrouds got the broken M:topmt for a F:topmt Punished Jno Farrier wh 12 lashes for contempt to his Officer AM Rec: our Water on bd Empᵈ Reeving & refitting the running rigging. [PRO ADM 51/4178]

This richly detailed description offers much information about the masting and rigging of a navy schooner. With the *Earl of Egmont* back at Port Royal by 5 October, new masts were fitted. It was found that the main boom was sprung.

Except for one cruise to Hispanola and the Bahamas in the spring of 1770, *Earl of Egmont* remained close to home for the next year and a half. Then from May of 1771 until November, she shuttled back and forth between St George's Cay in the Gulf of Honduras and Pensacola to the north. On 8 July 1771, Lieutenant Botham wrote a long report to Commodore Mackenzie from St George's Cay. This letter offers a fascinating account of the problems encountered in that area.

When Botham arrived at St George's Cay on 14 May, he was asked by the settlers to demand the return of 'the Slaves, who had run or been taken from their Settlements, & were in the Possession of the Govr of the Spanish Province of Jucatan. Agreeable to your orders I have attempted to redress this Grievance by demanding a Restitution of their Property, the loss of which has incapacitated many of them from following their Occupation' [PRO ADM C05/119]. Another complaint that the Lieutenant received was that the Spanish Governor was restricting the logwood works to the Honda, New, and Balise Rivers where trees for

logging operations had become scarce. When the inhabitants wanted to move 'to other parts of the Bay, which from having been unfrequented will yield Wood in greater plenty,' they had been 'molested by the Spaniards from Baccalar, and with the Loss of Property driven from their new Settlements.'

The Spanish Governor of Merida had written to the British asking 'them to return some Spanish Indians who had left his Province during the time of a Famine Occasioned by vast swarms of Locusts which destroyed all their Grain, & by which 40,000 Indians were starved to death.' This put Botham in an ambiguous situation since at the same time that he was demanding the return of slaves to the British settlers, he had to make a refusal to return the Indians sound reasonable. These negotiations were complicated by the fact that the Spanish Governor claimed an inabilty to translate the English communications. Botham believed this to be just a subterfuge but was unable to have his messages framed in Spanish because 'the only Person who could write Spanish, & used to negotiate all Business with their Province is dead.' Furthermore, the Lieutenant anticipated that even if he could get the Spanish to agree to his demands and 'promise Satisfaction for the Injury to amuse me, when I am gone the Person aggrieved will not receive the least Reparation.' In short, policing of this remote corner of the Empire was a practical impossibility under the circumstances.

The British subjects in Honduras were hardly ideal citizens. Botham felt that 'altho there are several of the most substancial People here, who are well disposed & wish for a power to preserve order among them, nevertheless the licentious & ungovernable Disposition of those whose Inclination is to live unconfronted (that they may commit all excesse with impunity) has ever prevailed hitherto.' He tried to convince the better citizens that by standing together they could 'subdue these Turbulent Spirits, but that they never can effect, for the continual Animosities subsisting between Individuals will ever pervert the Happiness & Welfare of the whole.'

Who would care to have been in Lieutenant Botham's shoes? Commander of a small, lightly armed schooner with a complement of just thirty men, he was charged with the reponsibility of bringing order to a lawless country surrounded by hostile Spaniards. Two of his own men stole a canoe with some equipment and deserted to Spanish territory where he was unable to retrieve them. He learned of four Englishmen in chains on board a Spanish *guarda costa* but was unable to help them. He noted that trade on the coast as indicated by ship arrivals had fallen off drastically although large quantities of high quality Logwood and Mahogany were on hand.

Earl of Egmont returned to Port Royal on 2 November 1771. Thereafter, she remained in the general vicinity of Jamaica until orders were received the following summer that she should sail for England.

Twin schooners for Jamaica: the *Earl of Egmont* and *Sir Edward Hawke.*

The twin schooners from New York, newly named *Earl of Egmont* and *Sir Edward Hawke*, remained together at Port Royal until November 1767. Admiral Parry advised their Lordships in the letter of 20 November that he had placed Lieutenant William Moulden in command of *Sir Edward Hawke*. Moulden replaced Charles Warburton who had originally been given the command on 23 October. The schooners finally separated when *Sir Edward Hawke* sailed on 14 November to start her own independent career. Sailing westward along the south coast of Jamaica, she turned in at the Black River where on the 19th Lieutenant Moulden 'found the water stinking sour and not fitt to drink therefore started it.' After a couple of days at Bluefields Bay, *Sir Edward Hawke* left Jamaica on the 22nd. She arrived at Pensacola on 7 December.

Most of the schooner's movements and activities have been gleaned from her log books which are still preserved in the London Public Records Office [PRO ADM 51/4342 (8,9,10,11,12)]. *Sir Edward Hawke* remained 'Moor'd in Pensacola Harbour' waiting for some kind of assignment during the rest of December, through January, and most of February in 1768. On the first of the year, she 'fired 3 Shot at a Sloop for hoisting improper Colours.' There was no indication that this might have been some kind of New Year's celebration. Most of the entries indicate that Lieutenant Moulden and his crew were simply marking time. On 8 February Moulden 'sent six Men with Hawsers and Grapnels to assist a Sloop that was on shore' and then 'hove overboard 200lb bread that was condemned pr survey.' The following day, there was a 'violent Squall with Thunder, Lightning & Rain.' They 'found several Vessels overset'. The schooner's boats were 'empd righting the Governors Schooner and a small Sloop'.

On 24 February, *Sir Edward Hawke* sailed to begin her work of assisting George Gauld with his survey. That spring while returning to Pensacola periodically, the schooner was positioned variously at the Pelican Islands, Hawkes Bay, and in the Mobile River. Her boats were often away with Gauld for days at a time. In June while at Pensacola, Lieutenant Moulden decided it was time to recondition his schooner. On the 8th, he sailed across the bay to Deer Point in company with the sloop of war *Druid*. There, *Sir Edward Hawke* was lashed alongside *Druid* while they 'got the guns out' and cleared 'the Schooner for heaving down.' On the 10th, '*Druid*'s Carpenters Empd Caulking the Deck.' Then on the 12th, they 'unrigg'd the lower Masts had a Survey on the Main mast which was condemned.' The men worked for several days cutting a new main mast only to find that it was 'rotten at the heart', and they had to start on another. Finally, a new main mast was installed on the 22nd and they were able to heave the schooner down for inspection of the hull. This problem with the main mast calls to mind the difficulty that Captain Kennedy reported in securing suitable spar material and the mishap which befall the *Earl of Egmont* the following year when her foremast broke off below the hounds.

Sir Edward Hawke continued to assist with the survey work for the rest of 1768. In July, she was at Ship Island and moving about as necessary. At the end of September, she went aground several times off Catt Island. She returned to Pensacola for a month and a half. Then from 3 December to 24 February 1769, the schooner was moored to the shore off English Point. During that period, the crew was occupied in cutting down trees to build a wharf. On 27 February, *Sir Edward Hawke* sailed with a convoy to Pedro Island where she remained until the end of March. She returned to Pensacola on 15 April, 1769.

At this point, there is a great void in the records until the thread of the story is picked up once more in the master's log on 10 September 1770 [PRO ADM 52/1783 (1)]. During that month *Sir Edward Hawke* was at sea in company with *Phoenix* according to the master, Benjamin Hickey. Whatever had happened in the meantime, it is evident that the schooner was no longer involved with the survey project. From 6 to 9 October, she was at Grand Turk Island in the Bahamas. There had been disciplinary problems. On the 3rd, Edward Morris was given 12 lashes for disrespect to an officer. John Bennet received 12 lashes for theft on the 4th. By 29 October, 1770, *Sir Edward Hawke* returned to Port Royal where she remained until 12 December. It would appear that she was a troubled schooner. On the 12th, Lieutenant Mason took command, and a lieutenant, midshipman, and 19 seamen were brought on board from the *Dunkirk*. After cruising the coast of Jamaica for four days, the midshipman and seamen were returned to the *Dunkirk*. The schooner then remained at Port Royal until March 1771.

On 11 March, Lieutenant Anthony Gibbes took command of *Sir Edward Hawke*. From 28 May to 17 June the schooner cruised in the vicinity of Jamaica, returning to Port Royal. Then in July, she was selected for a special 'cloak and dagger' mission. The account of this mission is based on information derived from three sources: the captain's log, a court-martial return, and correspondence between the Admiralty and the Secretary of State [PRO ADM 51/4342; PRO ADM 1/5305; PRO CO 5/119]. On 3 July, while *Sir Edward Hawke* was lying at Port Royal, Lieutenant Anthony Gibbes received orders to sail her to Grand Baru in the Rosario Islands. This is near Cartagena off the coast of South America. Gibbes was instructed to house the schooner's guns and make her appear as much as possible like a merchant vessel. Arriving at night or in the very early morning, he was to land a seaman belonging to the *Dunkirk* who knew the place. With the greatest secrecy, the seaman was to deliver a letter to the brothers Pachecos whom he knew by sight, having seen one of them when he came aboard the *Earl of Egmont* on a previous occasion. After the letter was delivered, *Sir Edward Hawke* was to put to sea and cruise off the place eight days; she was then to return to Grand Baru and pick up the answer to the letter in the same circumspect manner. This answer was to be addressed to Captain Hay of the *Carysfort*. The schooner was to carry the message to the Isle of Forte (Isla Fuerte) which lay about 90 miles southwest of Cartagena, where Captain Hay would be waiting with his ship. Lieutenant Gibbes was ordered: 'you are to keep a proper guard and look out that His Majestys Vessel may not run into any kind of Danger, or his Majestys Colours suffer any disgrace from the insults of Guarda Costas by surprize or otherwise.'

These well laid out plans went sadly awry in their execution. On 6 July, a midshipman and eight men from the *Dunkirk* came aboard and *Sir Edward Hawke* put to sea. On the 16th, land was sighted. By this time, they had tried to disguise the schooner by getting down the topsail and crossjack yards, striking the topmasts and housing the guns. On the 18th, they were close in shore, but very uncertain of their position. 'The man from the *Dunkirk* believed to be Isle Rosario, at 3 PM find the entrance shut up by a Reef that breaks all across the Supposed entrance. Put about in 11 fms Water, as we stand out this man believed he sees Rosario.'

Wandering along the coast on the 23rd, they thought that they recognized the neighborhood of Cartagena, but the appearance of the high land did not look right. When a sail was sighted, they tried to close to ask their position. However because of the schooner's reduced sail area she was unable to overtake the vessel. On the following day, they were able to close a *guarda costa* to which they sent a boat to learn their position. They were treated with courtesy, and the Spanish captain advised that Cartagena was twenty leagues to leeward. He suggested that if *Sir Edward Hawke* would accompany him to Boca Chica he would assist her to get wood and water. Gibbes apparently did not realize it at the time but the captain of the *guarda costa*, *La Pastora*, was suspicious and wanted to keep the schooner under surveillance. The two vessels set sail for Boca Chica, but the faster Spanish vessel was soon out of sight.

Sir Edward Hawke sighted Cartagena on the following day, but Gibbes was afraid to enter the harbor without a pilot. Knowing where they were finally, they sailed to Rosario Island where they anchored on the 28th. A canoe came out with a letter; apparently the occupants were recognized, and Gibbes turned over the letter that he had brought. The schooner was supplied with wood and water. On the 29th, they sailed for Jamaica, strangely forgetting the rendezvous with the *Carysfort*.

In the meantime when *Sir Edward Hawke* failed to appear at Boca Chica, the captain of *La Pastora* reported the affair to his superiors. He was convinced that the schooner was a smuggler, and reported that she was laden with bale and other goods. Two other *guarda costas* were sent after *Sir Edward Hawke*. They overtook her more than 12 leagues from the coast and out of sight of land. There on the high seas, they had no right to detain and search the schooner. They came close within hail and demanded to know what Gibbes was doing there. Dropping the pretences of disguise, he hoisted his colors and identified his vessel as a British

A trading schooner moored alongside a wharf. From the Colonial Shipyard diorama.

man-of-war. The Spaniards refused to accept this identification, and ordered him to send a boat or they would fire on him. The Spanish sloops mounted twenty guns each; nevertheless, Gibbes started to prepare for action, but was dissuaded by the master, John Hardcastle. Hardcastle went over to the nearest *guarda costa* where he was treated with indignities and sent back with orders that *Sir Edward Hawke* should accompany the sloops into Cartagena.

The three vessels arrived at Cartagena on 1 August. *Sir Edward Hawke* and her crew were not molested there and were allowed to wood and water. On the 15th, the *Carysfort* arrived in search of them. The Spaniards told Gibbes he could leave, but threatened to impose penalties if he ever dared to come within twelve leagues of their coast again. He sailed on 7 August and reached Jamaica on the 17th. On his arrival, Lieutenant Gibbes was put under arrest by orders of Sir George Rodney. On the 26th, he was tried by court-martial for having permitted such insult to the English flag. He was found guilty and dismissed the service.

Rodney sent two ships to Cartagena to present protests to the authorities. These protests came to naught with the various authorities prevaricating, claiming they knew nothing of the incident, or had no jurisdiction in the affair. Nothing could be done to bring the *guarda costas* to account and Gibbes was left to shoulder the blame. Rodney reported all this to the Lords of the Admiralty with great indignation which was recorded in the Admiralty Board Minutes for Friday 1 November 1771:

> A Letter was read from Sir George Rodney, Commander in Chief at Jamaica, giving account of an Insult offer'd by the Spaniards to the *Sir Edward Hawke* Schooner, and of the Steps taken in consequence thereof; and the Earl of Sandwich communicated to the Board, a Letter he had received from Sir George on the same subject; Resolved that copies of both be sent to the Earl of Hillsborough, for His Majesty's information. [PRO ADM 3/79]

A new log book was started on 27 August. It was signed by Lieutenant John Cowling who replace Gibbes as commander of *Sir Edward Hawke*. On 1 October, John Stevens replaced Hardcastle as master. For the rest of that month they cruised in the vicinity of Jamaica. Then the schooner extended her range and the period from 17 to 29 December found her at the Dutch possession of Curaçoa. On arrival there, she had gone ashore but hove off satisfactorily. Back at Kingston in January, David Atkinson joined as master; from then until June 1772, she cruised around Jamaica with lengthy layovers at Port Morant, Savanna la Mar, and

Port Royal. On 10 June, Richard Trotten took command and *Sir Edward Hawke* was careened for inspection and repair at Port Royal.

The Admiralty Board Minutes for Saturday 7 March 1772 had recorded:

> Resolved that Orders be sent to Sir George Rodney, Commander in Chief at Jamaica, to send home the *Earl of Egmont* & *Sir Edward Hawke* Schooners, if they are fit to proceed the voyage, else to put them out of Commission abroad. [PRO AM 3/79]

Sir Edward Hawke sailed for England on 6 July. The *Earl of Egmont* followed on the 22nd. They arrived at Portsmouth in September, two weeks apart. Thus the two schooners were reunited at the conclusion of their careers in the Royal Navy.

On 13 September, 1772, the Navy Commissioner at Portsmouth wrote to the Navy Board:

> I have received your Letters, of the 11th instant; And as desired by one, will write to the Commanders of the *Sir Edward Hawke* Schooner and of the *Earl of Egmont* Schooner on her arrival at this port, forthwith to prepare and send me, a Complete Set of Pay Books & ca when they have so done, and their prepared Muster Books are sent down to examine them by, I will forthwith pay them off. [National Maritime Museum POR/F15]

Sir Edward Hawke was paid off on the 22nd, and the *Earl of Egmont* which arrived on the 20th was paid off on 6 October. On 16 October the two schooners were taken into the South Dock at Portsmouth where they remained for a month. Then, they were moved into a holding area for an extended period.

On 26 July 1773, the Portsmouth Dockyard Officers reported on a survey that had been made of the two schooners. They advised that a 'Midling' repair with an estimated cost of £200 0s 0d apiece would be required to restore them. The Navy Board Minutes for the following day noted that the master shipwright and his assistants at Portsmouth had recommended that *Sir Edward Hawke* and the *Earl of Egmont* should be sold out of the service. The Lords of the Admiralty then gave orders to that effect on 30 July with instructions for 'the Officers of each yard to send us an Inventory of their Furniture & Stores (except the Schooners Sails & Anchors if small anchors are wanting) with the Value thereof, & of their Hulls'[PRO ADM 106/2589]. On Wednesday 11 August 1773, *Sir Edward Hawke* was sold to Samuel Holmes for £60 0s 0d, and the *Earl of Egmont* went to William Woolcombe for the same amount.

CHAPTER SIX

Sultana
the Smallest of Them All

The schooner *Sultana* has become popular in model building circles as a very attractive subject. Howard Chapelle produced a set of plans for model builders which has been used in conjunction with a detailed wood hull kit. Unfortunately, no one took the time to research the history of the schooner and publish the findings which would have forestalled a number of errors which have since been perpetuated. *Sultana* makes a lovely authentic model, but she should be recognized for what she was. At 52^{68}/₉₄ tons burthen, she seems to have been the smallest schooner ever entered on the Navy List. The smallest of the original six schooners purchased for the Navy, rated at 90³/₉₄ tons, was the *Magdalen. Sultana* was the only one of the Navy schooners investigated for this book which was not deemed large enough to mount carriage guns; her armament consisted solely of 8 swivel guns mounted along the rails, and the many models that have been built with cannon on the deck are, unfortunately, incorrect.

The first mention of *Sultana* in the Admiralty records appears to be a letter directed to the Navy Board from the Lords of the Admiralty.

Gentn   12 Feb 1768
    Sir Thomas Hesketh having made a Tender to us of a North American Schooner of sixty five tons which he thinks exceedingly well adapted for the Service of Cruizing against the Smugglers, We do hereby desire and direct you upon arrival of the said Vessel in the River, to cause her to be surveyed, and to report to Us whether she is fit to be purchased for the Service abovementioned. We are &c
Navy Board   Hawke   C Townshend   J Buller
[PRO ADM 2/237 p425]

This order caused the schooner to be brought into the dock at the Deptford Yard for a survey. The results of this inspection are to be found in the Deptford Yard Letter Book:

Honble Sirs,   Deptford Yard 2d March 1768
    In pursuance of your Warrant of the 27th past, We have taken a Careful Survey of the *Sultana* Schooner in Mr Randall's Dock, tender'd by Sir Thomas Hasketh to the Right Honble the Lords Commissrs of the Admiralty, and send you an account of her Qualities Condition and Dimensions, with our Opinion of the Value of her Hull Furniture & such Stores as may be proper to purchase with her, and have taken off her body, which Draught Accompanys this.
    Has the Character of being a good Sailor, Single Bottom, Built at Boston in New England Six Months ago, Appears well wrot & put together, the Beams are Double Kneed with lodging Knees and requires some additional Bolts; Rother wants Repairing & Bottom to be Caulk'd wants other small works to be done; has no Swivel Stocks for Guns.
    Her Dimensions are as follows Vizt

	ft	in
Length on the Range of the Upper Deck from the aft side of the Rabbit of the Stem to the Fore side of the Rabbit of the post	50	4½
Length of the Keel for Tunnage	38	5⅛
Breadth Extream	16	0¾
Depth in hold	8	4
Burthen in Tuns 52⁶⁸/₉₄		
Depth in the Waste	1	0½
Rise of the Fore part of the Quarter Deck	1	8
D° after rise	0	3
Length of the Quarter Deck	22	11
Rise of the Fore Castle	1	2
Length of D°	10	3
Length of the Great Cabin afore	7	9
Steerage	7	9
Height of the Great Cabbin afore	6	0
abaft	6	0

Breast Hooks under the Deck 3 No Sided 7in, and 7 bolts each.

Upper Deck Beams Sided 10in and Moulded 7 in, Kneed with two Lodging Knees each sided 6in & 4 Bolts each.

Quarter Deck Beams 4in Square & Kneed with one Lodging Knee each with 3 bolts.

Forecastle Beams Sided 7in and Moulded 6 ins and Knee'd with Two Lodging Knees each, & sided 6in Floor Timbers Sided 9 ins.

SULTANA	Hull			Mast Booms Gaff &c			Total		
	£	s	d	£	s	d	£	s	d
Value of the Mast &c Hull	237	5	0	24	16	6	262	1	6
Furniture & Stores as per Inventory							30	7	6
							292	9	0

And in our humble opinion she is a proper Vessel, fit to purchase for his Majestys Service,
We are

honble Navy Board   Honble Sirs Your &c
[PRO ADM 106/3315]   EC AH WP

The inventory of stores included just four sails which gives a clue regarding the original masting and sparring of the schooner. There were two 'Studing Jib' sails, a 'Fore sail' and a 'Main sail.' Among other items listed, there were two 'Hencoops' valued at 12s, a 'Sounding Rod' at 1s, and three 'Hatch Bars' worth 10s 6d.

On 8 March, the Lords of the Admiralty gave orders to the Navy Board that Sultana should be bought for the Royal Navy. They asked for recommendations regarding the 'number and nature of Guns and Complement of Men it may be proper to establish on her' [PRO ADM 2/237 pp494-5]. On 3 May 1768, the Navy Board advised that the schooner had been purchased. They suggested a complement of twenty-four men, and an armament of eight swivel guns [PRO ADM 106/2199 p40]. On the following day, their

Lordships acknowledged this communication. They ordered that the new schooner should be registered on the list of the Royal Navy by the name of Sultana. Sultana was to be 'established with a Complement of Twenty five Men and Eight Swivel Guns.' The Navy Board was further ordered to put her into condition for Channel service and to notify them when she was ready to receive her crew [PRO ADM 2/238 p5].

At the end of June, the officers at Deptford Yard notified the Navy Board that Sultana had been 'Undock'd from the Single Dock' [PRO ADM 106/3315] and was ready to receive her men. This information was relayed to the Lords of the Admiralty on 1 July. Their Lordships then issued an order to the Dockyard Commissioner:

My Lord   13th July 1768
  Having order'd a North American Schooner which the Navy Board have purchas'd to be employ'd in cruizing against Smugglers, to be register'd in the List of the Royal Navy by the Name of Sultana, we signify the same for your Lordships information, and are to desire you will cause her to be established with Eight Swivel Guns, and that they be put aboard her upon her arrival in Gallion's Reach, together with such a proportion of Ordnance Stores as may be proper for her in foreign Service, the same to be delivered into the Charge of the Lieut, who is appointed to command her, who is to indent for the Stores committed to his Charge; and to pass an account in the usual method.

         We are &c
The most Hone   Ed Hawke
The Marquis   Townshend
of Granby   Piercy Brett
[PRO ADM 2/238 p69]

Sultana's log book records began on 15 July 1768 [PRO ADM 51/4358 (5,6,7,8,9)]. The officer named to command her was Lieutenant Inglis who remained with her until she was paid off to be later sold out of the service. On the 13th, the Lords of the Admiralty had instructed the Navy Board to fit her out 'at Deptford for a Voyage to North America' with 'four months of all Species of Provisions except Beer of which she is to have as much as she can conveniently stow' [PRO ADM 2/238 p68]. Lieutenant Inglis advised their Lordships that the little schooner did not have much room to stow the beer. He asked that he be supplied with brandy instead. They amended their order on the 27th to the effect that Sultana should 'be supplied with three weeks Brandy' [PRO ADM 2/238 p88].

On 18 July, David Bruce came on board Sultana to serve as master. Bruce kept his own daily journal of the schooner's activities [PRO ADM 52/1455]. It abounds with atrocious spelling, yet it offers an interesting running account which is worth following for the remainder of 1768. Sultana was hauled out of the dock at Deptford on the 19th and moored alongside the Brad-

ford sheer hulk. There the masts were set in place, and the men kept busy with the rigging. Bricklayers, shipwrights, and joiners continued to work on board. The crew received and stowed stores and took on water. On the 28th, the anchor cables were bent, the records of stores completed, and the crew mustered preparatory for sailing. The following day, they picked up their small boat and returned the harbor boat that had been borrowed. On the 30th, they cast off from the hulk and sailed down river to Galleon's Reach. There on 2 August, 16 half hogsheads of beer were received and 5 empties were returned. The next day, the schooner sailed on down to Gravesend where 4 half barrels of powder were taken on board.

On 5 August, *Sultana* sailed once more and anchored in the Nore. Here they remained for thirteen days with the crew working on various details to make ready for sea. The carpenter made cleats for the masts and shrouds for use in belaying the running rigging. On the 11th, he shaped a square sail yard. They sailed to the Downs on 18 August, and remained there until the 24th. This slow progress down the Thames to the open sea served to familiarize the crew with their new vessel in addition to allowing time to complete preparations for the voyage.

On 25 August, they brought their boats on board and made sail, turning out of the Downs to start the voyage to North America. The way was long and arduous, taking almost two months for them to arrive at an anchorage at Halifax, Nova Scotia. On 31 August, the crew listened to the lieutenant as he read the Articles of War and an Abstract of the Act of

Sultana. From the Colonial Shipyard diorama.

Parliament for the payment of seamen's wages. This form of entertainment was offered five more times during the voyage. 9 September, the little schooner 'Shiped a Great Deal of water & the Sea Runs highe.' This too was repeated several times. On the 16th, they 'Spak a French Ship from Newfund Land Bound to Bayonne.' The carpenter was employed in repairing the small boat on the 18th. On the 29th, they spoke another French ship on its way to France. On 7 October, they 'spake a Brige from Newcastle to Halifax.' It was not noted whether the brig passed them up or vice versa. A sail in the north-west and one in the south-west were sighted on the 20th. The next day they 'Spak the Sail proved to be a schooner from the Banks of Newfoundland Bound to Cape Ann.' From here on realizing that they were nearing their destination and approaching shoal waters, they sounded the depth periodically and noted the composition of the bottom.

On 23 October, *Sultana* 'Spak his Majestys Schooner the *St Lorance* Lieutn Dundas Commander from Boston Bore away with her for Halifax Harbour the Land proved to be Cape La have of the Land of Novey Scotea.' Next day on reaching their destination, they hoisted out their boats which 'Towed us up to Halifax' where they found themselves 'Riding near his Majestys Sloop *Viaper (Viper)*' and they observed the arrival of 'his Majestys Ship *Lansustiance (Launceston)*.' On the 25th, *Sultana* 'Rec'd 4 Tuns of Shingle Ballast, 2 casks of Bread, one Firkin Butter a Quartr of Beef.' It will be remembered that this was the period when Commodore Hood, headquartered in *Launceston*, was concentrating his forces at Boston to subdue the disorders that had erupted there during the previous summer. Orders were given for *Sultana* and *St Lawrence* to sail in company to join the squadron at Boston Harbor. On the way, *Sultana* lost contact with the other schooner. On 4 November, she 'Spak a Schooner from Martinca Lading Mallasas Bound to Saliam.' Two days later, she located the entrance to Boston Harbor, and on the 8th, she got 'out Botts & towed up to Boston', anchored near Castle Island and 'Ships *Marmade (Mermaid)* Glasgow *Sinagel (Senegal)* Binatio *Bever (Beaver)* & *Hoop (Hope)* Schoonr.' Bruce noted in his journal that '9 ships with Troups' arrived on 10 November.

There was time then to give *Sultana*'s hull a little attention. On the 12th, 'haul'd a Shore the Schoonr at Castle Island Beach & Scroubed her Bottom at 2 AM Indivered to heve off but the Tide did not Rise highe a Nughe at 9 Floged Thomas Richie with one Douzon of Lashass for Drunkness & Negleck of Duty.' The next day, they were able to free *Sultana* from the beach; and on the 14th, they 'blak'd the Bends & pay'd the Side with Virnish of Pinne.'

On 15 November, Commodore Hood arrived in the move to transfer his headquarters as Commander in Chief of the North Atlantic Station to Boston for the winter. Bruce recorded this event in his journal: 'The Fort & all the shiping Salouted Commondor Houde at ½ past 2 Came to anchor his Majestys Ship *Rumney* & *Gaspey* Schoonr.' On the following day, Hood called for a conference of the ship's officers to be held on board his flagship, *Romney*. 'Man'd Ship for the Geniarl Going on board of the *Rumney* as Did all the Ships of the Fleet the Botts Employed in Landing the Troups out of the Transports.' As one result of this conference, *Sultana* received an assignment. She was to be stationed at the entrance to the harbor to act as a pilot boat for incoming vessels. On the 18th, she sailed from Boston and 'Spak his Majestys Schoonr the *Hoop (Hope)* & relived her off her Station.' *Sultana* anchored in Nantasket Road off George Island.

The little schooner remained on this station until 3 December. On 19 November they 'Sent the Cutter to Boston with the Midshipman & the weekly Accompt to the Commander.' That day and for several days thereafter, they experienced 'Hard gales & Squaly with Rain.' The cutter did not return. On the next day, Bruce noted that several sloops and schooners had been driven from their anchorages; and *Sultana* was having troubles of her own. On the 23rd, the winds started to moderate, and the cloudy skies brought some snow. At 9 am, they 'Sent the Bott to Boston to Inquire for the outhr Bott at 10 A:M Found the people onboard of the *Marmad* & the Botte Stove mostly to [pieces] Do Brought the people Down to Nantasket Road.' On the following day, they saw 'a Sail in the SE Do Bore away & Spak her provd to be the *Dolphian* Transport with Troops. ... Assisted her in to Boston Harbour.' For the rest of the month and up until 3 December, the weather was so severe that it was all they could do to maintain their station in Nantasket Road. On the 4th, they sailed up the south channel and anchored in Boston Road. For several days then, they took on water, boatswain's stores from the *Romney*, and purser's stores from the contractor in preparation for a cruise with *Senegal*. The 'stove cutter' was sent on board *Senegal* to be carried to their destination, Rhode Island.

On 8 December, *Sultana* 'Came to Sail at Noon Gott out of Boston Harbour in Company with his Majestys Sloop *Sinagel*.' On this voyage, the schooner lost contact with *Senegal* for a day; but on the 13th, she 'Joined Company with his Majestys Sloop *Sinagel* Employd Going in Before the *Sinagal* at 4 [pm] Came to anchor in Road Island Harbour in 2½ fathm....*Sinagal* Got a Ground at 6 A:M *Sanagal* Got up to the proper Road Between the Town & Fort.' This situation sounds like a duplicate of the one in 1764 where *St John* and *Squirrel* were involved. The two naval vessels remained at this anchorage from 14 until 24 December, with very little activity.

On the 25th, *Sultana*'s people 'Seized the *Royal Charlots* Bott with 8 cases of Ginn. . .went on board the Brig & Found the Customhouse officer on Shor Do

Sultana at Philadelphia.

Seized the Brig with all her takling & Left an Officer on board with 3 men & caled up her hacthes for the Benifit of his Majesty.' This was *Sultana's* first seizure, and her crew went at it with vim and vigor. On the following day, they unbent the brig's sails and searched for contraband in the hold. They 'Moored the *Charlot Brige*' with the assistance of some men from the *Senegal* on 27 December. They 'Struck Top mast & yards of Brig & unrove the running rigging' on the 28th, and 'sent inventory to the Collector of Newport Road Island.' With the brig thus dismantled, things were quiet for several days. Then on 2 January, 'Thomas Ricthe & William Chapman Carred the prize Botte on Shor & Left her & the Owners of the Brig *Charlota* Stole her from the warffe.'

The remainder of this chronological account is told by references to the records kept by Lieutenant Inglis in his log books [PRO ADM 51/4358 (5,6,7,8,9)]. For the rest of the winter and throughout the spring of 1769, *Sultana* remained in the vicinity of Rhode Island. On 14 January, wood was taken on board, and they 'Set up some Half Hogsheads that we was oblidged to shake on the Passage from England.' The next day, they received some hogsheads of rum. Then on the 18th, 'the Carpenter sent on shore to repair the Cutter with the Carpenter of the *Senegal* ... Sent 6 Cases of Gin from the Schooner to the Collector of His Majestys Custom house which was Seized out of the *Charlott Brigg*' on 23 January. The final outcome of *Sultana's* seizure action was that the brig *Charlott* was restored to her owners except for the gin and some earthenware on the 28th. Throughout the log, there are frequent references to the searching of vessels for contraband.

John Huxley, a crew member, died on 24 February. *Sultana* ran ashore at Providence on the 26th but got off without damage. During March and April, she moved about the bay, returning to Newport periodically. However in the middle of April, she had sailed from 'Tarpan Cove' for a three day stay at Martha's Vineyard. By the end of June, Lieutenant Inglis had received new orders. Stopping at New York from 1 until 4 July, he then sailed on down the coast and up the Delaware until he arrived at Philadelphia on the 12th. On the 17th, *Sultana* 'Fired two Gunns at a brigg to make her strike a Pendant she had hoisted.' This action resulted from a point of naval etiquette. Navy vessels flew a pendant at the mast head as a means of identification. For a merchant vessel to hoist a pendant in the presence of a man of war was an impertinence and could cause a confusion of identity. Numerous notations of such occurrences appear in the little schooner's log books. It is possible that her small size prompted others to taunt her in this way, and it quite naturally aroused resentment in Lieutenant Inglis and his crew.

Near the end of July, *Sultana* moved back down the Delaware and out into the Atlantic. 11 August found her at Halifax where she remained for seventeen days while being refitted and provisioned. At the end of August, she sailed once again, arriving at New York on 6 September. While there, her cutter broke away from the stern but was recovered the next day. Then she sailed south, and reached Hampton Road in the middle of September. *Sultana* cruised in and about the mouth of the Chesapeake Bay for the next six months. Lieutenant Inglis noted her presence during that period at Cape Lookout, Cape Fear Harbor, in the Elizabeth and James Rivers, at Norfolk, and various anchorages in the Chesapeake. Inglis observed the arrival of the schooner *Magdalen* from England on 2 December. In April, *Sultana* sailed to Philadelphia carrying two madmen and two women from Hog Island. After a lengthy stay there, she returned to Hampton Road by 26 April. On 21 May, Lieutenant Inglis had his schooner heeled over on a beach in the York River, and her bottom was scrubbed. She remained on her station in the Chesapeake Bay until the middle of August 1770 when she sailed for Halifax.

Sultana reached Halifax on 24 August, and stayed there until the 7th of the following month when she was sent to Boston. On 20 September, she sailed for Halifax carrying urgent orders. The Lords of the Admiralty had sent instructions for Commodore Hood to move the headquarters of the North Atlantic Station to Boston permanently. In October, *Sultana* sailed to Hampton Road, but returned to Rhode Island by 1 November. She was then stationed in Long Island Sound, on a range from Newport to New York. At Newport, Rhode Island, on 17 April 1771, she 'Rec'd the King's Money to be Carried to Boston.' The following day, Lieutenant Inglis 'fired a way $3\frac{1}{2}$ pounders at a sloop to make her hall down a pendant she had hoisted.' *Sultana* reached Boston on the 19th, and 'Sent the Boat on Shore with the King's Money' the next day.

Sultana returned to the New York area in May. She made stops of various duration at such points as Sandy Hook, Great Egg Harbour, New York, 'Statten' Island, and in the North River. In the middle of August, *Sultana* was moved to a new station. She arrived at Philadelphia on 13 August. Except for one voyage to Boston in the fall, she remained in the Delaware River for the ensuing year although she did venture down to Cape May for a week in June of 1772. On 2 September 1771, Lieutenant Inglis 'fired away $2\frac{1}{2}$ pounds to bring to a ship from Liverpool & to make them haul down a pendant they had hoisted.' Most of the time the schooner was noted as being at Philadelphia, Newcastle, Chester, or 'Gloster Point.' In July 1772, they scrubbed *Sultana's* bottom at Billingsport. Finally at the end of August, orders were received that she should return to Boston. She arrived there on 9 September and this marked the end of her service off the coast of North America.

In 1772, Rear Admiral John Montagu was Commander in Chief of the North Atlantic Station at

Boston. He wrote to Philip Stephens in London to explain his action in returning *Sultana* to England:

> Boston 8th October 1772
>
> The *Sultana* Schooner having been out of England upwards of Five years and is much out of repair, I have sent her home that her Company may be paid their Wages, and for their Lordships to dispose of her as they please. I beg you will inform their Lordships that the Schooner was Built for a pleasure Boat for a Gentleman at Southampton but not answering his purpose she was purchased for Government by orders of Sir Edward Hawke, and sent out here, she is by no means fit for this Station being too small and not able to encounter the heavy Gales of wind upon this coast, especially in the Winter Season. But as Lieut Inglis has been in her most part of the time she has been in this Country, I beg leave to refer their Lordships for his Opinion & Character of her. [PRO ADM 1/484]

This letter raises some interesting questions about *Sultana*. It implies that Sir Edward Hawke had taken advantage of his position to do a favor for a friend. Nepotism and preferential treatment for friends and associates were common practices in those days. They still are of course, but in the eighteenth century it was an accepted fact of life which hardly called for subterfuge or concealment. Sir Edward Hawke was the greatly honored and respected hero of Quiberon Bay. His squadron had dealt the French a decisive defeat during the Seven Years War, and from that time on, his recognition and fame were assured. In 1765, he had been promoted to the rank of vice admiral and appointed First Lord of the Admiralty. He held this pre-eminent position until January 1771 when he retired to private life.

Admiral Montagu seems to have suggested that Sir Edward did Sir Thomas Hesketh a special favor in buying *Sultana* for the navy. In 1768 when the schooner was surveyed, there was no evidence of any dissent to the proposed purchase; but then, who would have been tempted to oppose the First Lord of the Admiralty if he had made his desires known? *Sultana*'s limitations were recognized from the very beginning: her crew was limited to 25 men rather than the standard complement of 30 for a schooner; her storage space was limited; the ½ pounder swivel guns that armed her were almost a joke. It speaks well for Lieutenant Inglis that he had managed to handle this onerous job for more than four years.

Sultana sailed from Boston on 11 October 1772. It was a rough voyage. On the 23rd, Inglis noted in his log:

> 43° 23' N, 14° 6' E of Cape Cod.
> Hard gales and squally Wr, with rain & a great deal of Sea the WSW board at 2 Shipped a Sea filled the boat Washed away the Companion & overset the binnacle

lay'd the Schooner on her beam ends Cut a way the boat and let her go Over board to save the schooner. She righted brought her to a gain Split the foot of the foresail.

The little schooner reached Spithead on 21 November. While at anchor there, Lieutenant Inglis recorded 'the schooner very leaky in her bows.' On the 27th, he wrote 'Shipp'd a deal of water, the Sea broke over the Schooner.' On 7 December, he turned the schooner over to the dockyard officers at Portsmouth and the following day, he 'Paid the Schooners Company their Wages.' The Lords of the Admiralty were still thinking in terms of having *Sultana* refitted for further service. On 24 November, they had ordered the Navy Board to have her 'laid up at Portsmouth, & her Hull put in good Condition for Service, as other necessary Works of the Yard will admit thereof' [PRO ADM 2/241 p441]. However once *Sultana* had been paid off, she was set aside as a problem of no great urgency.

It will be remembered that the schooners *Sir Edward Hawke* and *Earl of Egmont*, lately returned from Jamaica, found themselves in the same predicament. Finally on 21 July 1773, the dockyard commissioners at Portsmouth acknowledged instructions from the Navy Board: 'Your Warrants received by the last Post, Directing the *Sir Edwd Hawke*, *Sultana* and *Earl of Egmont* Schooners to be surveyed on float & their condition reported' [NMM POR/F15]. The report on the survey of the three schooners was made on the 26th [NMM POR/D/19]. *Sultana* was 'in want of a small repair to make good' at an estimated cost of only £70 0s 0d.

The decision to sell *Sultana* in spite of the relatively low cost to recondition her is indicative of the fact that the authorities realized she was of limited value to the Navy. The master shipwright at Portsmouth and his assistants initiated the suggestion, and on 28 July, the Lords of the Admiralty authorized the sale of *Sultana*. The three schooners were auctioned off on 11 August 1773. *Sultana* went to John Hook Jr for £85.

When *Sultana* was originally surveyed for the Navy, her lines were taken off and recorded in two drawings; these Admiralty Draughts were dated at Deptford Yard 21 June 1768 (They are filed under Regd Nos 4521-2 Box 64 in the collection preserved at the National Maritime Museum). Except for the absence of figurehead and stern elevation views, they give a well-detailed plan of the schooner's hull; the dotted lines indicate her alterations for navy service. There was an unusual arrangement of shallow cubicles along each side and reaching forward from the quarterdeck to provide 'cabin' space for the seamen. Each of the eight cubicles was 6ft long with 27in of head room under the deck beams and an average of 3ft in width. The main cabin and officers' cabins provided 5ft 6in of head room under the quarterdeck beams. The small drawing

59

(Regd No 4522 Box 64) is a plan view of that 'berth deck' arrangement. The sheer plan of *Sultana* shows 12 swivel gun stocks along the side, but the records repeatedly report her armament as 8 swivel guns which must have been moved about as the circumstances required.

Sultana provides the subject for a lovely model which can be produced from these authentic plans. However, she should not be represented as a typical merchant schooner purchased for the Navy. Sir Thomas Hesketh misrepresented her with a rating of 65 tons; the Navy calculated the correct tonnage to be just $52^{68}/_{98}$. The model maker should recognize her as a yacht or 'pleasure boat' converted for use by the Royal Navy. Within her limitations, she had been of good service.

CHAPTER SEVEN

Halifax 1768-1775
Prologue to a Revolution

There were two commanders on the North Atlantic Station who might be thought of as having had the greatest influence on the story during the period of our interest in the Royal Navy colonial schooners. Rear Admiral Colville was the first of these since it was his responsibility to purchase the first six of the vessels and direct their initial employment in the service. The second was Commodore Samuel Hood. The latter had an unusually long life and a lengthy active service in the Royal Navy, which spanned a period of 54 years including the three 'world' wars that England engaged in during the eighteenth century. Born in 1724, he entered the Navy in 1741, retired from the service in 1794 with the rank of admiral, and died in 1816 with the title of viscount.

Biographies of Hood impart many details of his activities during the Seven Years War, the American Revolution, and the early years of the wars with Republican France; the three years that he was commander on the North Atlantic Station and the ensuing ten years while his career was in temporary though prolonged eclipse are however almost completely neglected. One account which covers seven closely printed pages relates simply that: 'In April 1767 he was appointed commander-in-chief in North America, with a broad pennant on board the *Romney*. On his return he commanded the *Royal William* Guardship at Portsmouth from January 1771 to November 1773'.

While commanding British naval forces in the North American colonies from 1767 to 1770, Hood found himself in a very delicate and compromising position. This was the middle period of the twelve years that led from the French and Indian War to the American Revolution. The sporadic protests and outbreaks of violence were coalescing into a more organized though still unacknowledged drive for freedom from the British domination which came to fruition in the War for Independence. Commodore Hood could hardly have anticipated the end results of this activity. He was charged with the duty of maintaining law and order in the area under his command. A report that he wrote to Philip Stephens provides a revealing picture of his situation:

Launceston in Halifax Harbour
July 11th 1768

Sir

The outrageous, and very extrordinary behaviour of the People of Boston becomes more and more alarming and cannot fail to give uneasiness at home; And as it must be agreeable to my Lords Commissioners of the Admiralty to know for certain how matters have gone, and how far the Force entrusted to me has been employed in support of the Commissioners of the Customs; I thought it my Duty in the most expeditious way to give you for their Lordships information a little detail of the Steps I have taken in consequence of the applications that have been made to me; And as the Friends to Government at Boston have repeatedly acquainted me that it is not safe to send Letters of a public nature from thence, I have ordered Lieut John Linzee of the *Launceston* to be the Bearer of this, which I hope their

Lordships will approve. On the 24th of March, I rec'd the Letter marked No 1 from the Commissioners which I have transmitted to you by two different opportunities, in consequence of it I prepared the *Romney* for sea, and she sailed hence for Boston on the 5th of May, accompanied by the *St Lawrence* Schooner; the *Hope* being then there. On the Appearance of the *Romney* before the Town, the Riot and Disorder seemed to Subside; but on a Vessel's being seized for illicit Trade Belonging to Mr Hancock (who is the richest man in the Country and the known abettor of Tumultuous proceedings) by the comptroller, a most numerous and violent Mob assembled and the Collector & Comptroller, with other officers, were beaten and wounded: the Collectors boat burnt, and other acts of a most violent nature committed. The lives of the Commissioners were threatened, and they were happy in taking Shelter by Stratagem on board the *Romney*, where they continued some days and afterwards landed at Castle William. From thence they wrote me the Letters No 2 & 3 by the *Beaver* which I sent back immediately, and she was followed next day by the *Senegal* – Capt Corner with the Two Sloops have guarded the Passes to Castle William Island, and prevented any attempts of surprising it. Governor Bernard by the Kings Command has acquainted the Assembly that his Majesty required it to rescind the Resolves of the last assembly and to protect & Support the Commissioners of the Revenue. This has been refused with the most scurrilous abuse on all his Majesty's Servants in England as well as those in America. The Governor gave a longer time to the assembly to reconsider the matter, which still refused, and it was dissolved on the 1st Instant. As you will see by his Excellency's Proclamation in the enclosed Newspaper, which contains the Messages between the Governor & the Assembly previous to its Dissolution. On the 6th Instant orders were received here to prepare a Temporary covering for the Six Comps of the 59 Regt on the Islands of Cape Breton and St John and the four of the 29th at the other outposts of this Province. Upon information of these orders from Col Dalrymple; I hastened the Equipment of the *Launceston*, as much as possible, and she is now ready for Service; not having been careened or done anything to for two years and a half; she wanted much repair, her sheathing was wholly destroyed by the Worm, and her bottom damaged in many places, I was therefore under a necessity to cause her to be new-sheathed. No 4 is a Letter I yesterday rec'd from General Gage, In consequence of which, I have sent a Shallop in Search of the *Glasgow* in the Gulph of St Lawrence, with orders to her Commander to proceed to Louisburgh, and bring from thence as many of the Troops, as he can take on board, I did propose sending the *Launceston* on this Service and to have ordered the *Glasgow* for those on the Island of St John; But Col Dalrymple having just been with me, and shewn me

his Instructions from General Gage, as well as Letters from Governor Bernard, and the Commissioners of the Customs; from which it is to be expected that a requisition of Troops will be made before the Junction of the whole Force in the Province can be effected; I shall therefore detain the *Launceston* here, and the Colonel will endeavor to hire small Vessels to go to the Island of St John. No 5 is a Letter I also rec'd yesterday from the Commissioners of the Customs.

The Schooner Mr Linzee comes in is about 80 Tons, which was built here the latter end of the year -65 by Subscription to serve as a Packet between Boston & Halifax, but the Proprietors being too numerous to agree in the management of her, she was sold last year, and the purchaser obliged to continue her as a packet for Twelve months, which he has complied with, and is now willing to sell her again. She cost above £900 before she put to Sea, is extreamly well built with the best materials, and is altogether a proper Vessel for his Majesty's Service to Cruise on this Coast, for the preventing illicit Trade; and as more Vessels of that sort are essentially necessary for that Business (which will be more fully made appear by the Commissr Letter to me No 6) especially as the situation of affairs at Boston requires the greatest part of the Force at present under my Command I therefore cannot help recommending the purchase of her to my Lords Commissioners of the Admiralty. Her Price is £550, which is exceedingly reasonable, considering the manner she is built, and fitted. If their Lordships think fit to cause her to be purchased, nothing is to be paid for the hire of her, otherwise I have agreed the owner shall have at the rate of £30 pr month. If she becomes the Kings, I beg you will prefer my humble request, to the Board, that Lieut John Linzee may be honoured with the Command of her; In whose room I have given an order to Mr Wm Boyce to act as a Lieutenant in the *Launceston* till their Lordships pleasure is known. No 7 is a Duplicate of my last Letter No 8 Letters from the Commissioners to Captain Corner with advertisements etc. And I should be wanting in Justice to Capt Corner was I not to desire you will acquaint their Lordships that he has acted in the Duty I sent him on to Boston with most becoming Zeal for the King's Service And with the utmost prudence and Discretion.

I am Sir
Your most obedient and
most humble servant
Sam: Hood

Philip Stephens Esqr
[PRO ADM 1/483 pp97-100]

Commodore Hood's long letter is well worth quoting in full because it offers at first hand an account of the first links in the inexorable chain of events which led directly to the American Revolution. The attempt to suppress smuggling brought on acts of such violence that it was deemed necessary to station troops in Boston in order to maintain order. The influx of soldiers with its attendant housing problems brought enforcement of the detested Quartering Act. The presence of troops created an atmosphere which brought on the 'Boston Massacre', The Boston Tea Party followed, only to be answered from England by the Intolerable Acts which closed the port of Boston. The final scene in this prelude to war was of course the attempt to control and confiscate arms and ammunition in the hands of the colonists with the confrontation at Lexington and Concord.

More pertinent to this story of colonial schooners is the fact that the letter provides an introduction to the schooner *Halifax*. *Halifax* is the vessel that Commodore Hood described and recommended for purchase by the Royal Navy. In carrying this dispatch and its associated documents to England, she became the harbinger of dramatic events to follow, a role that could only be appreciated in retrospect. Lieutenant Linzee arrived at Portsmouth around the end of August 1768 and turned his dispatches over to the authorities. The Lords of the Admiralty passed Commodore Hood's suggestions on to the Navy Board which in turn sent orders on 9 September to Richard Hughes, the Commissioner at the Portsmouth Dockyard. He acknowledged their instructions 'directing the officers to survey the Schooner sent from Hallifax, by Commodore Hood, and to report whether she appears to be a proper Vessell, to be purchased for the service; and send a draught, of her &ca with their opinion of her Value' [NMM POR/F14].

Proper identification of the *Halifax* in this account with the Admiralty Draught of the little schooner is awkward because it becomes necessary to contradict information published in Howard Chapelle's books. For one reason or another, there is no date on the 'Hallifax' drawing which is the basis for this investigation. In his book *The History of American Sailing Ships*, Chapelle identified *Halifax* with a schooner which was part of a squadron under Lieutenant Henry Mowatt that bombarded Falmouth, Maine in 1775. At the time he wrote his description, Mr Chapelle was apparently unaware that there had been two schooners with that name. The first *Halifax* was destroyed in February 1775 and replaced by another schooner rechristened, as Admiral Graves noted, with the same 'name to continue that of the late *Halifax* lost near Machias.' In his later book *The Search for Speed Under Sail*, Chapelle refers briefly to *Halifax* as 'a New England schooner bought in 1775,' and then gives the statistics that appear on the Admiralty draught. This statement if true would make a fiction of the *Halifax* story as related here. Since the drawing is undated, some other source was required to make positive identification of the schooner bought in 1768 with the drawing.

The solution to this quandary was found in the Portsmouth Dockyard report of the survey made on *Halifax*. This document is preserved in the National Maritime Museum. It should be noted that the dimensions given in this report duplicate those found on the drawing in all details:

Portsmouth Dockyard Officers' Reports
27th September 1768
In obedience to your directions of the 9th instant pray leave to acquaint you that we have taken a schooner from Halifax, hired by Commodore Hood, into a dock and having surveyed and made a draught of her herewith send her principal dimensions and scantlings as also the value of her hull, Masts, Yards, Furniture and Stores. And pray leave to observe that she appears to be well built, is about two years old, schooner rigg'd and has the character of being a good sea boat and of carrying a stiff sail are therefore humbly of the [opinion] she may be a proper vessel to be purchased for the service she was hired for Viz:

Principal Dimensions:	ft	ins
Length of the Range of the Deck	58	3
Length of the Keel for tonnage	46	10½
Breadth Extream	18	3
Depth in hold	8	10
Burthen in Tons		No 83 4/94
Depth of the waist in Midships	1	0¾
Height of the cutting down in Midships	0	9½
Scantlings:		
Timbers sided at the Keel	0	10
Timbers sided at the top of the side	0	6
moulded at the Floor Heads	0	6¾
between the floor heads	0	4⅞
at the top of the side	0	4¼
Room and space of the timbers	1	9
Plank of her bottom	0	2

	£	s	d
The Hull measures 83 4/94 tons @ £3-15-0 per ton	311	8	2¼
Masts, yards etc.	20	8	0
Boats	4	10	0
Rigging with blocks	6	16	0¾
Ground tackle	27	12	9
Anchors	11	5	3
Sails	23	16	7½
Other furniture	0	18	11
	406	15	10

Roger Gastrill   Thos Cosway   T Bucknall
Thos Snell   John Henslow
[NMM POR/D/17]

The drawing which was made as a result of this survey has been preserved with the collection of Admiralty draughts at the National Maritime Museum [Regd No 4594, Box 64]; it is the most complete of the four drawings with which this book is concerned, and the one best qualified to represent a typical colonial schooner design of the period. Actually, two schooners are detailed. Solid lines delineate the *Halifax* as she was originally built to serve as a packet while 'ticked' lines show how she was altered at Portsmouth for service as a navy schooner. On the drawing the name was spelled with two 'l's, but although the double letter is encountered occasionally on other documents, the great majority exhibit the usual correct spelling for 'Halifax'.

The survey was sent to the Navy Board. They in turn reported to the Lords of the Admiralty in a letter dated 30 September. It was their opinion that it would be more practical to buy the schooner for £550 than to pay the £30 per month rental for her use. On 12 October, their Lordships, Hawke, Palmerston, and Yonge at that time, instructed the Navy Board to proceed with the purchase of *Halifax*. They also asked to be informed 'what Number and Nature of Guns and Complement of men may be proper to establish on her' [PRO ADM 2/238 p190]. Lieutenant Linzee and his men who had remained with the schooner had run short of provisions, so on the 13th their Lordships ordered the Navy Board to supply them with provisions 'for ten People at whole allowance for Seven Days' [PRO ADM 2/238 p191]. This suggests that *Halifax* had sailed from America with a crew of ten men. Finally with all the particulars determined, the Lords of the Admiralty ordered the *Halifax* to be commissioned as follows:

Gentn   19 Octr 1768

We do hereby desire and direct you to cause the North American Schooner, which you were directed to purchase for his Majestys Service by our Order of the 12th Inst to be registered on the List of the Royal Navy by the name of *Halifax* and established with the Number and Nature of Guns and Complement of Men mentioned on the other side hereof.

You are to cause the said Schooner to be fitted out at Portsmouth for a voyage to North America, manned with the aforesaid Complement of Men, victualled to six months Beef and Pork and four Months of all other Species of Provisions except Beer, of which she is to have as much as she can conveniently stow, and a proportion of Brandy in lieu of the Remainder and to be stored for foreign Service.

We are &c
Navy Board   Ed Hawke   C Townshend   P Brett
[PRO ADM 2/238 pp195/6]

The reverse side of this order listed the following armament and crew to be furnished to *Halifax*:

Carriage Guns	three pounders	6
Swivel Guns		8
Complement of Men		30

The said Complement to consist of

1 Lieut in Command at	£0 5s 0d a day	
1 Second Master and Pilot	3 10 0 a month	
1 Midshipman		
1 Clerk and Steward to the Comg Officer		
1 Boatswain's mate		to be allowed
1 Gunner's Mate		6th Rates pay
1 Carpenter's Mate		
1 Surgeon's Mate		
1 Servant to the Lieut		
And the rest to be Seamen.		

Commodore Hood's request was honoured, and John Linzee was given command of the newly acquired navy schooner. His log book records for *Halifax* began on 22 October 1768. It is interesting to note at this point that Lieutenant Linzee was Hood's brother-in-law. Susannah Linzee had married Samuel Hood in 1749 while he was temporarily unemployed by the Navy and on half-pay. She was the daughter of Edward Linzee who was the mayor of Portsmouth for several years. Her brother, John, was serving under Hood in the *Romney* when the commodore saw a chance to give him a boost up the ladder with the command of *Halifax*. Officially established as her commander, Lieutenant Linzee was then able to oversee the alterations made to the schooner throughout the rest of October and the first week in November.

These changes included elevating the cabin platform to provide more storage space below, raising the line of the bulwarks with openings provided for the carriage guns, and a new railing with six swivel gun stocks raised around the after half of the deck. Although *Halifax* was allotted eight swivel guns, there is no positive identification on the drawing to show where more than six might have been mounted. The exterior changes altered the schooner's profile so much that it would have been difficult to recognise her as the little packet she had been. Moreover, there was a drastic change made in her sparring and rigging. A suggestion of this is found in a letter from the dockyard commissioner to the Navy Board which was dated 23 October: 'Your letter of the 21st instant is received. And the Warrants that came therewith, directing the Halifax Schooner's Fore & Main Masts, to be shortened four feet each: and fit her with proper Topmasts, to carry Topsails &c' [NMM POR/F14]. This information indicates that *Halifax* had been fitted originally with pole-headed masts carrying fore-and-aft sails only. This was typical of privately owned schooners manned with small crews, When the Navy took them over and provided a crew of thirty men, squaresails were a natural addition to the rig.

On 9 November 1768, Commissioner Hughes advised the Navy Board that 'yesterday afternoon . . . the *Halifax* Schooner was put out of the South Dock.' This apparently indicated that the major alterations had been completed. The schooner remained in the harbor until 3 December when she was towed out and moored at Spithead. On that occasion, a packet of dispatches for Commodore Hood was delivered to Lieutenant Linzee. Linzee's log book [PRO ADM 51/3867 (4)] entries offer a record of these and subsequent movements as he set about returning to North America.

Halifax did not sail from Spithead until 3 January 1769. It was to be a long and tortuous passage which proved difficult even though a southerly route was followed. On the 18th, Linzee had seaman McDunnack punished with a dozen lashes for 'uncleanness'. While the square sail was being set on the 24th, it was split and replaced with the main topsail. The main topmast was carried away on the 30th, and some spars, sails, and rigging were lost. *Halifax* arrived at Funchal, Madeira on 2 February where she found the *Tryall* and 26 merchant ships. She stayed there for several days before resuming her westward voyage. On 28 February Linzee brought to a sloop by firing a shotted 3 pounder. He learned that she was from Virginia and bound for Antigua. Swinging northward, he finally reached Martha's Vineyard on 21 March. He had to fire 15 three pounders and 2 swivels to secure a pilot. Three days later, *Halifax* arrived at Boston and saluted Commandore Hood in the *Romney*. This brought Lieutenant Linzee's log book record to a conclusion for reasons that can be best explained by the following letter:

Romney in Boston harbr April 8th 1769
Sir

I beg you will be pleased to acquaint my Lords Commissioners of the Admiralty, that the great fatigue Lieutenant Linzee had to encounter with in his Passage to America in his Majesty's Schooner the *Halifax*, has affected his Constitution to such a degree as to render him unequal to such active Duty. I have therefore at his request removed him into the *Romney*; Appointed Lieut Saml Scott (who is a Friend of Lord Palmerston) to be Commander of the Schooner; and placed Lieut Thos West in the *Beaver* in his room which I flatter myself their Lordships will not disapprove of.

   I am Sir
   Your most obedient
   humble Servant
   Sam: Hood
Philip Stephens Esqr
Admiralty

     [PRO ADM 1/483]

As this story of *Halifax* progresses, it will be noted that command of her proved to be a traumatic experience for most of the lieutenants who succeeded to the position. Lieutenant Scott was no exception. It will be remembered that Lord Palmerston was one of the three Lords of the Admiralty who signed the order for the purchase of *Halifax* on 12 October of the previous year. Hood apparently considered that his action in appointing Scott to command the schooner was a wise political move because of the Lieutenant's friendly relationship with his Lordship. Samuel Scott began his log book entries on 28 March 1769 at Boston [PRO ADM 51/4211 (1)]. The next day, *Halifax* was hauled ashore to have her bottom cleaned. She remained at Boston until 1 May when she moved out to Nantasket Road for a couple of days. The rest of the month was spent cruising off Cape Ann to intercept merchant vessels.

On 5 May, Lieutenant Scott examined the brig *Sally*. Her captain was John Whilly who said he was 35 days out of Glasgow, bound for Boston; Scott impressed one man from her crew. On the 8th, the schooner *Success*, Captain Thomas Parsons, was examined; she was 28 days out of Dominica and one man was taken from her crew. On the 23rd, Lieutenant Scott impressed two men from the schooner *Cicero* coming into Boston from St Nicholas. This sort of activity continued until 28 May when *Halifax* returned to Boston. She remained in the bay for several weeks thereafter, alternating between Boston Harbor and Nantasket. Then on 17 June, the schooner sailed for Halifax with a sergeant and nine men of the 64th Foot on board. Arriving on the 23rd, she remained there for five days and then returned to Boston. During the months of July, August, and well into September, *Halifax* continued to cruise off the coast stopping merchant vessels for inspection. Periodically, she laid over at Marblehead, Plymouth, or Boston for a couple of days to take on provisions. On 11 September a deserter from the 64th Foot was taken on board in Boston Harbor. Then on the 15th she sailed for Halifax to be inspected and refitted.

The schooner stayed at Halifax from 25 September until 20 October. On 10 and 11 October, *Halifax* was hove down for inspection and cleaning. Sailing from Halifax, her new orders directed her to the Delaware River and Philadelphia where she remained from 10 November until the end of the month. John Atkinson died on the 10th. *Halifax* wintered in Wilmington Creek from 3 December until 19 March 1770. On 13 December, while moored off the town of Wilmington, Scott noted that there was 'a great deal of Drift Ice in the Creek' then 'at 2PM a Shallop drove foul of us and broke our Cabbin Windows.' The next day, he warped *Halifax* alongside the wharf at Wilmington. Several days were spent in unrigging, and removing anchors, booms, yards, cables, and other weighty objects to the wharf so as to lighten the schooner and heave her up as clear of the ice as was possible. Thereafter, observa-

Halifax entering Boston Harbor.

tions were limited essentially to the weather conditions and the receipt on board of provisions for the crew.

With the arrival of warmer weather in March, *Halifax* sailed up to Philadelphia where she stayed until the 26th. Then she moved down the river and returned to Boston by 16 April. For the rest of that month, throughout May, and most of June, *Halifax* was stationed at Boston with intermittent tours of duty at Nantasket and off Cape Ann. On 21 June, she sailed for Halifax carrying 30 barrels of pitch. The schooner was at Halifax from 27 June, to 17 July. During this period, Lieutenant Scott and his crew became embroiled in a bizarre chain of events which judging from the records were never fully explained. The muster book entries for August and September attempted to bring order out of the chaos but failed to clarify many strange factors. It was such an unusual situation that a composite of those records is worth recording here.

Halifax Muster Book, August & September 1770 [PRO ADM 36/7254]

No	Name	Entered	Born	Age	Rating	Disposal
5	Robert Carnaby	25 Oct 68 Portsmouth	Shadwell London	49	AB	Ran 13 July 70 Halifax
11	John Briscoe	28 Oct 68 Portsmouth		40	AB	Ditto
13	William Brien	29 Oct 68 DRAGON	Plymouth	22	Clerk	Discharged 30 Sept 70
14	John Crispan	30 Oct 68 Portsmouth	Bristol	24	AB	Died 27 July 70 at Sea
21	Patrick McDunack	15 Nov 68 Portsmouth	Kildare	36	AB	
25	Samuel Cousins	19 Nov 68 Portsmouth	Portsmouth	21	AB	Discharged Halifax 30 Sept 70 in lieu.
26	Joseph Anthony	19 Nov 68 Portsmouth	Madiera	41	AB	Discharged Boston 4 June 70
27	Robert Byrne	19 Nov 68 Portsmouth	Dublin	22	AB	Died at Sea 30 July 70
34	Samuel Scott	28 Mar 69 BEAVER			Lieut	Discharged Superceeded 12 Aug 70
35	John Lowe	28 Mar 69			Lt Serv	Ditto with his master
36	William Childs	2 Apr 69	Kildare	25	AB	Died at Boston 3 Aug 70
37	John Peirce	21 Apr 69 Boston			2nd Master	
38	William Gray	21 Apr 69 Boston	Portsmouth	20	AB	
40	Lewis Sheddin	13 May 69	Fifeshire	16	AB	Disch 23 May 70 at Philadelphia
49	John Wilson	22 July 69 ROMNEY	Fifeshire	31	AB	
50	Peter Francis	do	London	24	AB	
51	Henry Butter	do	Middlesex	17	AB	Disch 15 July 70 ROMNEY
52	Gilbert Jabbicombe	23 July 69 ROMNEY	Devonshire	40	AB	Ran at Boston 1 June 70
53	Andrew Martiano	do	Naples	36	AB	Ran at Boston 1 June 70
55	Thomas Rothburne	24 July 69 VIPER	Exeter	28	AB	
56	John Bond	do	London	24	AB	
58	Nathaniel Baily	27 June 69 Boston	Virginia	28	AB	Died 14 July 70 Halifax
59	William Mathews	29 July 69 Boston	Bristol	24	AB	Ran 13 July 70 at Halifax
60	Robert Roberts	22 Aug 69 YOUNG ABRAHAM Schooner	Carnarvon	22	AB	
61	Edward James	10 Sept 69 BRIGHT WILLIAM	Cheshire	23	AB	Disch 26 Feb 70 in lieu.
62	Patrick Graham	8 Oct 69	Edinburgh	25	Mid	
64	Ambrose Shareman	19 Oct 69 Halifax	Dublin		Surg Mate	
65	William Smith	11 Nov 69 Philadelphia	Boston	36	AB	Ran 3 Aug 70 Nantucket
66	Samuel Parsons	1 Dec 69 Wilmington	London	23	Carp Mate	Ran 3 Aug 70 Nantucket
67	David Davidson	28 Dec 69		25	AB	
68	Connought Nortson	27 Feb 70	Norway	24	AB	
69	James Tripe	24 Mar 70	Exeter	23	AB	
70	John Adams	2 June 70	Plymouth	24	AB	Ran at Boston 3 Aug 70
71	Abraham Young	2 June 70	Exeter	27	AB	Ran at Boston 3 Aug 70
72	Jeremy Bigg	13 Aug 70 SENEGAL			Lieut	
73	Michael Thompson	13 Aug 70 Halifax			Lieut's Servant	

The earliest evidence in these records from which trouble for *Halifax* might have been predicted was the desertion of two seamen who 'ran' at Boston on 1 June. A month and a half later shortly before the schooner was due to leave Halifax for Boston, three more men ran. The next day, 14 July, Nathaniel Baily died in an unusual accident. With *Halifax* tied up alongside the careening wharf, he 'fell overboard and was drowned in bringing on board a Basket of Shot.' Lieutenant Scott had carried out musters and made reports on 26 June and on 9 July. They showed a full complement of 30 men. Apparently this aroused the commodore's suspicions because Hood himself held a muster on the 15th. This report showed a total of 26 men which was to be expected under normal circumstances with the loss of four men in the previous two days. However, the suspicion remained that there were other irregularities such as reporting desertions long after the fact and possibly hiring men to stand in as substitutes at the muster. This would enable the commander to maintain a clear record and continue drawing rations for a full complement.

Halifax sailed for Boston on 17 July. During this passage which lasted fifteen days, Scott recorded the deaths of two men. Then on 3 August 1770, William Childs died in Boston Harbor. Lieutenant Scott's log book entries end on that date. The Lieutenant, his servant and four of the crew disappeared at the same time. Some of the dates and places that appear in the muster records are questionable and reflect the fact that there was considerable confusion in trying to reorganize the records. Hood was expecting to be relieved of his command with the arrival of Gambier that fall and had yet to move his headquarters permanently from Halifax to Boston. The problem followed him back to England as evidenced by the following letter:

Sir   Portsmouth Novr 6th 1770
I beg you will be pleased to acquaint my Lords Commissioners of the Admiralty that I mustered the crew of his Majestys Schooner *Halifax* commanded by Lieut Samuel Scott on the 15th of last month [note: this is obviously an error on Hood's part since the events took place in July and August] in the harbour of Halifax, and she sailed immediately for Boston; a few days after I received information that seven of the men

mustered by me, as part of her complement, were not belonging to her but hired for the purpose of Answering to fictitious names. His Majesty's Ship *Fowey* being then under orders for Boston, I acquainted Capt Robinson with the affair, and directed him to send the *Halifax* to me, on his arrival and upon Lieut Scott's hearing of it – conscious I imagine of not being able to stand the inquiry – he absented himself from his duty; and as Capt Robinson could not see, or hear of him, for four days, he sent the Schooner to me; and on her arrival, and receiving Capt Robinson's Letter; I removed Lieut Jer[emia]h Biggs from His Majesty's Sloop *Senegal*, to the Command of the *Halifax*, and gave a Commission to Mr Morgan Richards to be Lieut of the *Senegal*, which I hope their Lordships will be pleased to confirm: He is a very deserving young man, and passed his examinations for a Lieutenant some years since.

> I am Sir
> your most obedient
> humble Servant
> Sam Hood

Philip Stephens Esqr
Admiralty
[PRO ADM 1/483]

Scott's log book stops on 3 August. The next captain's log book in the series does not start until 4 October. However, the master's journal which continued uninterrupted serves to reveal the schooner's movements during the missing two months [PRO ADM 52/1267 (4)]. *Halifax* sailed from Boston 4 August 1770; She arrived at Halifax on the 12th. It is noted in the muster records that Lieutenant Scott and his servant were discharged on that date. This could only be a paperwork ploy to clear the books. No evidence has been found that Scott was ever apprehended or court martialled for his actions. Jeremiah Bigg (or Biggs) took command on the 13th. In August, he cruised to 'Pascataway' and then down to Boston. In early September, *Halifax* sailed up to 'Passmaquoddy' and from there returned to Halifax by the 22nd. She sailed for Boston under her newly appointed commander, James Glasford, whose log book entries begin the following day at sea on 4 October 1770.

Examination of the muster book records reveals a number of fascinating details to supplement those already noted. 73 men had served in *Halifax* during a period of 21 months since leaving England. By 1 June, there were only 8 men left from the original crew that had sailed from Spithead. By the end of September, there was just one left; Patrick McDunack, who had been punished for 'uncleanness' on 18 January 1769, had outlasted them all. One might also speculate about the reported deaths, even that of Nathaniel Baily. It could be that Scott entered them fictiously in his records to cover up unreported desertions in an attempt

to clear his books. There is not much available to fairly assess his character. His penmanship is clean cut – almost of a 'copper plate' appearance. His entries were meticulous with very few misspelled words and suggest an intelligent, well-educated person. The mystery of whether he was a devious monster bringing death and disaffection to his crew or a well-meaning individual trapped in an impossible set of circumstances is wide open to speculation.

Hood had sailed for Boston on 2 October to relocate the headquarters of the North Atlantic Station. He turned over his command to Commodore James Gambier on the 10th and sailed for England four days later. *Halifax* also was scheduled to return to England. This may explain why Lieutenant Glasford replaced Biggs after he had held the command for only two months. In any case, the little schooner was tainted with some measure of disgrace for which she could hardly be held responsible. She remained at Boston for the rest of October. On the 26th, the crew painted her. On 1 November, they 'struck two guns and all swivels down into the hold' and sailed for England. *Halifax* arrived at Falmouth on 5 December. The next day, the crew remounted the guns and swivels that had been stowed below. They sailed over to Plymouth on the 8th and *Halifax* remained there for most of the following three months. On 9 March 1771, Lieutenant Abraham Crispin relieved Glasford as commander, but the schooner still stayed in the vicinity of Plymouth until well into June.

Finally, on 9 June *Halifax* sailed for Boston carrying dispatches to advise Commodore Gambier that Rear Admiral Montagu was coming to replace him as commander of the North Atlantic Station.

> You are hereby required and directed to proceed forthwith in His Majesty's Schooner under your Command to Boston in New England and having delivered to Commodore Gambier the Pacquet you will herewith receive for him you are to put yourself under his command and follow his orders, or the Orders of the Commander in Chief for the time being of His Majesty's Ships in North America, for your further proceedings. Given &c 30th May 1771.
>
> > Palmerston
> > Lisburne
> > A Hervey

Lieut Abm Crispin
HALIFAX
[PRO ADM 2/97 pp119-120]

Halifax did not arrive until 27 August. Her news was stale since Montagu had reached Boston on the 13th and already relieved Gambier. In contrast to her earlier history, the following two years of the schooner's career make dull reading. Most of the time was spent in the Massachusetts Bay area although she was stationed at Rhode Island for the last three months of 1771. Then again *Halifax* was stationed at Rhode Island from the middle of February 1773 until 8 May. On 11 April 1773 Lieutenant Jacob Rogers took command. His penmanship was so poor that the log book records he kept are almost illegible. He left Rhode Island in May and returned to the Massachusetts coast. While cruising from place to place, *Halifax* stopped in at such locales as Picataqua, Falmouth, Pecks Island, Hope Island, and Brunswick. While at Brunswick, the master's journal notes that she was 'Hauled ashore to examine the bottom' and the crew was employed in 'Caulking the butts ends which we found very open' [PRO ADM 52/1823 (6)]. *Halifax* returned to Boston on 26 March 1774 to stand witness in another strange episode.

The master's journal records that on the 27th Midshipman Williams was confined for neglect of duty. Admiral Montagu ordered Lieutenant Rogers put under arrest and the midshipman was relieved. A court-martial was held on board the *Active* at Boston on 18 April 1774 [PRO ADM 1/5306]. The presiding officers were George Talbot, captain of the *Active* acting as President, Thomas Symonds, Thomas Jordan, James Ayscough, and George Montagu. The officer on trial was Lieutenant Jacob Rogers. Listed as witnesses were: Donald Furzer, John Williams, Midshipman; Richard Mortley, Boatswain; Edward Showers, Carpenter; John Elliot, captain's servant; Read, Master; Patrick McDonach, Cook; and James Frazier, Gunner. The charges brought against Rogers were: mistreating the ship's company, misappropriating stores, and faking the log.

The evidence which was presented comprised a long and varied list of abuses: instead of buying candles ashore, Rogers had them made from 1 cwt of ship's tallow; he had exchanged ship's slops ashore for fowls; sheets of tin had been sent to a tinsmith who had made half of them into a dripping pan, kettle, and boiler for the use of the Lieutenant's family while keeping the rest in payment for his services; wood cut by the ship's company had been sent to his house; the men were given short rations of rice, and Rogers calculated 9 ounces to the pound when supplying cheese; for a week, he had the fire put out daily at noon. The men who had been cutting wood ashore came aboard wet to the waist and could not dry themselves by the fire. It was claimed that the fire was put out to save wood so he could send it to his house. He had struck his servant in the face and made him bleed while he was serving at the table. He came on board one night at about 8pm and sent for the cook; as the cook had turned in with no fire to keep going, he took a little while to come up. He claimed to be sober, but there was some evidence that he had been a little drunk. In any case, Rogers had him triced up in the shrouds with an iron bolt in his mouth and kept him there until midnight. McDonach (McDunack?) was unable to speak for several days because his mouth had been so lacerated. On one occasion when *Halifax* had been ordered on a cruise, the schooner spent three nights anchored behind

islands. The Lieutenant claimed that it would be easier to catch smugglers that way. However in order to keep the Admiral from finding out that his orders had been disobeyed, he had made log entries as though the schooner had been at sea. On 2 September 1773, an entry had been made in the log that a boat had been overset and all her gear lost. This was pure fiction. On 27 December 1773, *Halifax* was struck by a heavy sea and a small amount of gear was washed overboard. The log book entry claimed falsely that a considerable quantity of meat had been lost.

Lieutenant Rogers was convicted of the charges and discharged from the Navy. It would appear that *Halifax* had hit a new low in her career as a Navy schooner. The court-martial proceedings did reveal one very interesting bit of information. The ubiquitous Patrick McDunack was still very much a member of the crew. For three and a half years he had been the only man still aboard who had sailed for Boston in *Halifax* way back in January 1769. He must have been blessed with an iron constitution and perseverance to match. On 21 April 1774, Lieutenant Joseph Nunn took command of the schooner, and it appeared that better days were ahead. Nunn was an officer of excellent reputation who had been serving in the *Active*. For obvious reasons that will appear shortly, there are no captain's log book records extant for the period of Lieutenant Nunn's command in *Halifax*. However the master's journal which continued until November and official correspondence relating to the schooner and her activities serve to fill in the picture.

On 22 April just four days after he had testified at Lieutenant Rogers' court-martial, Donald Furzer, the surgeon's mate, died. On the 28th, *Halifax* moved out to Nantasket Roads. Five days later, she sailed for Halifax, arriving on 10 May and remaining there for the rest of the month. On 9 June, the schooner returned to Boston and stayed there except for short cruises along the coast for the rest of the year. On 12 December, Captain William Maltby wrote to Admiral Graves after his ship, the *Glasgow*, had gone aground on the rocks at Cohasset in Boston Bay that Lieutenant Nunn in *Halifax* had come to his aid. *Glasgow* had lost her rudder and was so badly damaged below the waterline that her pumps were barely able to keep her afloat. With help, she was able to reach Boston by the 14th for a survey and necessary repairs.

As tensions continued to rise, the British authorities became increasingly concerned about concentrations of arms and ammunition in the hands of the colonists. Admiral Graves at Boston was worried about the possibility of such supplies being smuggled in by sea. He wrote to Philip Stephens:

In this idea I have order[ed] the *Gaspee* Brig, lately returned from protecting the Fisheries in the Bay of Chaleur and Gaspee, with the *Halifax* Schooner to be stationed from Cape Elizabeth on one side of Casco

Bay to Passamaquody harbour, and have given their Commanders Directions to take every opportunity of Winds and Weather to move suddenly from place to place, without their Intentions being previously made known to any person, by which means they will in the Course of this Season visit the greater part of the Harbours within the Limits of their Stations; and although they may not be successful in seizures, yet I apprehend the Knowledge of their being on the Coast may prevent considerable Importations of smuggled Goods and Arms and Ammunition.

At the end of December, *Halifax* was temporarily relieved of this duty to carry some repaired sails to the *Scarborough* at Piscataqua. On 8 January, Graves wrote in a report to Philip Stephens that 'The *Halifax* Schooner is so very leaky and out of Repair, and is in such continual want of patching to make her swim, that she is totally unfit for any Service but to be at Anchor, which I have directed her to do this Winter, and in the Spring intend to have her surveyed; she is a very bad low Vessel, and so extremely wet and uncomfortable to the Seamen that no consideration will keep them belonging to her.' Nevertheless because there was a shortage of small vessels of her type available to the Navy, *Halifax* continued with her assigned duties until fate stepped in to take a hand.

Lieutenant Nunn wrote a report to Vice Admiral Graves which describes the conclusion of the *Halifax* story.

Sir   Boston March 1st 1775

The 15th February at three O'Clock in the Morning I sailed from Cranberry Harbour, with His Majesty's Schooner the *Halifax*, intending to put into Machias to take a Pilot for Passamiquody, the Pilot we then had Onboard not being acquainted with the Coast further than Machias; At half past twelve the Pilot being deceived in the Land, run the Schooner upon a Ridge of Rocks off Sheep Island, three Leagues from Bucks Harbour near Machias, the Vessel going at that time seven Knots and a half with a fresh Gale at WSW – the Rudder was immediately knocked off on the Vessel striking – I then ordered the Mainsail to be lowered down, hoping to force her off with the Head Sails; upon Sounding we found she had sued three feet forward and surrounded with Rocks, that had three feet less Water on them that She drew – I then ordered the Sails to be furled and the Boats hoisted out, to save what Provisions and Necessaries we could for our Subsistance – At six found the Tide had left the Vessel dry upon the Rocks, with her Starboard Side bulged, seeing it was impossible to save her, we with much difficulty got ashore upon Sheep Island where we encamped, at seven came on a very hard Gale of Wind with Frost and Snow; – At 8 the Sea broke over the

Halifax (right) and *Chaleur* on the stocks. From the Colonial Shipyard diorama.

Mast Heads and overset the Vessel. We saw no more of her till day break, when we found she was beat to pieces, nothing but Masts appearing upon the Water, we at the same time saw the Yawl was stove to pieces on the Rocks; – At 8 in the Morning it was more moderate, and finding we were upon an uninhabited Island, I thought it necessary to embrace the first Opportunity of sending the Boats to the Main to endeavor to find some Vessel or Boat, to carry us off the Island, having but one Boat, the loss of which must have cut Us off from any resource, and the Master being an entire Stranger on the Coast, did not think it prudent to risque the Boat without the Pilot, who I ordered to go, cautioning the Master at the same [time] to prevent his escape from him – At nine the next Morning the Master returned with A Small Schooner from Buck's Harbour, where he informed me the Pilot made his escape from him, at half past ten embarked for Bucks Harbour.

As a Detail of what occured afterwards would be to tedious to insert at present, I must beg leave to refer to the enclosed Journal of our Proceedings from the time we left Cranberry Harbour, to our arrival in this Port. I am, Sir [&c]

Josh Nunn

[PRO ADM 1/485]

A court-martial was convened on board the *Somerset* at Boston on 9 March 1775 to enquire into the loss of *Halifax* [PRO ADM 1/5307]. The evidence presented was essentially the same information as had been offered in Lieutenant Nunn's report to Admiral Graves but with the addition of a few interesting details. At the time the schooner struck, the crew had been preparing to anchor as the pilot, who was at the tiller, expected to be in the harbor in another half hour. At low tide with the schooner high and dry, it could be seen that the hull was too seriously damaged for there to be any hope of saving her. As the tide rose, *Halifax* broke up rapidly. The next day when the boat was sent for help, the pilot believed that Bucks Harbour was just around the headland; but instead it was found to be nine leagues distant. While the men from the boat were thawing themselves out in a house at Bucks Harbour, the pilot managed to make his escape. The woman of the house then directed them to where her husband was located about three miles up the river in a small schooner, and the following morning, the schooner went out to Sheep Island and brought off the rest of the crew. The next day, they all went on to Machias where a sloop was found to carry them to Boston.

The court decided that the loss of *Halifax* was due entirely to the incompentence of the pilot. Lieutenant Nunn and his ship's company were acquitted of any responsibilty. The next month, hostilities broke out, and the British found themselves beseiged in Boston. Nunn was sent to England with dispatches for Lord Dartmouth. He arrived in London on 10 June. On 24 July, the Admiralty gave him command of the cutter *Folkestone* with orders to deliver dispatches for Admiral Graves in Boston. Before sailing however, he discovered that the cutter was too leaky and out of repair to make the voyage, and the dispatches were sent by another vessel. Then on 9 September 1775, Lieutenant Nunn took command of the schooner *Magdalen* at Portsmouth and sailed for North America. The American Revolution was in full swing by this time. November found Lieutenant Nunn and the *Magdalen*, the last of the original six schooners purchased for the Royal Navy, involved in the successful defense of Quebec.

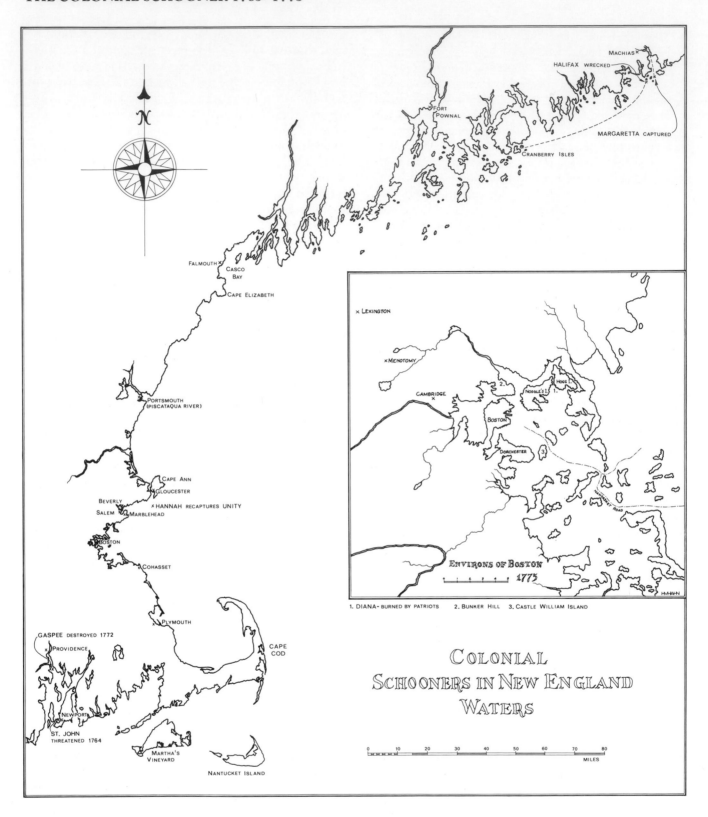

MACHIAS ×

HALIFAX WRECKED

FORT POWNAL

MARGARETTA CAPTURED

CRANBERRY ISLES

FALMOUTH ×

CASCO BAY

CAPE ELIZABETH

× LEXINGTON

× MENOTOMY

CAMBRIDGE ×

2. NOBLE'S I. HOGG I.

1.

BOSTON

PORTSMOUTH (PISCATAQUA RIVER)

DORCHESTER 3.

NANTASKET ROAD

CAPE ANN
GLOUCESTER

BEVERLY
SALEM × MARBLEHEAD × HANNAH RECAPTURES UNITY

BOSTON

COHASSET

ENVIRONS OF BOSTON 1775

H. MAHN

1. DIANA – BURNED BY PATRIOTS   2. BUNKER HILL   3. CASTLE WILLIAM ISLAND

PLYMOUTH

GASPEE DESTROYED 1772

× PROVIDENCE

CAPE COD

NEWPORT

ST. JOHN THREATENED 1764

MARTHA'S VINEYARD

NANTUCKET ISLAND

COLONIAL SCHOONERS IN NEW ENGLAND WATERS

0   10   20   30   40   50   60   70   80

MILES

CHAPTER EIGHT

George Washington's Navy-1775

The *Halifax* assignment to patrol the coast of Maine as an attempt to prevent the smuggling of arms and ammunition was but a small part of the pattern that developed during the latter part of 1774 and early 1775. Increasingly aware of the imminence of armed conflict with the Sons of Liberty, British Authorities sought to stave it off by curtailing the quantities of munitions held by the provincials or vulnerable to seizure by them. Many of the leaders considered that the colonies were in a state of rebellion long before the opening shots were fired at Lexington. On 14 February 1775, the day before *Halifax* came to grief, Major John Pitcairn, who was in command of the marines at Boston, wrote to Lord Sandwich in England: 'I think many of the people of this country begin to think they have gone too far . . . all the friends to Government are of opinion that vigorous measures at present would soon put an end to this rebellion.' Pitcairn displayed the usual British contempt for the capabilities of the colonials, some of whom on the other hand were so puffed up with self-righteousness as to consider themselves invincible. Pitcairn closed his letter in a note of frustration and with the rather irrational statement: 'I mean to seize them all and send them to England.'

Two months earlier at Portsmouth, New Hampshire on 14 December 1774, a mob had raided Fort William and Mary and carried off from 200 to 220 barrels of gunpowder. The next day, a large party returned under the leadership of John Sullivan and took out 16 cannon and 60 muskets. They left behind about 20 cannon that were too large for easy removal. John Wentworth, a governor who was relatively well-liked by his people, was forced to request help from Admiral Graves at Boston. *Canceaux* arrived on the 17th; and when *Scarborough* came in the next day under Captain Andrew

Barkley, they set about safeguarding the remaining armament left in the fort and on nearby islands in the harbor. It was while *Scarborough* was engaged on this mission that *Halifax* carried the repaired sails to her.

Winter weather brought with it a precarious truce. However on 26 February, the transport *Sea Venture* carried 140 men under Lieutenant Colonel Alexander Leslie from Castle William to Marblehead. General Gage had been informed that cannon and other military stores were to be found at Salem. He decided that soldiers should be sent to seize them. Colonel Leslie and his men marched the five miles to Salem from Marblehead only to find that the citizens had been warned in time to move the cannon beyond a draw bridge which had then been raised. Moreover, the British found themselves faced by a large crowd which included a sizeable body of armed men. Neither side was prepared to make the decisive move that would have precipitated a general conflict. The episode concluded with the British troops marching back to their transport without the cannon they had come for.

In need of small vessels to carry dispatches, Vice Admiral Graves hired the schooner *Margueritta* and furnished her with a crew, supplies, and armament taken from his flagship *Preston*. She was sent to the Piscataqua on 30 March with orders for Captain Barkley still commanding there in the *Scarborough*. With her name anglicized to *Margaretta*, the little schooner was to play a memorable role in the days to come. Down in Rhode Island, Thomas Gilbert of Freetown was forced to flee for his life to a British man of war on 10 April after he had tried to recruit colonists to the King's cause. On the 15th, Lieutenant Thomas Graves, commanding the schooner *Diana*, took into his custody 8 cannon, 6 cohorns, and 45 small arms along with shot and equipment for the cannon from Fort Pownall on the Penobscot River. This left the frontier fort almost defenseless with Indian country close by. On the 20th, Henry Colins in the schooner *Magdalen* landed 20 men at 3am with orders to seize gunpowder stored in the magazine at Williamsburg, Virginia. Their return three hours later with 15 half barrels of the powder was followed by news of an outraged citizenry. However, the die had been cast on the day before at Lexington.

The British forces in Boston soon found themselves encircled by a horde of partially-trained, informally-officered, indifferently-equipped Minutemen and militia which had finally found a vent for the uncertainties and frustrations that had mushroomed over the years. Boston proper, which at that time was practically an island with just a narrow strip of land connecting it to the mainland, was impregnable to such a force when defended as it was by trained troops. On both sides, there was indecision in selecting a course of action. The situation was so new and lacking in precedent in some ways. The result was a stalemate. The colonials were still petitioning Parliament and King George for reconciliation and some accommodation of their grievances. It would be many months before they would finally realize that the English government would make no compromises. The British military leaders in Boston hesitated to take offensive action at a time when there might have been some chance of throwing the provincial forces into complete disorder. The punishment they suffered during the retreat from Concord had taught them a bitter lesson.

Boston Harbor was serrated by inlets, fed from several rivers and dotted with numerous small islands, all of which were navigable or readily reached in shallow draft vessels or small boats. The British held firm control of the harbor with their warships and Boston itself with their troops. However, there was considerable activity around the fringes while both sides avoided a major engagement. The Americans constructed some floating batteries with the intention of bombarding Boston. One of those came to grief when a cannon burst while firing on the town. Whaleboats manned by experienced oarsmen to mount forays on the islands were used to remove livestock and destroy crops that the British might have used to supply their garrison. Near the end of May, the provincials raided Noddle's Island by wading across at low tide. While trying to repel them, the schooner *Diana* came under heavy fire from a large force of patriots on the mainland. She ran ashore after her crew was forced to desert her. The rebels salvaged the four 4 pounders, 12 swivel guns, and any articles of value that could be carried off before destroying the Navy schooner by fire. The British countered these activities of the Americans with their ship's boats, and whaleboats and armed gondolas of their own.

The Americans began capturing British vessels that could be converted to their cause. In May after Ethan Allen and his Green Mountain Boys had taken Ticonderoga, they moved on to Skenesborough where they seized Major Skene's schooner. After the little vessel had been armed with cannon, Benedict Arnold sailed her up Lake Champlain, and an armed sloop was captured at St John's. This small naval force then held command of the lake for the time being.

On 26 May, Admiral Graves gave orders to Midshipman James Moore, commanding the schooner *Margaretta*. He was to convoy sloops belonging to a Mr Ichabod Jones to Machias and protect them while they loaded fuel and lumber to supply the garrison at Boston. At the same time, he was to retrieve the cannon that Graves understood had been salvaged from the wreck of *Halifax*. Those people at Machias having the guns in their possession were to be reimbursed for their trouble.

Margaretta arrived at Machias on 2 June with two sloops. It appears from one account that Ichabod Jones tried to take advantage of the show of force represented by the Navy schooner to enforce his terms for trading provisions to the inhabitants in exchange for lumber. He succeeded in arousing the animosity of those he was trying to deal with and refused to trade with those who had opposed him. On Sunday, 11 June, Moore and his second in command were on shore in the town meeting house, when they became alerted to the approach of a group of armed men. Fearing for themselves and the safety of the schooner, they jumped out of a window and managed to board *Margaretta* before the growing mob could reach them. At first Moore tried to recover the two sloops that had been seized, but soon found that he had his hands full just trying to save the schooner. After an extended running fight during which the schooner had her booms and gaff carried away in a jibing maneuver, the pursuers in a commandeered sloop and schooner overwhelmed the *Margaretta*'s crew. Midshipman Moore was fatally wounded while the Machias patriots were acquiring an armed vessel which could be used for privateering.

The stalemate at Boston was disturbed when the patriots decided to fortify Bunker Hill in an ill-advised and poorly planned move. The British countered this foolishness with a suicidal frontal attack on 17 June, and then allowed the surviving provincials to escape across the narrow Charlestown neck when their ammunition ran out. This costly British 'victory' was nothing more than a defensive move which would be nullified when the Continental Army was finally able to mount the cannon from Ticonderoga on Dorchester Heights in March 1776.

News of Lexington and Concord with the resultant siege of Boston brought a sense of urgency to the Second Continental Congress which was convened in Philadelphia on 10 May. In its initial stages, the affair at Boston was a local, New England action. However, the representatives from the other colonies recognized it as a joint responsibility. Still, the United States of America was a thing of the future envisioned by few if any of the delegates. Although assembled in a common cause, they were not responsible to a central authority. Their loyalties were reserved for their respective provincial connections. An army organized on that basis would have been a disaster.

John Adams has been given credit for his statesmanship in effecting the appointment of George Washington to be Commander-in-Chief of 'the grand American Army.' This was a shrewd move that helped to unify the divergent interests of the thirteen colonies. The New Englanders displayed so much jealousy and dissension within their own ranks that the acceptance of the appointment of a 'foreigner' to command them is surprising. Washington's qualifications for the position by virtue of his character and experience were evident to the delegates to the Second Continental Congress. Yet, it could be doubted that any of them realized the absolute perfection of their choice which was to be confirmed throughout the trying times that followed. Washington accepted the commission in a most modest and self-deprecatory manner, but he had been angling for it and must have felt in his heart that he was taking on a job for which he had been predestined. The appointment was made on 18 June, in Philadelphia. Washington assumed command of the army at Cambridge on 2 July.

Washington was faced with an awesome responsibility. He was expected to organize an army from scratch which would be called upon to challenge the military might of the strongest country of his time. The 'army' that he had inherited was undermined by the customs of short-term enlistments and the popular election of officers. Most of his 'liberty'-loving men were not prepared to concede that they might have to accept certain responsibilities in exchange for the enjoyment of those liberties. In addition to handling the personnel problems, he needed to search out ways and means to make continued British occupation of Boston untenable. Henry Knox was sent to Ticonderoga to see about transporting the much-needed artillery that could force the issue.

One glaring weakness in the British position which was readily apparent to General Washington was their absolute dependence on supplies brought in by sea. Within a few days of his arrival, he had not only inspected the troop encampments but had reconnoitered the 'sea coast east of Boston.' The thought of disrupting the enemies' supply lines with the use of armed vessels must have occurred to him without need for prompting. That this course of action had not been taken earlier tends to emphasize the lack of coordinated leadership that existed before Washington's arrival. It is true that the Royal Navy controlled Boston Harbor and its approaches. Escort protection for transports and supply ships was provided; but as subsequent events proved, there were loopholes in this pro-

tection. Even where ships were under convoy, it was not uncommon for unfavorable weather conditions to scatter them. Already patriot vessels such as those at Machias were operating along the coast of Maine as privateers. Admiral Graves termed them 'pirate vessels' and continued to apply that epithet indiscriminately to the schooners which later were fitted out and commissioned for service in 'George Washington's Navy.'

Washington estimated that there was a total of 12,000 British troops, marines, and Tories shut up in Boston. The serious problem of food supply that this posed led to a number of complicated intrigues. Vice Admiral Graves wrote to Captain George Vandeput of the *Asia*, in New York:

Sir   Boston July 18, 1775

As every stratagem must be used to procure provisions at this Juncture, the Contractor for the Navy at Boston' has ordered his Correspondent Mr Wm McAdams at New York to charter a Vessel from 80 to 100 Tons, and to put on Board her Bread, Beef, Peas, Oatmeal, and Rice. These Provisions are to be consigned to John Grant Esqr Spanish Town Jamaica, and the Vessel of course will be cleared for that place. No person in New York can possibly know but she really is intended of Jamaica, not even Mr McAdams himself, who is ordered to write an Account of his proceedings on this Business, And to draw upon London for the Amount. When this Vessel so laden goes down the River you must seize her, and putting a sufficient Strength on Board send her to Boston; but I desire this may not be done till she is at the Hook, that the knowledge of this transaction may not get to New York and prevent our future Success, for which Reason all the People and the Master must be sent hither. If the *Kingfisher* could sail at the same time with the provision Vessel, and alter her destination at Sea, it would be better and blank Letters directed to Jamaica might be put on board her early from your Ship, so that no Suspicion would arise of your detaining her upon any supposed Exigency of Service. I am &c

Sam Graves

The person who helped Washington to create his own naval force to supplement the army was Colonel John Glover. He commanded the Marblehead Regiment which was designated as the twenty-first regiment in the newly organized American army. As an initial contribution, Glover had his own schooner, *Hannah*, to offer for use in testing the feasibility of the project. It began on or around 1 August 1775, with the refitting of *Hannah* at Glover's wharf situated in the town of Beverly, Massachusetts. This was just four weeks after Washington had arrived on the scene.

John Glover was most certainly the sort of man Washington was looking for when he took command, one who could assume responsibility and get results.

They were close in age, with Glover forty-two to his commander's forty-three, a factor which should have given them some rapport. Glover was a self-made man. His carpenter father had died when he was four and his widowed mother had raised John and his three brothers under impoverished circumstances. From this meagre start, Glover had done what would have been impossible under the contemporary social system of the mother country, England. Learning the trade of shoemaker, or cordwainer as it was known, he had opened his own shop. This shop was soon expanded to include the sale of strong liquors. How the making of shoes related to the sale of rum might be hard to understand in this day and age, but it enabled the entrepreneur to pyramid his holdings until he was in a position to own his first schooner, the 60-ton *William*, by 1763. From this point on, the typical American success story became a fore-gone conclusion. By the 1770s, John Glover was an eminently prosperous merchant and had raised himself to the highest level of society in Marblehead.

On 19 April, 1775, Glover was second-in-command of the Marblehead Regiment when an unusual circumstance elevated him to the position which made subsequent events and recognition more probable. His commander was Jeremiah Lee. On the evening of the 18th, Lee and two fellow members of his local committee of safety and supplies were meeting with Samuel Adams and John Hancock at a tavern in Menotomy. The three Marblehead men elected to stay the night at the tavern. Early the next morning, they were awakened by the approach of the British on their way to Lexington. Lee and his friends hastily left their room for a nearby field to avoid being caught by a search party of soldiers. This precipitous act left them poorly dressed for protection from the early morning chill. Jeremiah Lee sickened as a result of this exposure, and died three weeks later. The command of the regiment was thus passed on to John Glover and he was commissioned as colonel in the Massachusetts army.

The inhabitants of Marblehead found themselves in an ambiguous situation fraught with danger. By and large, they were rabid patriots with a goodly number of radicals among them. However, the town was in an exposed position on the sea coast and especially vulnerable to reprisals from British warships. The people had to walk a tightrope to avoid punishment while their men were serving in the rebel cause. Colonel Glover's schooner, *Hannah*, had been on a trading voyage to the West Indies when hostilities broke out. Since Glover and his regiment were delayed in leaving for the encampment at Cambridge, he was able to keep an eye out for her return. The situation was critical since the British sloop-of-war *Merlin* was blockading the Marblehead harbor. On the afternoon of 6 June, *Hannah* was sighted outside the harbor flying Glover's house flag, white with a blue diamond. Glover rowed out to meet her at the same time that a boat from the naval vessel was sent to stop her from entering the harbor. *Hannah*'s captain, heeding the owner's instructions, sailed on into Marblehead. By some strange quirk of fate, the British did not react to this show of defiance and both *Hannah* and the intrepid colonel escaped unscathed.

In 1774, Glover had purchased a wharf in Beverly, Massachusetts, across the bay from Salem. As described by the deed which has been preserved, it was 'a certain parcel of upland and flat ground being situated in said Beverly with a warehouse, coopers shop and wharf and pump.' Glover continued to maintain his place of residence in Marblehead but moved his business operations to these newly acquired facilities which had cost him 'sixty-five pounds lawful money.' When it was decided to alter *Hannah* for the experiment in arming vessels for use in intercepting British supply ships, she was sent from the vulnerable, open Marblehead harbor to Beverly. Here she could be worked on in relative safety, making good use of Glover's wharf and the skilled workers available at that location.

There is considerable documented information to be had about people connected with the *Hannah* venture, some of which identifies and confirms events with which the schooner was connected, but virtually nothing relating to her appearance. To determine the rental charges for her services, she was rated at 78 tons. Glover was to be paid at the rate of one dollar per ton per month. That is the only clue to her physical appearance. A long list of the men who worked to convert *Hannah* has been compiled from contemporary records which indicated that the labor charges were not inconsiderable, but it does not offer details of the alterations that were made. It would have been necessary to pierce her bulwarks for a pair of 4 pounders on either side and to provide mountings for ten or a dozen swivel guns. Normally sailed by a crew of no more than six men, she was asked to accommodate a number six times that many, a requirement which must have necessitated considerable alteration. This work went forward throughout the month of August.

On 24 August, a sailing master, a master's mate and four seamen were hired at Beverly. The balance of *Hannah*'s crew was selected from the Marblehead regiment which was by that time encamped at Cambridge. The thought of manning a naval vessel with soldiers would seem absurd if it were not remembered that the men chosen for this service had been sailors beforehand. Having accepted Glover's offer of *Hannah*, General Washington also undoubtedly followed his suggestions in the selection of officers and crew. Nicholson Broughton, who was commander of the 5th Company in Glover's regiment, was named Captain. Glover's 20-year-old son, John Jr, who commanded the 9th Company, was assigned to *Hannah* as a lieutenant. About three dozen enlisted men made up the rest of the crew that was to man the little schooner.

HMS *Nautilus* in pursuit of *Hannah*.

The most significant document to be used in establishing *Hannah*'s claim to fame is the one by which Washington commissioned Captain Broughton. The instructions incorporated into this commission which was drawn up by Colonel Joseph Reed, Washington's secretary, were intended to cover all aspects of *Hannah*'s mission and provided a precedent for subsequent operations. Addressed to Captain Nicholson Broughton and endorsed by General Washington, they read:

2 Sept

1st. You being appointed a Captain in the Army of the United Colonies of North America, are hereby directed to take the Command of a Detachment of said Army and proceed on Board the Schooner *Hannah*, at Beverly, lately fitted out & equipp'd with Arms, Ammunition and Provisions at the Continental Expence.

2nd. You are to proceed as Commander of Sd Schooner, immediately on a Cruize against such Vessels as may be found on the High seas or elsewhere, bound inward and outward to or from Boston, in the Service of the ministerial Army, and to take and seize all such Vessels, laden with Soldiers, Arms, Ammunition, or Provisions for or from sd Army, or which you shall have good Reason to suspect are in such Service.

3rd. If you should be so successful as to take any of such Vessels, you are immediately to send them to the nearest and safest Port to this Camp, under a careful Prizemaster, directing him to notify me by Express immediately of such Capture, with all particulars and there to wait my farther Direction.

4th. You are to be very particular and diligent in your Search after all Letters and other Papers tending to discover the designs of the Enemy, or of any other Kind, and to forward all such to me as soon as possible.

5th. Whatever Prisoners you may take you are to treat with Kindness and Humanity, as far as is consistent with your own Safety. Their privat Stock of Money, and Apparall to be given them after being duly search'd, and when they arrive at any Port, you are to apply to the Committee, or to anny Officer of the Continental Army stationed at such Port for a Guard to bring them up to Head Quarters.

6th. For your own Encouragement and that of the other Officers and Men, to Activity, and Courage in this Service, over and above your Pay in the Continental Army, you shall be entitled to one third Part of the Cargo of every Vessel by you taken, and sent into Port, (military and naval Stores only excepted, which with Vessels and Apparell are reserved for the publick Service) which 1st third Part is to be divided among the Officers and Men in the following Proportions. Captain 6 Shares, 1st Lieut 5 do, 2nd Lieut 4 do, Ship's Master 3 do, Steward 2 do, Mate 1½ do, Gunners Mate and Serjt 1½ do, Privates 1 Share each.

7th. You are particularly charged to avoid any Engagement with any armed Vessel of the Enemy, though you may be equal in Strength, or may have some small Advantage; the Design of this Enterprize, being to intercept the Supplies of the Enemy, which will be defeated by your running into unnecessary Engagements.

8th. As there may be other Vessels imployed in the same Service with yourselves, you are to fix upon proper Signals, and your Stations being settled so as to take the greatest Range, avoid cruizing on the same Ground. If you should happen to take Prizes in Sight of each other; the Rules which take Place among Private Ships of War, are to be observed in the Distribution of Prize-Money.

9th. In case of retaking the Vessel of any Friend to the American Cause, I will recommend it to such Person to make a suitable Compensation to those who have done such a Service; but such Vessels are not to be deemed as coming within the Directions respecting other Vessels.

10th. You are to be extremely careful and frugal of your Ammunition, by no means to waste any of it in Salutes, or for any Purpose, but what is absolutely necessary.

By this document, *Hannah* can be accorded recognition as the first armed vessel officially commissioned in the service of the thirteen colonies by a central authority. It would be nice to report that her captain and crew could serve as models for latter day Navy men. Judging from his record as captain and, later, commodore in Washington's embryo fleet, Nicholson Broughton could be viewed as an inept bumbler or a piratical scalawag. During *Hannah*'s brief career, Captain Broughton showed himself far more solicitous of the welfare and convenience of his fellow Marbleheaders who comprised the crew than with diligent application to the instructions by which he was supposedly bound. The crew behaved no better.

In his book *George Washington's Navy*, William Clark has provided a most entertaining account of *Hannah*'s 'inglorious career.' In late August 1775, thirty-six privates with their two lieutenants marched from Cambridge to Marblehead on what must have seemed like a lark. These sailors-soldiers-sailors had been released after two months of tedious army duty to return home to wives, families, and sweethearts before embarking on a cruise which they had reason to hope would bring them wealth in the form of prize money. Since *Hannah* was not quite ready to sail, they enjoyed a short furlough at home before crossing over from Marblehead to Beverly where the little schooner was waiting.

Hannah finally sailed for her first cruise on the morning of 5 September. Two days later, Broughton made his first report:

Glouster September 7, 1775
To his Excellency George Washington Esq Captain

General in and over the Confederate Army of the united Colonies in America
May it please your Excellency

I beg leave to acquaint your Excellency that I sailed from Beverly last Tuesday at 10 oClock with a fair wind, proceeded on my Cruise; on the same day about 5 oclock saw two ships of War, they gave me Chace, I made back towards Cape Ann but did not go in, next morning I saw a ship under my lee quarter she giving me Chace I run into Cape Ann harbour, I went out again that night about sunsett, and stood to the southward, next morning saw a ship under my lee quarter I perceived her to be a large ship, I tac'd & stood back for the land, soon after I put about & stood towards her again and found her a ship of no force, I came up with her, hail'd & asked where she came from, was answer'd from Pescatugua, & bound to Boston, I told him he must bear away and go into Cape Ann, but being very loth I told him if he did not I should fire on him, on that he bore away and I have brought her safe into Cape Ann Harbour, and have deliver'd the ship and Prisoners into the hands & care of the Committee of Safety for this town of Glouster, and have desired them to send the Prisoners, under proper guard, to your Excellency for further orders.

Also have sent the Captain of the ship we took for your Excellencys examination, and I shall proceed immediately in the further execution of your Excellencys orders And am your Excellencys (&c.)

Nicholasson Broughton

It is easy to imagine the glee with which the crew responded to this initial success. Captain Broughton undoubtedly inspired his fellow townsmen with visions of the prize money which would soon be lining their pockets. The disillusionment which was soon to follow plunged the profit-seeking 'patriots' into serious trouble.

Unity, as the 260-ton ship described above was named, was controlled by a seven-man prize crew from the British warship, *Lively*, when *Hannah* appeared on the scene. She had belonged to a loyal patriot named John Langdon and, as such, could not be claimed as a legitimate prize. Article Nine in Broughton's instructions very clearly covered such a case. However, he was determined not to let this chance for prize money elude his grasp. He wrote a letter to Washington in which he made a number of allegations to the effect that *Unity*'s cargo was not legitimate. He suggested that she was in fact engaged in furnishing supplies to the British. The arguments did not hold water, and *Unity* was released to her owner. While these negotiations were going on, *Hannah* apparently lay idle in Cape Ann Harbor at Gloucester.

When the crew learned that its expectations had gone a-glimmering, a full-scale mutiny developed under the leadership of one John Searle. It required a detachment from Cambridge to quell the uprising and return the crew to camp under custody. As was promised under Article Nine of his instructions, Washington had fully intended to seek some recompense for *Hannah*'s officers and men as a reward for the retaking of *Unity*. However the mutinous action of the crew altered those intentions. He wrote to Langdon:

Sir,   Camp at Cambridge September 21 1775

E'er this you must have heard of the taking, and retaking of your Ship; and of my ordering it to be delivered up to your agent . . . I have promised the Officers, to wit. Captn Broughton, Lieut Glover, & another Subaltern whose name I cannot recollect that I would recommend them to your notice & compensation . . . I should have done the same thing in behalf of the men (for you must know the Vessell which retook yours was fitted out at the Publick expence, & manned with soldiers for a particular Expedition) but for their exceeding ill behaviour upon that occasion . . . I was obliged to send for, and bring them here Prisoners instead of prosecuting a scheme I had in view with the People of Halifax, & I hope to bestow a reward of a different kind upon them for their Mutinous behavior . . . With very great esteem, I am &c.
To the Owner of the Ship *Unity*

A month later in a letter to Colonel Reed, John Glover acknowledged that he had 'received the present which Capt Langdon made to the Officers on board the Schooner he thinks it very genteel.' The crewmen, on the other hand, were court-martialled and sentenced to punishment:

[Extract]   Head Quarters, Cambridge, September 22, 1775.
Parole Lynn   Countersign Marblehead
The undernamed Prisoners, try'd by a General Court Martial for 'Mutiny, Riot and Disobedience of orders,' are severally guilty of the Crimes, wherewith they are accused, and the Court upon due Consideration of the Evidence, do adjudge that the prisoner Joseph Seales receive thirty-nine lashes upon his bare back and be drum'd out of the Army, and that the prisoners, John Gillard, Jacob Smallwood, John Peltro, Samuel Grant, Hugh Renny, James Jeffery, Charles Alcrain, Samuel Hannis, Charles Pearce, James Williams, John Kelly, John Bryan and Philip Florence, do each of them receive Twenty lashes upon his back and be drum'd out of the Army – The prisoners Lawrence Blake, Samuel Bodin, John Besom, Benj Bartholomew, Francis Ellis, Joseph Lawrence, John Sharp, John Poor, Joseph Fessenden, John Foster, John Lee, Lawrence Bartlet, Philip Greatey, Peter Neivelle, Samuel Parsons, Jeremiah Dailey, Francis Greater, Richd Pendrick, Robert Hooper, Anthony Lewis, Nicholas Ogleby, and Thomas Metyard; be fin'd Twenty Shillings lawful money each.

Joseph Foster, Joseph Laurence and Joseph Tessenden, being recommended by the Court Martial, as proper objects of mercy, The Commander in Chief is pleased to remit their fine, and to order the sentence upon all the others, to be put in Execution at Guard mounting, tomorrow morning – Those upon Prospect Hill to receive their punishment there; the rest at the main Guard.

Except for the first cruise which has been described, there is no positive documentation which identifies *Hannah* by name to help in tracing her subsequent movements. Those movements can be followed by inference from information found in contemporary records to form a basis for the story that has been commonly accepted. Captain Broughton is known to have resumed cruising in a schooner near the end of September. There is no evidence to show that this was not *Hannah*, nor is there any indication that his cruising met with any success. In a letter to Glover dated 17 October, Colonel Reed noted 'We are told that our Vessels make a Practice of running in every Night when they have been out & the Men come on Shore – This must be rectified.' Such behavior has been ascribed to Broughton with no direct identification to back it up, but it does seem probable from what is known of his character. A well-documented event took place on 10 October in which it has popularly been assumed that *Hannah* played a leading role.

HMS *Nautilus* arrived at Boston from Rhode Island on 5 October. On the 8th, Admiral Graves 'ordered the *Nautilus*, as being by much the best going Vessel of any then at Boston' to cruise for eight days in an attempt to capture rebel privateers. Her commander, Captain John Collins, had suffered an embarrassment just a month earlier. He was accused of being lax in his duty while *Nautilus* was blockading the Delaware River in August. A court-martial was held on 11 September and he was sentenced to a reprimand and loss of six months of personal pay. This experience must still have been rankling him when he sighted an armed schooner in Salem Bay on 10 October. Although that schooner was not named in the records, it is generally accepted to have been *Hannah*.

Nautilus, rated at 314 tons, carrying a crew of 100 men with her armament of 16 six pounders, was a Goliath to *Hannah*'s David with no prospect that the little schooner's four 'pop guns' would serve as a lethal sling shot. When *Nautilus* gave chase, *Hannah* headed for the harbor at Beverly. When Broughton saw that the faster man-of-war would cut him off before he could reach safety, he changed course and ran the schooner onto a sand bar about a half-mile short of his goal in order to avoid capture.

High water mark had been at 11:58am. By the time the chase ended and *Nautilus* was able to approach *Hannah*, the water had receded, leaving the schooner well aground. *Nautilus* nosed her way into the shallow waters while her captain debated ways and means for destroying *Hannah*. Meanwhile taking advantage of their position, the Marbleheaders were removing to safety the precious armament which was so hard to come by in the colonies.

Nautilus was within easy range when a quirk of fate took a hand in *Hannah*'s story. The wind and ebbing tide caused the sloop-of-war to drift uncontrollably onto a mudbank. Her hull careened at an angle which made it impossible to bring her guns to bear. All thought of sending a detachment of his ship's boats to set fire to *Hannah* had to be discarded. The schooner was high and dry and the men ashore had rallied to fire with muskets and swivel guns at any sign of British activity.

Nautilus herself was now in a precarious position. Across the narrow bay on Salem Neck, a large force of patriots had set up some four pounders and brought them to bear on the hapless sloop. Those cannon had about four hours in which to inflict considerable damage before the tide rose and Captain Collins was able to haul his command out of its predicament by use of a stream anchor. In his haste to escape from the threat of being captured by a proposed boarding party of rebels, the British commander cut the cable and left his best bower anchor behind. It is interesting to recollect that *Nautilus* was recorded as having had trouble with running aground and losing anchors ten years earlier in the Mississippi River.

Lieutenant John Barker, a British officer stationed in Boston, recorded his impression of the events at Beverly in a diary, under the date of 22 October:

> . . . The *Nautilus* Capn Collins come in; in chase of a Privateer she drove her ashore and run aground herself, but got off again with the lost of 1 man killed and 1 wounded; coming into this harbour she run aground again, and was with great difficulty got off in two days; she now lays between this Peninsula and Noddles Island, . . .

From the patriot viewpoint, the *New England Chronicle* also described the action:

> Cambridge, October 12.
> Last Tuesday one of our Privateers from Beverly, having been on a Cruise in the Bay, was followed, on her return into Port, by the *Nautilus* Man of War. The Privateer run aground in a Cove a little without Beverly Harbour, where the People speedily assembled, stripped her, and carried her Guns, &c ashore. The Man of War was soon within Gunshot, when she also got aground; she however let go an Anchor, and bringing her Broadside to bear, began to fire upon the Privateer. The People of Salem and Beverly soon returned the Compliment from a Number of Cannon on Shore, keeping up a warm and well directed Fire on the Man of War for 2 or 3 Hours. and it is suposed did

her considerable Damage, and probably killed and wounded some of the Men; but befor they could board her, which they were preparing to do, the Tide arose about 8 o'Clock in the Evening, when she cut her Cable, and got off. Some of her Shot struck one or two Buildings in Beverly; but no lives were lost on our side, and the Privateer damaged very little if any.

From this account, it could be assumed that the schooner was floated off the sand bar at the next high tide and moved to the protection of Beverly Harbor. Her identification as *Hannah* has been questioned with the unproven hypothesis that *Hannah* was off on another mission. However, there is documentary evidence that indicates the schooner was available and in the vicinity at the time of the encounter with *Nautilus*. For those who do not have ready access to archives of contemporary documents, the continuing series of books, *Naval Documents of the American Revolution*, is a superb source of information. It has provided most of the authentic detail in this chapter. In volume 2, there are direct and indirect references to suggest *Hannah's* whereabouts.

On 9 October, in a letter to Washington the very day before the *Nautilus* episode, Glover and Stephen Moylan wrote:

Colonel Glover has given the strongest proofs of his good oppinion of the Schooner commanded by Captain Broughton, he has ventured his brother & his favorite son on board of her, however Lest any blame may lay with him, if any Misfortune shoud happed (which God avert) he will be pleased to have the Captain & his Company removd to a vessell of better fame for Sailing, we have for this purpose hired a schooner from Mr Stevens of Marblehead, She is noted for her good qualitys, & will be ready to take in the *Hannahs* Company & Stores in 12 or 14 days the extra Sails &c on board the Later will serve for her, she is taken up on the same terms with the other two, 4/p ton month or 5/4 Lawful money.

It is interesting to note that of all the vessels commissioned for George Washington's navy, *Hannah* appears to be the only one that was not rechristened with a name more suitable to her new calling. Is it possible that she fell into such disrepute because of her poor showing that she became simply referred to as 'that schooner'? This is how Glover mentioned her on 22 October, when he acknowledged Langdon's gift to her officers. In ending his letter of 20 October, to Glover and Moylan, Colonel Reed suggested 'If you think any Good Purpose would be answered by it, you can send out Colonel Glover's Schooner 'till the Substitute is got ready.' In any event, the name 'Hannah' seems to have disappeared from the records as pertaining to the schooner in question.

Shipping records have been discovered that identify

a schooner owned by John Glover in 1774 and named *Hannah* which was rated 45 tons. If this rating and identification of the schooner were correct, it would mean that a vessel smaller than little *Sultana* had been manned with the absurdly large complement of about 40. It will be remembered that *Sultana* was allowed only 25 men, 5 less than the standard crew for a Royal Navy schooner. There are indications that ship owners in the colonies registered their vessels at much lower tonnage than was determined by standard calculations. It was probably a 'shrewd' Yankee trick to save on customs expenses. As an example, when Admiral Colville purchased *Chaleur* in 1764, the owner reported her tonnage as 90 at a time when it would have paid to boost the figure to get a better price [PRO ADM 1/482 p362]. Her 'Kings tonage' was calculated at 117. *Hannah's* true rating may have been slightly inflated at 78 tons to increase the rental charges but she was certainly larger than 45 tons.

Hannah's debut had resulted in a modicum of success with the recapture of *Unity*. However, the project to arm vessels began to stagnate in the month of September. It had turned sour with the mutiny on *Hannah*, the loss of precious time, the trial and need for punishment of the mutineers, and little to show for it all. The Massachusetts House of Representatives was considering 'the Propriety of fixing out Armed Vessels for the Defense of [their] Sea-Coast', but they deferred to General Washington's judgement in the matter. Then early in October, John Hancock in Philadelphia wrote to Washington that two brigantines loaded with munitions had left England for Quebec in August. He asked the General to send two armed vessels in an attempt to intercept the British supply ships. This revitalized the project.

Time was of the essence. If suitable armed vessels had been available, they should have sailed immediately. As the events transpired, the two schooners, *Hancock* and *Franklin* did not sail until 22 October, more than two months after the supply ships had reportedly left England. Broughton had been given command of the little expedition with the rank of commodore. John Selman was second in command, sailing in his own schooner *Eliza* which had been renamed *Franklin*. It is doubtful that they could have reached the Gulf of St Lawrence before the objects of their search had passed up the river. Their actions once they did reach those waters verged on piracy. They ignored Washington's orders concerning the proper treatment of local inhabitants. They seized vessels that later were judged as not proper prizes and released to their owners. They brought respectable citizens back as prisoners to Washington's great embarrassment. He found it necessary to apologize and return them to their homes. When faced with a reprimand for these unseemly acts, Broughton and Selman simply resigned from the service.

However, the machinery had been set in motion. Plymouth was selected as a second base for fitting out armed vessels. Agents were appointed in various ports to receive and supervise the disposition of captured ships. Washington rapidly expanded his 'navy' through the medium of his agents, Glover and Moylan, and his secretary, Colonel Reed. The little fleet that he initiated continued in operation through the year 1777, long after Washington left the scene. A total of 55 vessels were taken. Most of them carried ordinary supplies, but a few were transporting the precious munitions and armament of which the patriot army was in such dire need. The most important and dramatic capture was the 250-ton brig, *Nancy*. She was taken on 28 November 1775, by Captain John Manley in the *Lee*. Her cargo of arms and ammunition was so invaluable that extraordinary precautions were taken to guard against the danger of recapture. It was unloaded at Gloucester and transported by land to Cambridge as expeditiously as possible. John Manley became one of the earliest American naval heroes for this and other exploits.

It has been suggested that the fortification of Dorchester Heights in March 1776 forced the British evacuation of Boston. Actually, the British had seen the folly of maintaining their hold on Boston long before that. Boston did not provide a suitable base of operations for prosecuting a war which had expanded to include the entire Atlantic Seaboard. General Howe had in fact received permission from England for the evacuation before the end of 1775. The inadequacy of available transport had condemned him, his troops and the civilian loyalists sheltering with them to a very lean winter. Considered in this light, Washington's navy might be given as much credit as the artillery from Ticonderoga for reinforcing the British desire to extricate themselves from a most inhospitable situation. When Manley captured *Little Hannah* on 9 December 1775, her cask of oranges, intended for General Howe, went instead to Washington's breakfast table.

CHAPTER NINE
The Drawings

So far, this book has been concerned with the history of colonial schooners. Since it is directed primarily toward model builders, the time has come to consider the construction of schooner models. The first and very important step in this process is the selection of a good set of plans. One of the finest sources for authentic ship's plans is to be found in the extensive collection of draughts produced by the British Admiralty which is now in the custody of the National Maritime Museum. Photostats of these original drawings can be ordered directly from the museum.

The Admiralty draughts are especially significant to modelers interested in the eighteenth century American-built ships which are represented in the collection. Without them, the graphic record of those ships would be very meagre. Howard I Chapelle provided general circulation and recognition for those plans in his many books. By identifying and presenting them in the continuity of history, he performed a service for model builders which cannot be too greatly appreciated. In the preface to his first book, *The Baltimore Clipper*, Chapelle credited Mr C Knight, the British Admiraly Curator, with searching out for him the plans of small sailing craft in the Admiralty archives. It is likely that Mr Chapelle first learned about the existence of contemporary drawings for colonial schooners at that time. He certainly made excellent use of them when they were introduced in *The History of American Sailing Ships* which followed.

The four schooner designs presented earlier in this book are an invaluable record of such vessels built in America during a particular period in history. Nothing had been learned from contemporary records which confirms the surmise that a special effort was made to record the lines of those schooners at that time, but it is interesting to note that all four draughts were made in 1768. Navy schooners were regularly sent to England for refitting, but the designs of others were not recorded unless there are still some draughts to be so identified. The rough plan for *Sir Edward Hawke* and the *Earl of Egmont* was copied for the record in April according to the notation on Captain Kennedy's letter. The drawing of *Sultana* was made in June, just two months later. The most complete plan of all was drawn for *Halifax* in September. It was the only one of the four which details the design of the stern. Finally, in November of 1768, *Chaleur*'s lines were set down along with a very important list of her mast and spar dimensions. The value of these plans is enhanced by the fact that they depict such an interesting variety of schooner design.

Another approach to the establishment of plans for building a model is an attempt to reconstruct the subject where no authentic design exists. To name a few examples, this has been done many times over in *Santa Marias*, *Half Moons*, and *Mayflowers*, and Charles G Davis did it most effectively for the popular *Lexington*. The purist may shun such models, but they do perform a useful purpose in bringing to life ships of special historic significance where there is no hope of recreating a true representation. Those models are reasonable approximations of the size and general appearance of their prototypes. Governed by these considerations, the first model project offered here will be a reconstrution of Colonel Glover's schooner, *Hannah*.

Hannah's tonnage was recorded as being 78 to determine rental charges for her service in George Washington's navy. As has been shown, registered tonnage of a vessel in those days is an unreliable means for establishing her size without corroboration from actual physical dimensions. This may have been due to different or faulty methods of calculation or possibly a deliberate falsification of the records. However, in view of the fact that *Hannah* was armed with four carriage guns and carried a crew of 40 men, the 78-ton rating is quite within reason; it would leave her five tons smaller than the navy schooner, *Halifax*, which was of no more than average size for those armed vessels. Marblehead, Colonel Glover's home town, was noted for its fleet of fishing schooners. This reputation prompted the British Admiralty to apply the term 'Marblehead schooner' to the new class of vessel instituted in the navy in 1764. In addition to their fishing ventures, the schooners were used to deliver their catch after it had been dried to markets where it could be exchanged for such products as sugar and molasses. It is reasonable therefore to assume that *Hannah* could have been such a vessel.

In his book on American fishing schooners, Howard Chapelle presents as plate 4 a reconstructed plan dated for 1785. This design suits the requirements for a model of *Hannah* as outlined above. While the sheer plan offers quite a different aspect, comparison reveals a close resemblance of the hull design to the lines found on the Admiralty drawing for *Halifax*. This similarity makes it possible to accept the reconstruction as suitable for a schooner built in the mid-1760s as *Hannah* was. On this basis, Chapelle's design has been modified and adapted to produce a reconstruction of *Hannah* to build the first model detailed in this book. The second model for which plans will be furnished and the construction described is *Halifax*. In contrast, this will result in a schooner model as nearly like the prototype as possible since the very complete contemporary drawing of the actual vessel is available.

Model builders who wish to attempt plank-on-frame models with subjects for which no detailed frame plans are available are faced with the problem of developing their own drawings. This proves a great deterrent to many otherwise excellent craftsmen. This book includes plans for building two schooner models by means of a special plank-on-frame technique which should serve as an introduction to the work with relatively simple examples. Once the ship modeler has built a plank-on-frame model, he is unlikely to return to solid, carved hull construction methods, and will want to be able to produce his own plans for later models. With this in mind, a review of the drawing process seems to be in order.

Strict adherence to theoretically correct drawing procedures is not required in laying out the lines for a good model; the skill, judgement, and accuracy required for good model work should suffice. Many of the confusing details which are valuable to the marine architect for building a full size ship are superfluous to the model builder. Buttock lines and diagonal sections can be ignored. Basically, all that is required to produce the model plans for a hull is a proved set of body lines which determine the shapes of sections at right angles to and at measured intervals along the keel, and the sheer plan which is a broadside view of the ship that determines the spacing of the body lines. The basic plan will be derived from photostats of contemporary draughts or reproductions of present day drawings which derive from such original material. Whatever the source, the process of reproduction is subject to distortion and inaccuracies which must be guarded against. The scale which appears on a drawing will serve to catch deviations parallel to it. In a reasonably good reproduction, these errors will not be great enough to disturb any but the most fastidious of draughtsmen, and for practical purposes, will not affect the quality of the model.

The proof of the body and sheer plans is in the waterlines that can be laid out from them. Those lines should 'fair up' as smooth, continuous curves from one end of the hull to the other with all the plotted points falling nicely on those curves. Most plans do not show these longitudinal curves for the shape of the hull above the actual waterline except for the topmost sheer line. However, the model builder will want to lay out 'waterlines' at regular intervals from the keel to sheer in order to establish the contours of the topsides. When waterline sections are drawn across the body plan, they should be spaced fairly close together. This will result in a large number of waterlines available to provide points for laying out the curves of the frames. Considerable variation is possible in curves where there are too few points to determine the shape. This shape should be sketched lightly freehand with a pencil line through the plotted points to show up the character of the curve. The smooth, finished line is then drawn with the aid of suitable French curves. A long, graceful 'ship's curve' will be required for the longitudinal hull lines where the curvature is slight.

Use of French curves to draw body lines and subsequently the frame shapes for a model could be questioned theoretically when Admiralty draughts are used as the basis. The body lines on the *Halifax* drawing, to cite an example, are made up in large part with circular arcs. The original drawing includes sets of horizontal and vertical lines which locate the centers for floor sweeps and lower and upper breadth sweeps. Nevertheless, it will be found that careful use of French curves will match up with the resulting lines and eliminate the tedious mechanical process of laying out and fairing up the circular arcs. Besides, the process by which the original drawing was created could be put to question. The lines were taken off a hull which had seen three years of service. In order to satisfy the conventions of his drawing procedures, the draughtsman then had to work in reverse to find the centers on his drawing which would produce circular arcs to fit the body lines developed from measurements of the hull. At best, the resulting drawing had to be something of a compromise though it is the best source that could be hoped for to use in recreating *Halifax*.

A primary purpose of this book is to present plans and describe the procedure for building plank-on-frame models by a special method. This method makes it easier to assemble the framework of the hull and hold it securely while being planked than the standard 'building-board' technique. The frames can be faired up both inside and out almost as easily as though they were formed from a solid block. In model building, it is generally considered wise to start with an unambitious project before tackling a complex one. The little schooner models presented here provide a modest challenge to the person wanting to build a plank-on-frame model for the first time. The initial subject, *Hannah*, requires no carving or other special work to complicate the process; the second model, *Halifax*, incorporates some of these complications to prepare a model builder for the more intricate work of constructing a frigate or ship-of-the-line built by the same methods.

As the plans for these models were drawn up, an attempt was made to design the component parts in true proportion to those in the prototype. The frames were designed with the 'sistered' or double construction with a stepped arrangement of floors and futtocks which provides strength and stability in the assembled unit. This is a compromise with the dockyard survey information for *Halifax* which suggests that the futtocks were joined end to end and diminished in thickness as they approached the sheer line. The model plans call for frames 9in thick spaced 12in apart which agrees with the 1ft 9in room and space recorded for *Halifax*. Thus, although it would be impossible to precisely duplicate the construction of the original schooner without much more detailed information the model design offers a close approximation.

The first step was to lay out the sheer plan with the various features of the hull. The body line stations were marked off perpendicular to the rabbet line of the keel and the body plan showing the shapes of those sections in the hull was drawn up. The body lines represent the shape of the hull under the planking as indicated by the fact that they extend into the rabbet. The waterlines on the original drawing can be discarded for model building purposes once it has been proved that the body lines agree with them. A new set of waterline planes should be drawn in on the new drawing from the rabbet in the keel to the highest point on the sheer plan. Then, the new waterline curves can be laid out below the sheer view using dividers to pick off dimensions from the body plan. This provides the foundation for the model's master frame plan.

At this point, the designer must arbitrarily locate the model's frames on the drawing with the room and space allowances that have been decided on. This arrangement can be made advantageously by locating the frames to facilitate model construction with an accommodation of changes in the sheer line and provi-

sions for windows or gun ports. Whole frames are marked off forward on the hull to a point where the waterlines indicate that the outside surface of the frame will become sharply angled to its sides. Here, cant frames should be fitted in using the same room and space allowance where they flare out at the deck level. The stern section is treated in a similar fashion with the last cant frames located as far aft as possible to carry out the lines of the hull. A decision has to be made regarding how far aft whole frames fitted to the top of the keel may be used. Beyond that point, deadwood mounted on the keel must be provided for fastening the half frames and cant frames. Half frames become necessary when the rise of the floor becomes so acute that is is no longer practical to make the frame in one piece. When the shape of the stem at the bow is drawn, deadwood must be included to allow for fastening the cant frames. This deadwood can be the same thickness as the stem itself because of the angle at which the planking enters the rabbet. However, the deadwood at the stern must be thinner than the keel by the thickness of two planks so that they can be fitted flush with the keel and stern post. The keel can be designed so that it will be notched to locate the whole frames. This will ensure both convenience and accuracy later on when the hull is assembled in the frame jig.

When the frame locations have been established on the waterline layout, the designs of the individual frames can be developed. First, a reference plane is located on the sheer plan parallel to the rabbet in the keel and as close to the top of the sheer line as is practical to allow for construction of the model on the frame jig. Extensions from the tops of each frame must protect beyond that reference line by the thickness of the material used to make the jig. Masonite $\frac{1}{4}$in thick is a practical choice for these small schooner models. A master guide sheet should be laid out on the drawing board to include the notched keel in section on a vertical centerline with the waterline planes and the reference line drawn in. Fine ink lines would be preferable for all of this work for the sake of accuracy and visibility.

For each frame, a piece of tracing paper is taped down over the prepared guide sheet. The centerline, reference plane, the rabbet which marks the bottom of the frame, and the notch and thickness on the keel are drawn on the tracing paper first. Then, the point where the frame crosses each waterline on the master frame plan is picked off with dividers as a dimension taken from the centerline and transferred to the individual frame sheet. Wherever the frame surface is not at right angles to its sides, there will be two points to plot on each side of the centerline. When all of the waterlines have been set off in this manner, the frame shape can be drawn in with the aid of a French curve. The top of the frame relative to the reference plan is located from the sheer plan. Frame extensions are drawn from those points parallel to the centerline.

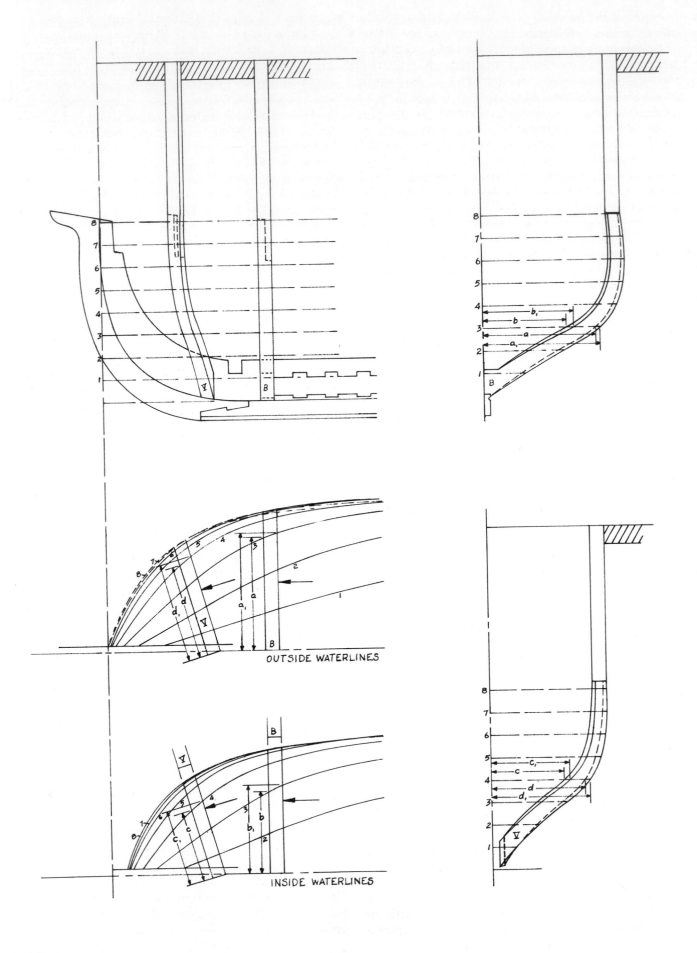

OUTSIDE WATERLINES

INSIDE WATERLINES

In order to maintain a continuity of shape from frame to frame, it is helpful to keep the previous drawing in place and superimpose another piece of tracing paper to lay out the next successive frame. Thus, when the frame is sketched in, the similarity of shapes can be observed and preserved as the family of curves grows. Cant frames require special treatment. Since the measurements are not made normally to the centerline of the keel, an arbitrary 'centerline' must be drawn perpendicular to the sides of the cant frame to provide a common reference line. The frame details considered so far furnish the patterns to be used in shaping the outside contours of the frames.

When the frames are assembled in the jig to form the hull of a model, annoying extra work can be avoided if the inside fairs up as well as the outside. This condition can be provided for by using a procedure that ensures the insides of the frames are drawn with as much care as the outsides. When the outside contours for all the frames have been laid out, every fourth or fifth frame along the length of the hull is developed further. Lines representing the insides of the frames are drawn to suit the model requirements for moulded dimensions. Those frame drawings are relocated over the guide sheet and the new lines are converted into a set of 'inside waterlines' superimposed on a plan view of the frame arrangement. Then, the complete set of frame drawings is reworked to add the inside shapes as determined from those inside waterlines. This entails considerable work at the drawing board, but it is amply rewarded when the model is built. When shaped accurately to the drawn patterns, the frames will fair up both inside and out.

The drawings can now be further developed to help in building the model. With the frame locations shown on the sheer view of the master frame plan, modifications can be drawn in to provide sills for the gunports and window openings and filler blocks as needed to complete the sheer line. The arrangement of transoms and stern frames along with miscellaneous timbers to complete the stern assembly can be laid out. The positioning of the stern frames will be governed by requirements for window openings. On the plans drawn for this book, the uppermost or 'wing' transom has its centerline located vertically at the point where the round tuck of the hull ends and the lower counter starts. This provides a fastening surface for both sets of planking. This transom is notched on its top surface to locate the lower ends of the stern frames and on the bottom at its transverse centerline to fit the top of the stern deadwood. All of these features can be located on the model from the drawing by transferring measurements taken from the reference line which represents the surface of the frame jig on which the model is built.

The sheer plan of *Halifax* shows the internal profile details which include the locations of the main deck beams. This sort of information can be added to the master frame plan to show the relationship of the deck beams to the frames in the model. This can then be projected onto a plan view and a design developed for framing the decks of the model with allowance for the various openings and reinforcements needed. If the deck is to be completely planked over, it may not be considered necessary to include the knees and other features which would have been found in the original vessel although some craftsmen enjoy doing that work just for its own sake and their personal satisfaction.

One more drawing is required to complete the preparations for building a hull by the method presented in this book. It is necessary to lay out the design of the frame jig on which the hull is to be assembled. Once again the plan view of the frame arrangement is needed. All of the drawing work described in this chapter is facilitated with the use of tracing paper. Once a particular plan has been established on paper, it is a simple matter to copy off needed details to develop a supplementary drawing. In this case, it is only necessary to mark off the notches to fit the frame extensions which were drawn on the individual frame details. This is done by measuring and marking off at the corresponding position on the frame plan as the bottom of the notch on each side of the hull. Those notches need not be more than 1/8 in deep, and the pattern for cutting out the opening in the jig can be completed on that basis. The extensions of the stern frames where they meet the reference plane should also be drawn in on this plan by projecting their locations from the sheer plan and the end view.

Ship modeling is generally noted for testing a person's patience. Preparing drawings for a model is certainly no exception to that rule. However, the exercise of care and patience in this preparation will simplify the model work that follows and make it much more pleasurable.

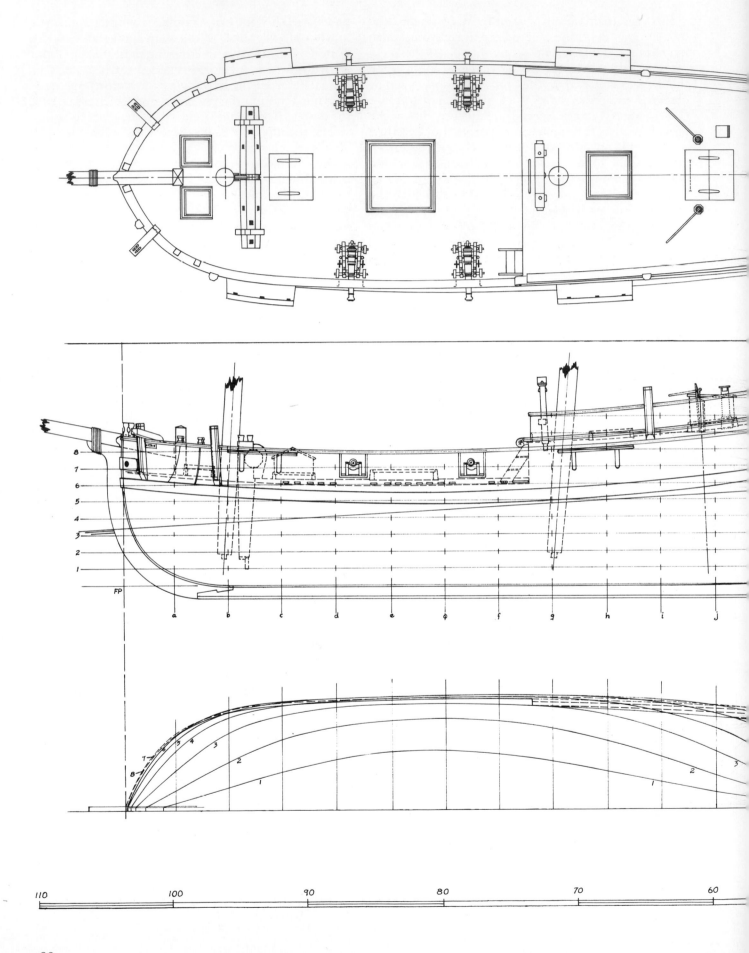

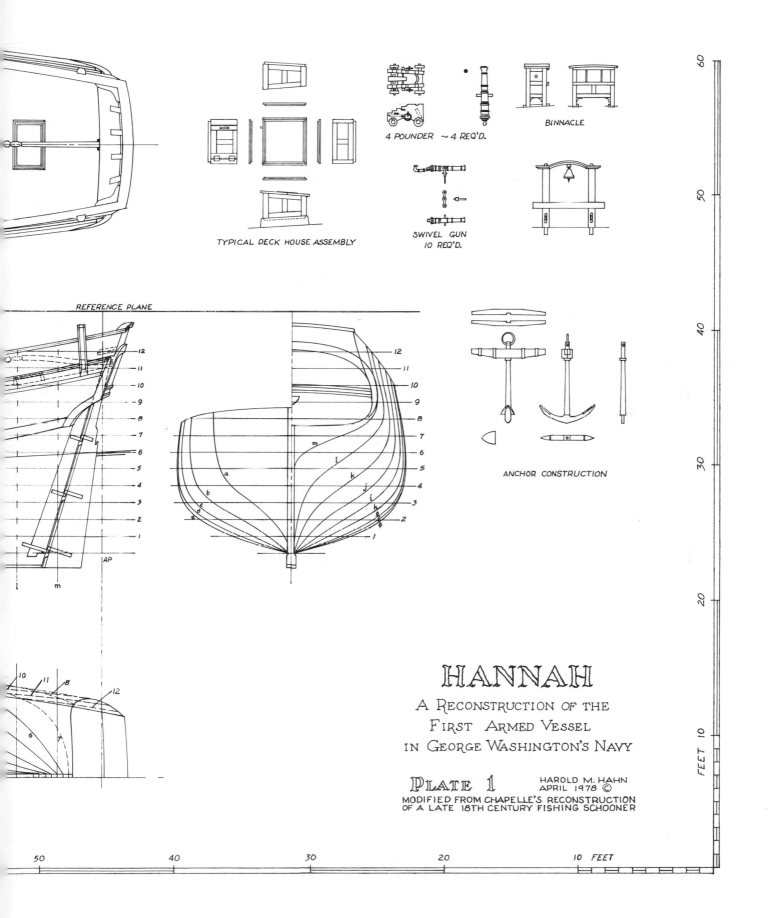

TYPICAL DECK HOUSE ASSEMBLY

4 POUNDER ~ 4 REQ'D.

BINNACLE

SWIVEL GUN
10 REQ'D.

REFERENCE PLANE

ANCHOR CONSTRUCTION

AP

HANNAH

A RECONSTRUCTION OF THE
FIRST ARMED VESSEL
IN GEORGE WASHINGTON'S NAVY

PLATE 1

HAROLD M. HAHN
APRIL 1978 ©
MODIFIED FROM CHAPELLE'S RECONSTRUCTION
OF A LATE 18TH CENTURY FISHING SCHOONER

50   40   30   20   10 FEET

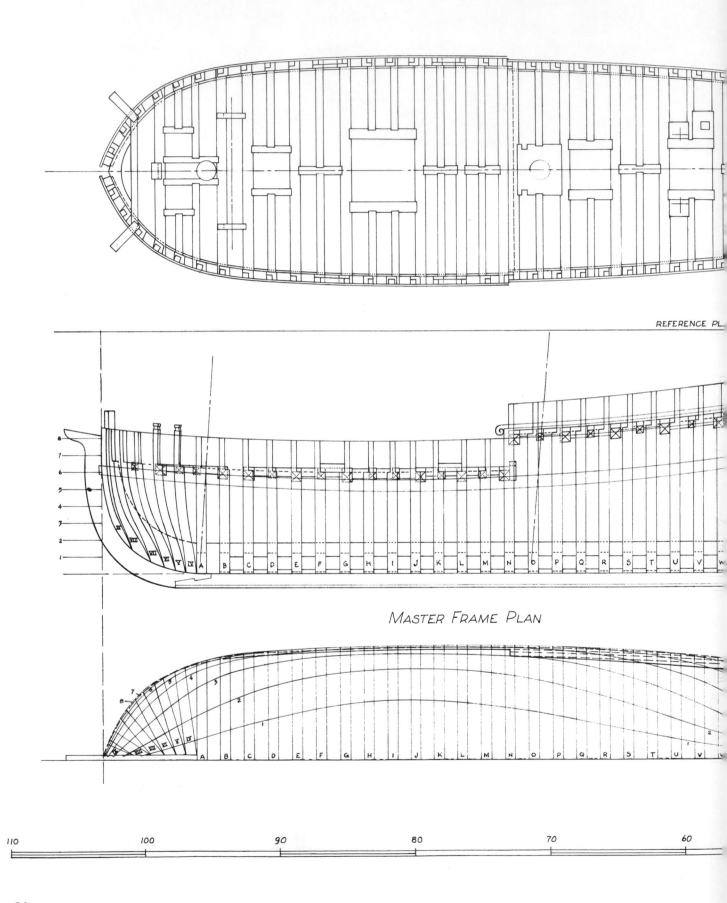

REFERENCE PL.

MASTER FRAME PLAN

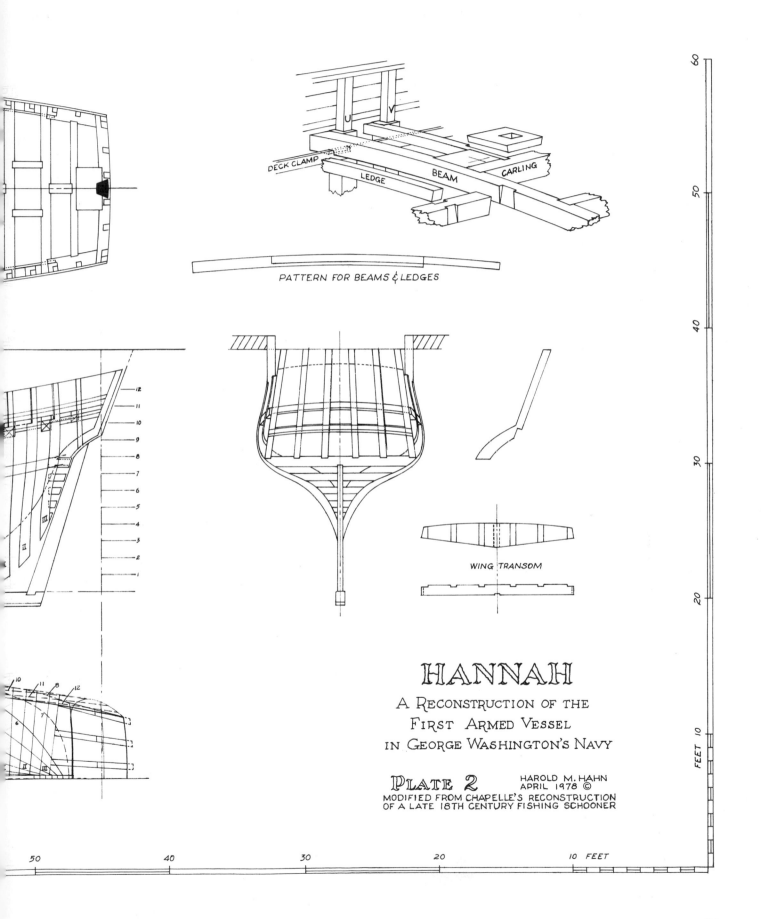

DECK CLAMP

LEDGE BEAM CARLING

PATTERN FOR BEAMS & LEDGES

WING TRANSOM

HANNAH

A Reconstruction of the
First Armed Vessel
in George Washington's Navy

PLATE 2

HAROLD M. HAHN
APRIL 1978 ©
MODIFIED FROM CHAPELLE'S RECONSTRUCTION
OF A LATE 18TH CENTURY FISHING SCHOONER

50   40   30   20   10 FEET

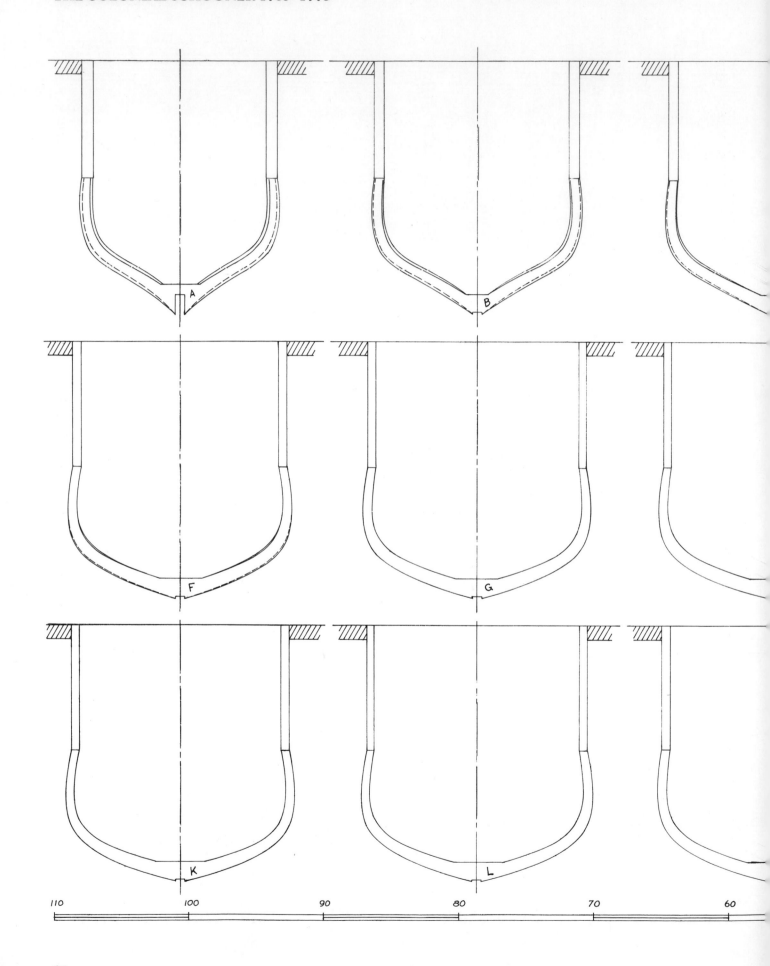

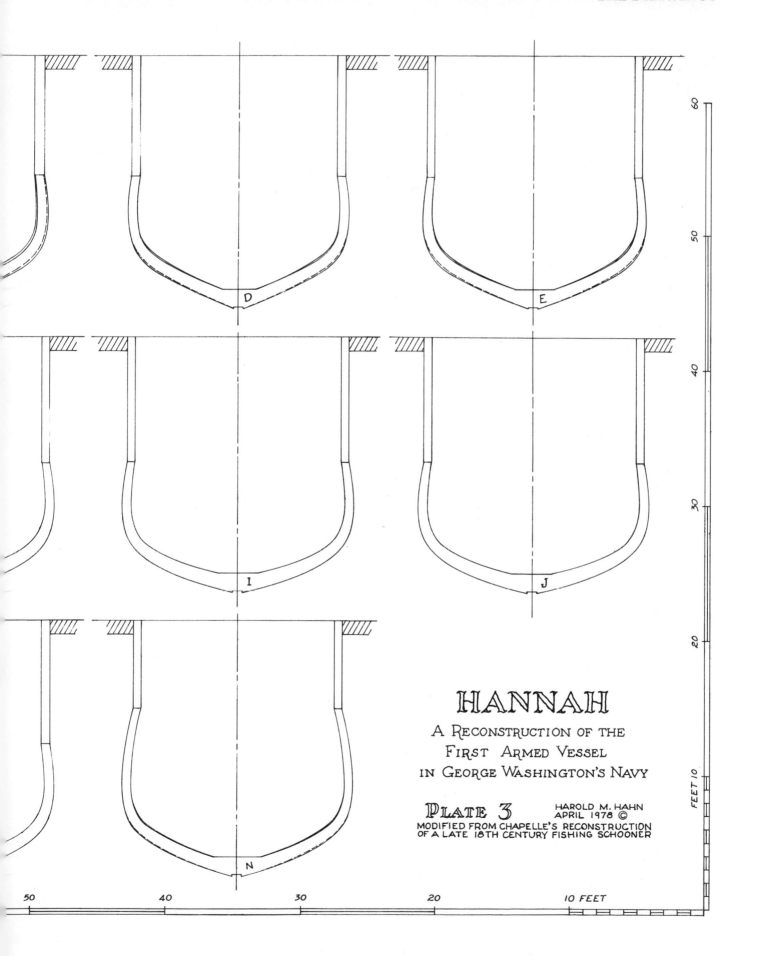

HANNAH

A Reconstruction of the
First Armed Vessel
in George Washington's Navy

Plate 3

HAROLD M. HAHN
APRIL 1978 ©

MODIFIED FROM CHAPELLE'S RECONSTRUCTION
OF A LATE 18TH CENTURY FISHING SCHOONER

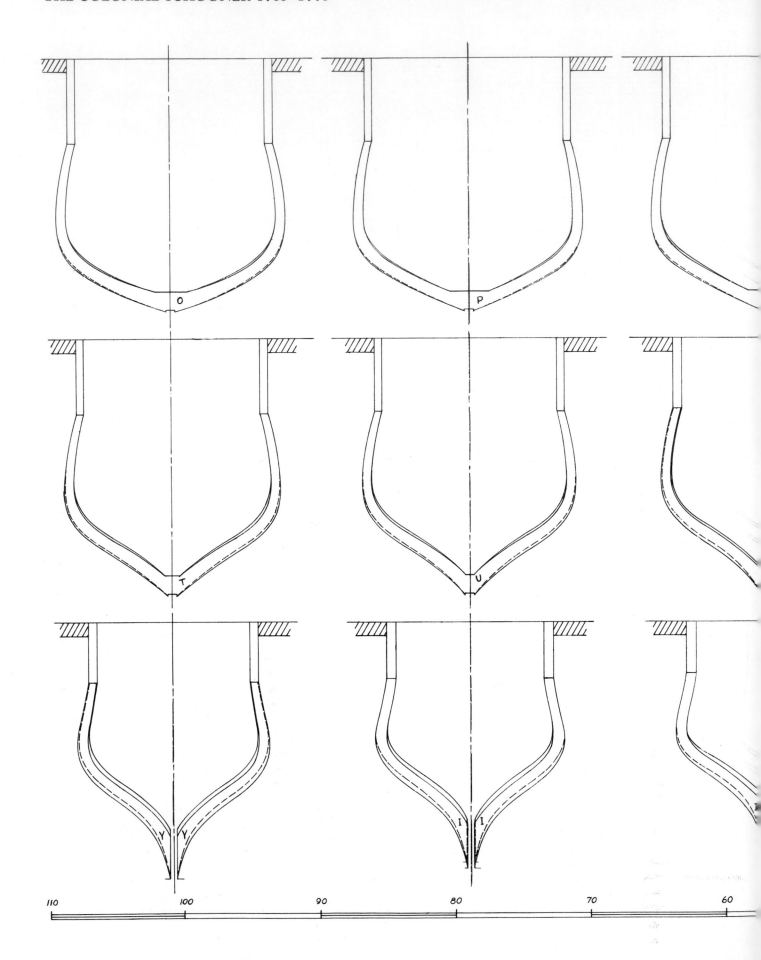

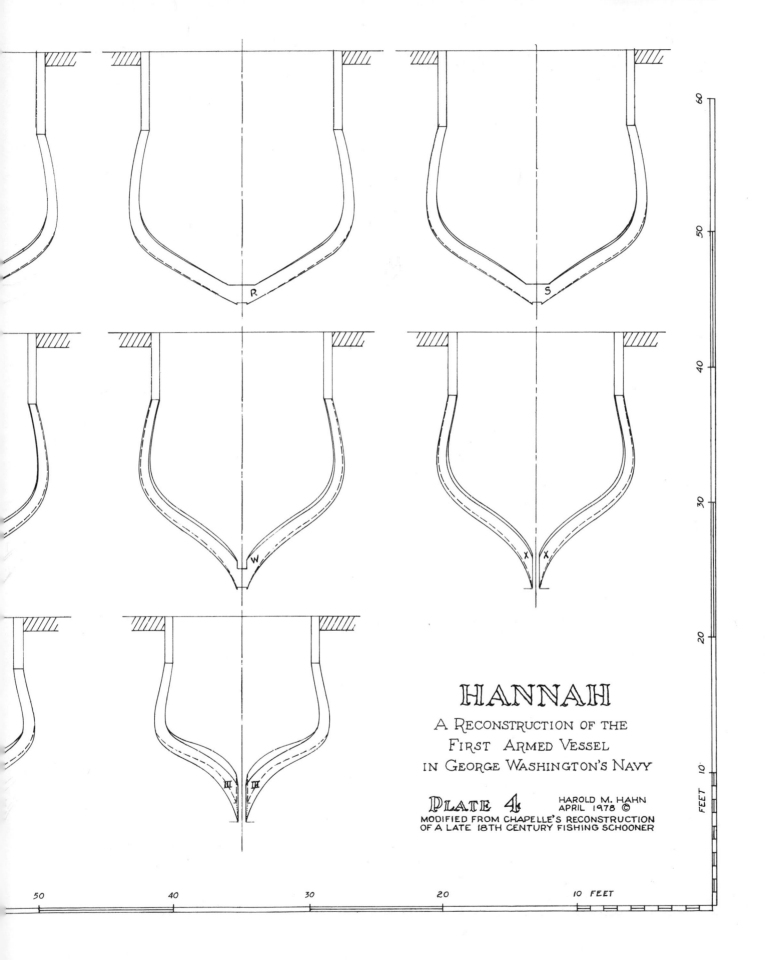

HANNAH

A RECONSTRUCTION OF THE
FIRST ARMED VESSEL
IN GEORGE WASHINGTON'S NAVY

PLATE 4   HAROLD M. HAHN
APRIL 1978 ©
MODIFIED FROM CHAPELLE'S RECONSTRUCTION
OF A LATE 18TH CENTURY FISHING SCHOONER

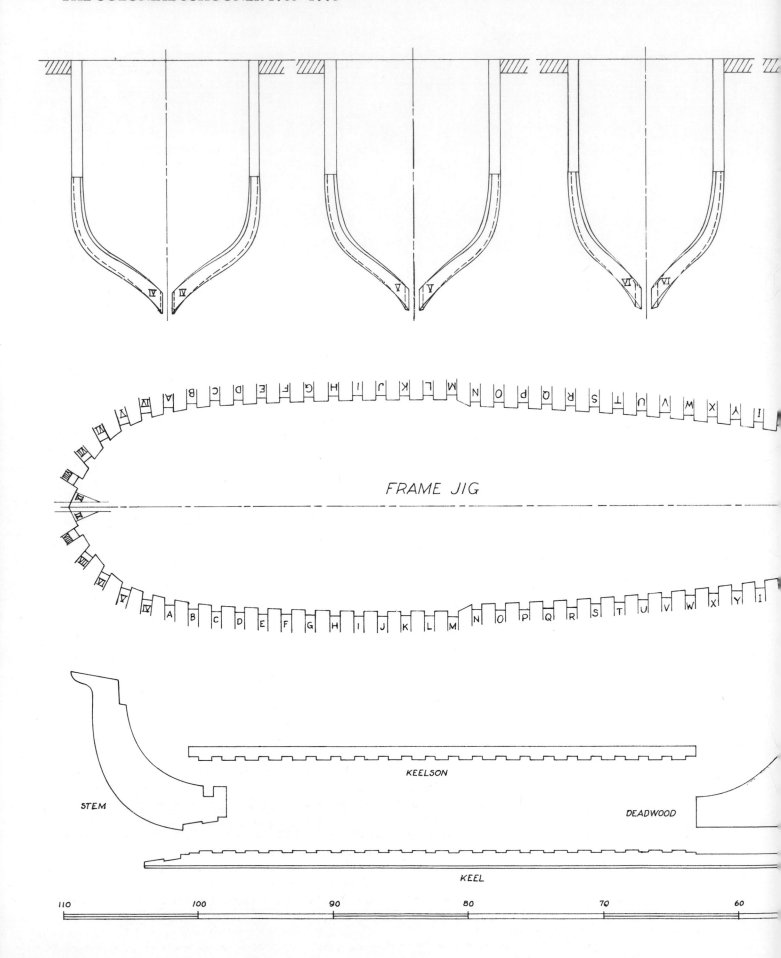

FRAME JIG

KEELSON

STEM

DEADWOOD

KEEL

110   100   90   80   70   60

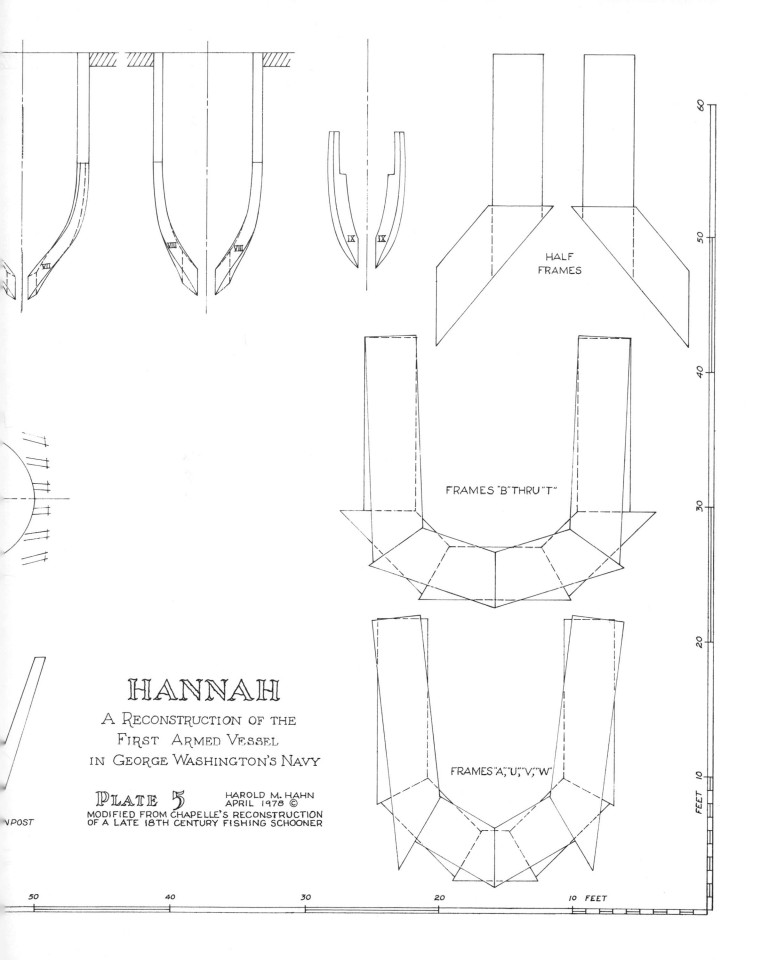

HALF
FRAMES

FRAMES "B" THRU "T"

FRAMES "A","U","V","W"

HANNAH

A RECONSTRUCTION OF THE
FIRST ARMED VESSEL
IN GEORGE WASHINGTON'S NAVY

PLATE 5   HAROLD M. HAHN
APRIL 1978 ©
MODIFIED FROM CHAPELLE'S RECONSTRUCTION
OF A LATE 18TH CENTURY FISHING SCHOONER

VII   VIII   IX

NPOST

50   40   30   20   10 FEET

60   50   40   30   20   10   FEET

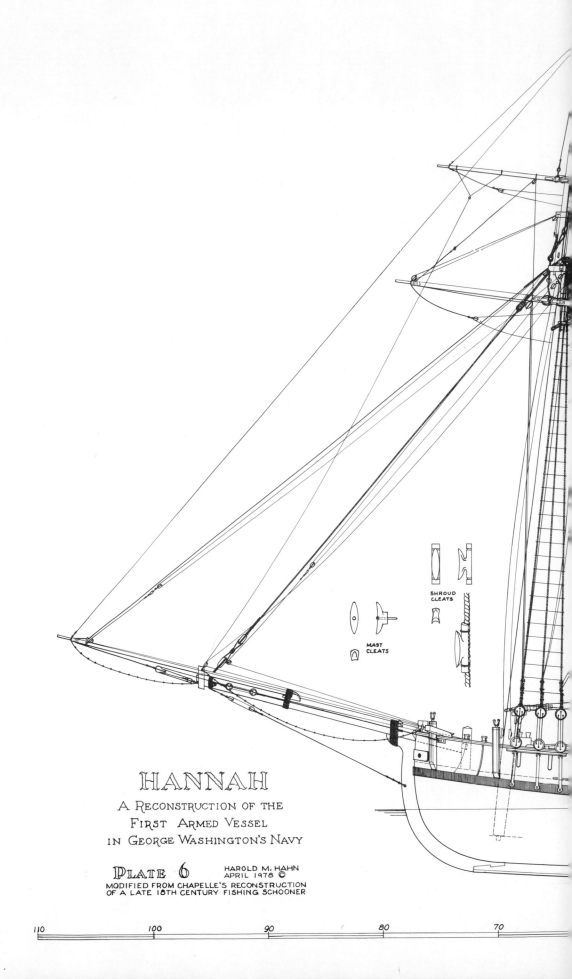

SHROUD
CLEATS

MAST
CLEATS

HANNAH

A RECONSTRUCTION OF THE
FIRST ARMED VESSEL
IN GEORGE WASHINGTON'S NAVY

PLATE 6   HAROLD M. HAHN
APRIL 1978 ©
MODIFIED FROM CHAPELLE'S RECONSTRUCTION
OF A LATE 18TH CENTURY FISHING SCHOONER

110   100   90   80   70

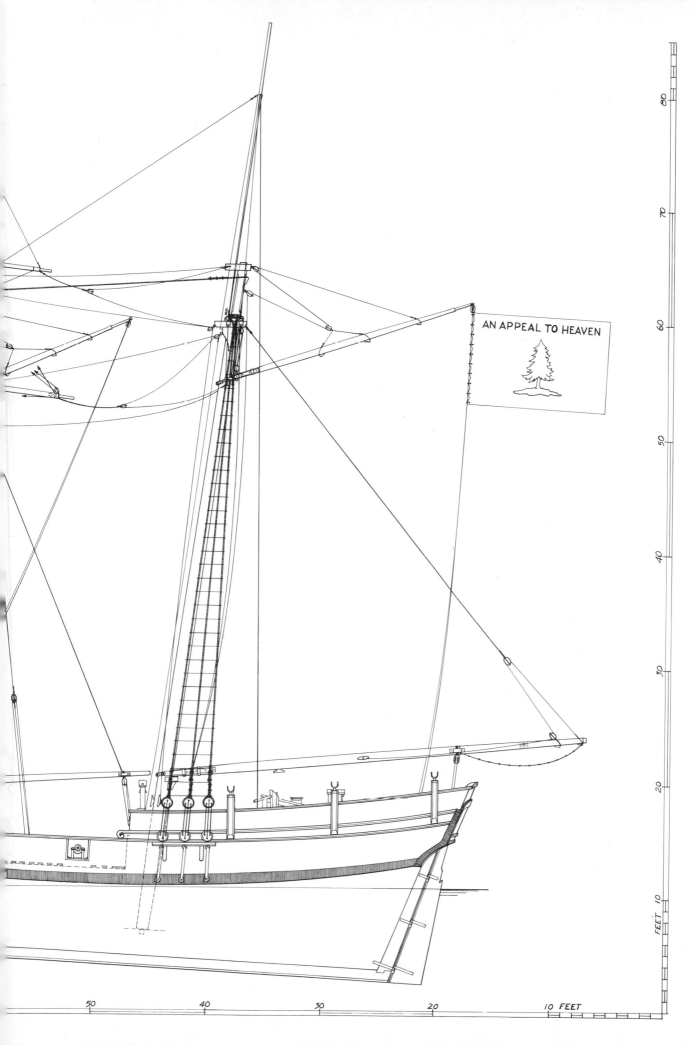

AN APPEAL TO HEAVEN

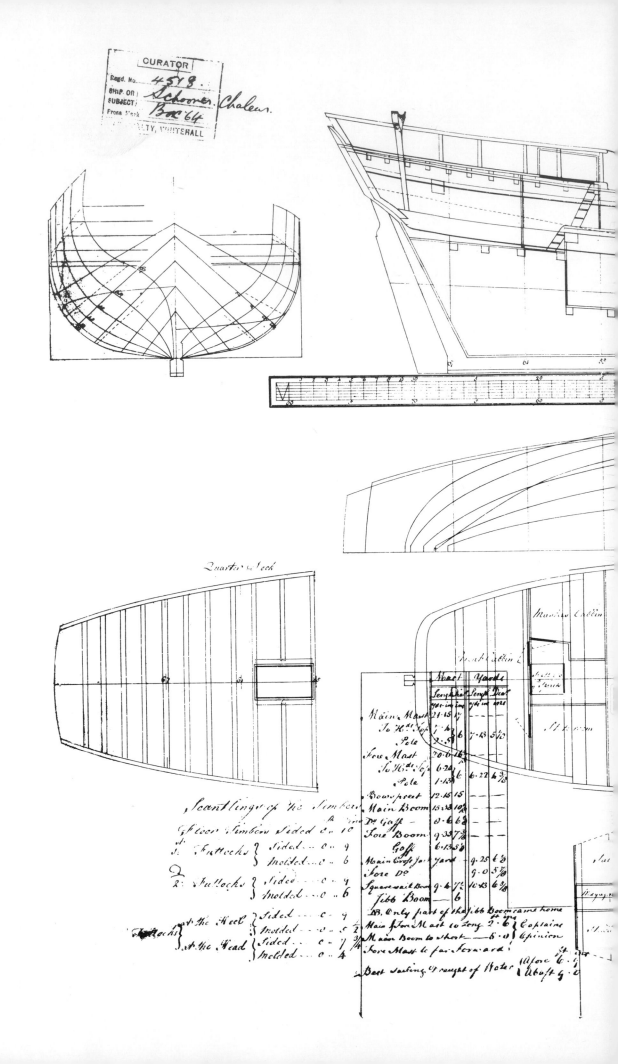

Quarter Deck

Scantlings of the Timbers

Floor Timbers Sided 0 . 10

1st Futtocks { Sided --- 0 . 9
              { Molded --- 0 . 6

2nd Futtocks { Sided --- 0 . 9
             { Molded --- 0 . 6

Futtocks { at the Heel { Sided --- 0 . 9
         {   { Molded --- 0 . 6
         { at the Head { Sided --- 0 . 7
         {   { Molded --- 0 . 4

	Mast		Yards	
	Length	Diam	Length	Diam
	feet-in	in	feet-in	in
Main Mast	21.15	7		
To Hd. Top	7.4	6	7.13	5½
Pole	2.5			
Fore Mast	20.0	6½		
To Hd. Top	6.24	6	6.22	6½
Pole	1.15			
Bowsprit	12.15	15		
Main Boom	15.33	10½		
Do Gaff	9.6	6½		
Fore Boom	9.35	7½		
Gaff	6.13	5½		
Main Cross Jack Yard			9.25	6½
Fore Do			9.0	5¾
Square sail Boom	9.6	7½	10.13	6¾
Jibb Boom		6		

N.B. Only part of the Jibb Boom came home

Main Fore Mast too long 2.6 } Captaine
Main Boom too short --- 5.0 } Opinion
Fore Mast too far Forward !

Best sailing Draught of Water { Afore 6.7
                              { Abaft 9.0

100

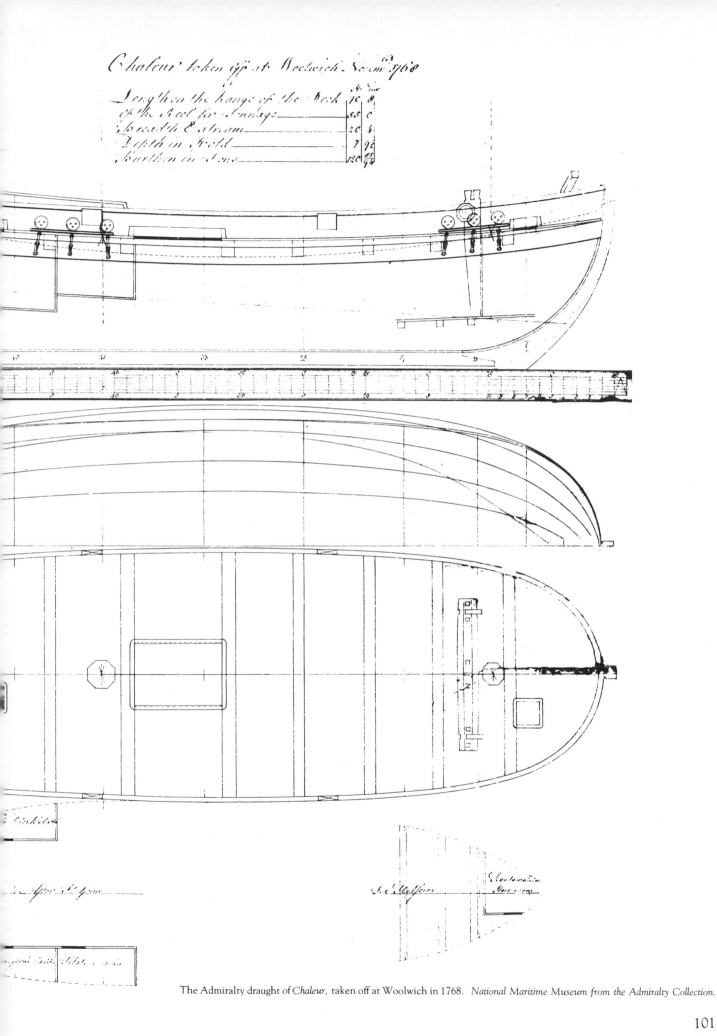

Chaleur taken off at Woolwich Novemr 1768

	ft	ins
Length on the Range of the Deck	70	8
of the Keel for Tonnage	55	0
Breadth Extream	20	4
Depth in Hold	7	9½
Burthen in Tons	120	85/94

The Admiralty draught of *Chaleur*, taken off at Woolwich in 1768. *National Maritime Museum from the Admiralty Collection.*

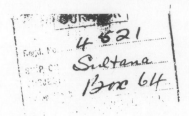
The Draught of his Maje

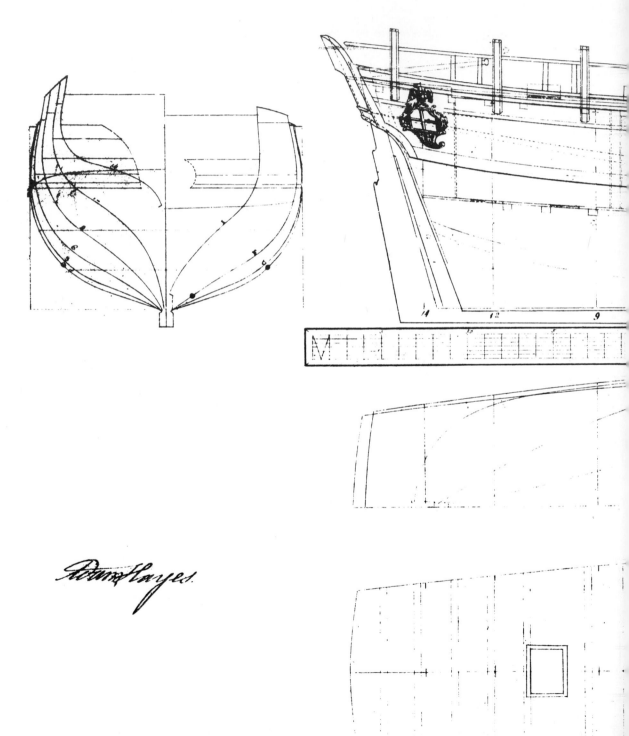

The Admiralty draught of Sultana.   National Maritime Museum from the Admiralty Collection.

Schooner *Sultana*, her Body taken off in Mr Randall's Dock, and as she was fitted here.

Length on the range of the Deck . . . . 50..6^{5 ft m}

        Keel for Tonnage 38.5/8

Breadth Extreem 16.0 3/4

Depth in Hold . . . . 8..4

      Burthen in Tonns $52 \frac{60}{94}$ Tons

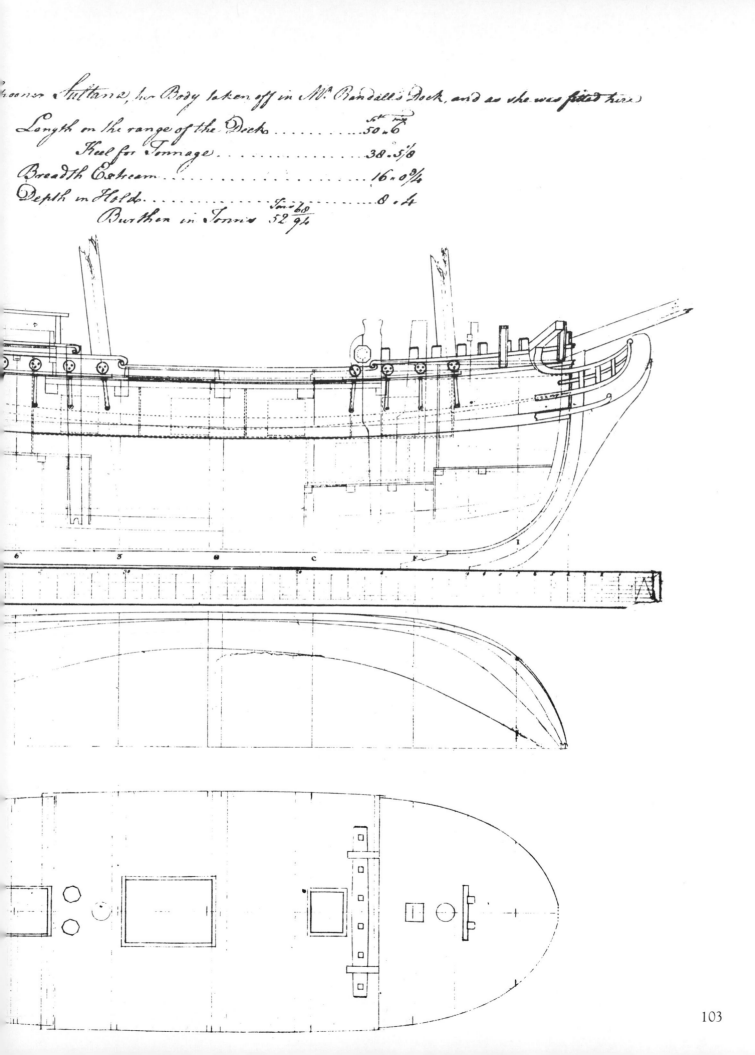

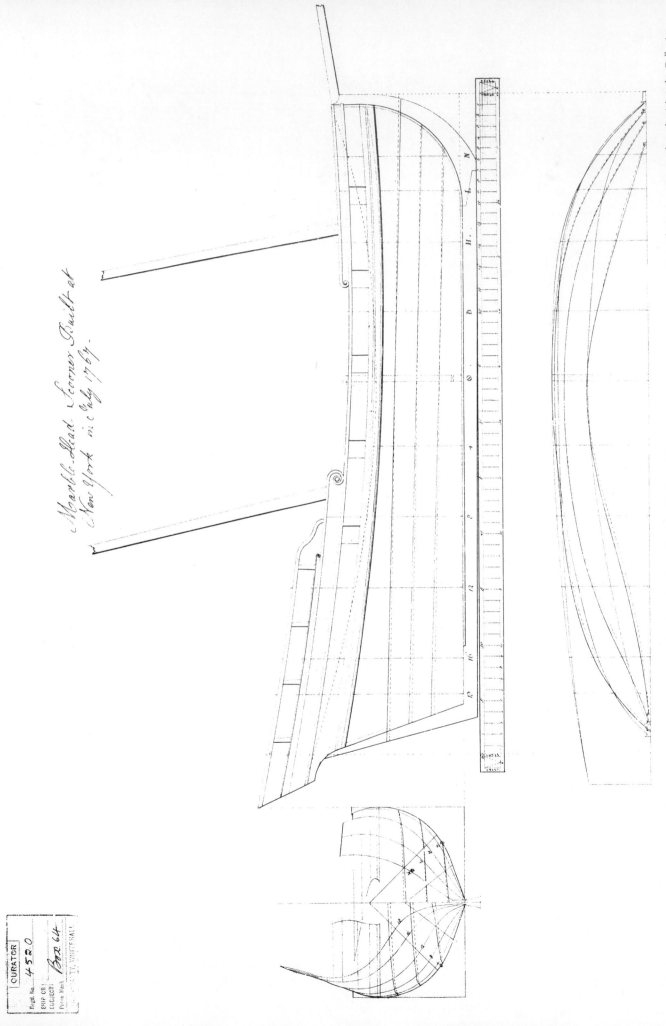

Marble Head Scooner Built at
New York in July 1767 –

National Maritime Museum from the Admiralty Collection.

Admiralty draught of a Marblehead schooner probably the *Earl of Egmont* and Sir *Edward Hawke* taken off in New York in 1767.

CHAPTER TEN

Framing Hannah's Hull

The model builder will be pleased to have completed the drawing work so that he can start cutting wood. Necessary though it may be, the task of drawing details for a model is not likely to be a favored occupation. The craftsman becomes impatient to start making sawdust in order to see his creation take form. The drawings for both *Hannah* and *Halifax* have been detailed to the extent that they provide patterns which can be copied, cut out and cemented to the wood to eliminate the need for tedious and sometimes inaccurate tracing to transfer the shapes. However, one more drawing procedure must be followed in preparation for making the frames which will be the first order of business.

The floors and futtocks for the frames could be drawn up individually, cut out as separate pieces, and painstakingly joined together as has been sometimes recommended. The method suggested and illustrated here is to cut frames complete from pre-assembled units which provide for a range of frame sizes within a given pattern. Reference to Plate 5 of the *Hannah* drawings will show that three patterns are sufficient to suit all the frames needed for this relatively simple model. The patterns are drawn to be used with strips of wood with a $^{15}/_{16}$in minimum width. (All dimensions are for plans drawn to a $\frac{1}{4}$in/ft scale). Some people may object to the wastefulness of this procedure, but more of them will be likely to appreciate the saving in time and effort that results. In order to design patterns such as these, it is a simple matter to lay the frame drawings (on tracing paper) on top of each other until it is determined what range of sizes can be accommodated for practical purposes in a given pattern. It can be seen that when a frame is cut from the assembled unit, in general, the grain of the wood will follow the curves to produce a strong and stable, though delicate-looking, piece. Two copies of the pattern will be required for each frame. While the Xerox copying process distorts an image and is unsuitable for accurate model work, it can be used to advantage to make copies of the patterns for the initial frame assemblies where some distortion can be tolerated.

Hannah has been selected for the first subject because of the simplicity of the model. The construction of *Halifax* is essentially the same but with some added complications that will be dealt with later. The frames of the model in 1/48 scale are designed to be $^{3}/_{16}$in thick. The pieces of wood that make up the frames must finish to one-half that thickness. Some allowances must be made for finishing operations, so it is suggested that strips be cut approximately 0.10in thick. The selection of wood will be determined by availability and the model builder's inclinations, but it is recommended that a close-grained hardwood be used. In the cases of the models which illustrate this text, *Hannah*'s frames were made of boxwood while those in *Halifax* are of Swiss pearwood. The tiny models made for the diorama used hard maple.

For obvious reasons, it would be convenient if the strips of wood used to make segments for the frame assemblies were smooth surfaced and of uniform thickness. This could be accomplished in a number of ways depending on the facilities or friendly help available. Perhaps the easiest and most economical way, if an 8in table saw is handy, is to make use of a 7in diameter veneer saw which is readily available commercially. The sides of the saw are ground with a taper below the teeth which have no set. The blade cuts a kerf just .070in wide thus making it economical on wood. When the saw is new and sharp, it will produce a

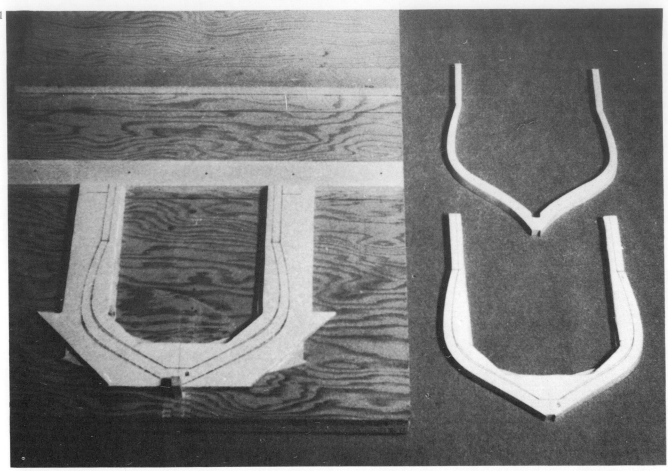

Cutting out the frames to the pattern.

perfectly smooth surface, and the fence can be adjusted close enough to the blade that it can cut strips of uniform thickness that are almost paper thin. Boards must be less than 1¼in thick since that is the maximum depth of cut to which the saw should be set. While the machine is set up to cut strips for the frames, it would be practical to cut all the material of the various thicknesses that can be anticipated for use in planking and framing the model.

Once the strips for making frames have been cut, a regular system can be used for cutting the many segments needed to make up the assemblies. A piece of ¼in masonite is fastened to the miter gage which is used to push material on the saw table for cross cuts. This masonite jig should be slotted with the shape of a given segment so that when a prepared strip is inserted and passed through the saw blade a piece of the correct size and shape is cut off. When that segment has a different angle at each end, there should be two slots on the side of the jig designed so that when one piece has been cut off, the strip can be turned over, inserted in the second slot and the next one cut without delay. If the strips are all of uniform width and the slots in the masonite jig are cut accurately, the job will go fast with excellent results. The veneer saw should be used for the smooth surface it produces so that the segments will butt together without any extra work required to fit them.

Each frame assembly pattern has two different arrangements of segments which, when glued together, will make a frame with staggered joints. Thus, two paper patterns will be required for each station. The segments should be rubber cemented to the paper with regular glue in the joints between pieces. Done on a flat surface, the pattern holds the unit in place while the glue sets in the joints. Until these sub-assemblies are glued together in pairs, they must be handled with some care to avoid breaking the pieces apart. The wood face should be leveled with a large sandpaper block. If the segments are of uniform thickness, this should be a minor operation designed to clean lumps of glue from the surface. When all the units for the frames of a given pattern have been assembled, those of one conformation should have the paper trimmed away from the outline. They can then be turned over and glued to the faces of the second set made to that assembly pattern. Some clamping arrangement will be required while the glue sets, and some provision made to prevent the units from sliding out of position when the pressure is applied. One positive method is to pin them together.

When the glue in the completed frame assemblies has set, the paper can be peeled off both sides. It may be a bit stubborn in spots where the rubber cement has taken hold better under pressure or where the glue has squeezed through, but for the most part the paper should pull or rub loose readily enough. A little scraping and sanding will clean the wood up in preparation for the next step. It is time to rubber cement the frame patterns to the wood. The drawings have dotted lines to indicate the back side of a frame as determined by the position from which it is viewed. It so happens that the procedure outlined below will reverse that position. If for some reason it is desired to keep the relative position of staggered joints the same from frame to frame, the various relationships should be studied to decide on which face of the assembly to cement the pattern. This consideration can be important in a model where it is necessary to cut into a frame to set in a sill or to reduce the thickness to make bulwark stanchions or other openings in the framework. If there is a joint close by, it should be on the cut side, leaving a solid futtock on the farther side for strength. Do not cut away the paper inside the 'U' of the paper patterns until they have been fastened to the wood. It helps to maintain the shape and the span across the extensions. Some outlines will come close to the edge of the double thickness of futtock material, so take care in positioning the patterns. The excess paper can be trimmed away with a razor blade or a sharp knife.

Before starting to cut out the frames, it would be advisable to make the keel and mark its notches with the letters that identify the frame locations. The keel should be about 0.17in thick at the middle but will taper to about $1/8$in at either end. For this reason, when the notches are cut in the bottoms of the frames, they should be fitted to their respective positions along the length of the keel. This should be an easy fit which will not be likely to bind up in the final assembly. There is a pattern for the keel in Plate 5 which can be cut out and cemented to the wood. Rubber cement is recommended for all of these applications because it will not cause the paper to lose shape like a water-based glue and the paper can be removed easily when the shape has been cut out. The residue of rubber cement can be rubbed off readily to leave the wood surface clean.

Photograph 1 shows three original, logical steps to be followed in cutting out a frame. For the first step, a simple jig has been made with a straight edge to represent the bottom side of the frame assembly jig which corresponds to the ends of the frame extensions. A square peg is set into the surface to represent the top of the notch in the keel at the correct distance from the straight edge. The frame assembly is first trimmed of excess material on the bottom edge. Then the notch which fits on the keel is cut out according to the pattern depth and with special care to keep it centrally located. Next, the ends are cut off close to the lines on the pattern for the frame extensions. The piece is tested in the spacing jig and trimmed equally on each side until it fits snug between the peg and the straight edge. It may seem that this is carrying caution to extremes, but it does not take much extra effort. It does

give some reassurance that the primary reference points have been conscientiously preserved so that the frames will fair up in the final assembly.

The second step is to cut the outside contours of the frames. They are carefully sawed, filed, and sanded smooth to the outside line to be square with the sides. The frames for these schooner models are small enough to be cut readily with a jewelers saw though a jig saw may be preferred. Where a bevel is indicated by a double line on the pattern, the outside surface should be blackened on the back side with pencil lead and the frame beveled to the dotted line. Care taken to avoid cutting into the blackened edge will maintain the correct shape on that side. It should be noted that in the design of the bow cant frames there are some twists in the contour which require special interpretation. Since bevels are cut to the dotted lines wherever shown on the pattern, the bevel should be cut to the back side of the piece when the inner line is solid. In effect, this treats the frame the reverse of the drawing convention used as mentioned earlier, but it does not affect the final result.

It is best to finish the outside surface, bevel and all, before cutting out the inside shape of the frame since that weakens the piece considerably. The procedure described above is followed when cutting to the inside lines except that the bevel indicated on the pattern by a solid line must be sketched in on the back side of the frame and the surface angled to suit. Again, watch the twist in the bow cant frames which can be confusing. The frames for the models pictured in this book were all cut out using the above procedures. When they were permanently set into the frame jig with the keel assembly, a minimum of correction was required to fair up the surfaces, both inside and out.

Eighteenth century ships were fastened together with wooden treenails, commonly pronounced trunnels. These pegs were about 1in to $1\frac{1}{2}$in in diameter and driven into holes bored through the parts to be fastened together. The ends were sometimes split for a wedge which could be hammered in to ensure that the trunnels would not work loose. The appearance of a plank-on-frame model can be made to look more interesting and authentic if it is trunneled. The assembly itself will also be made more secure when it is drilled and pegged together. These considerations can be applied to the frames just completed if they are trunneled on each side of every futtock joint. The wooden dowels used should be slightly smaller in diameter than the drilled holes, making a close, sliding fit. The end of the dowel is dipped into some slow-setting epoxy glue before being pushed into the hole. When the glue has hardened permanently, the projecting ends can be sliced off with a razor blade or sharp chisel. The frame can then be sanded on its sides until the $3/16$in design thickness is reached. This can be done by laying a sheet of 100 grit garnet paper on a flat surface and rubbing the frame across it. When the wood is close to size, a

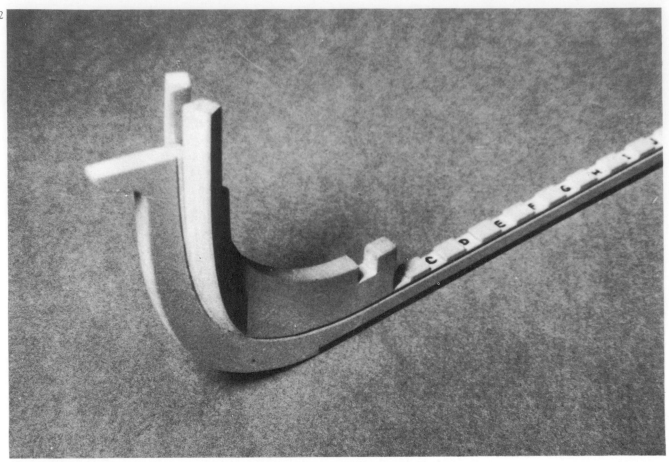

The assembly of the keel and stem with the knighthead pieces fastened to the deadwood.

finer paper should be used to finish the surface.

Since trunnels are to be used extensively in these models, some thought should be given to a method for making the fine dowels that will be needed. The frames for *Hannah* were trunneled with dowels .028in in diameter which were set into holes made with a number 69 (.0292in diameter) drill. Finer dowels will be required for the planking operations that come later. Split bamboo has been commonly recommended for trunneling models, but boxwood dowels were used for the models pictured in this book. They were produced by pulling initially square strips through a draw plate until the desired diameter was reached. The draw plate was made from a piece of soft, sheet steel. A row of holes was drilled using the complete range of drills graduating in size from number 60 down through number 80. These holes were countersunk on one side of the plate with larger drills so that the length of the actual hole through which the dowel was to be pulled would be only about $1/64$in. This was done to reduce the drag on the wood and thus the force needed to pull it through the hole. This tensile force is also kept to a minimum by using every hole in sequence.

When the wood strips are prepared, every effort should be made to select straight-grained stock and to cut it in the direction of the grain. Cross-grained sections make for weak spots in the strips which, especially in the smaller diameters, are vulnerable to break-age. It is difficult to tell the direction of the grain in boxwood; but if a straight piece known to have been cut from the outside of the tree trunk can be found, the conditions will be met. The veneer saw should be used to cut flats close in thickness to the finished dowel size. Square strips can then be sliced off the edge of a flat while it is clamped under a steel straight edge. A sharp, new razor blade should be used for this operation, because a dull blade would force its way through the material and damage the fibers of the delicate pieces.

The square strip is prepared for the drawing operation by sanding one end to a taper which will allow it to pass through the smallest hole to be used in forming the dowel. It should project about $\frac{1}{4}$in so that it can be gripped between the thumb and finger. The strip is first drawn through the largest hole that will produce fine shavings from it. It should be inserted on the flat side of the hole opposite the countersink to take advantage of the square cutting edge. The end is best grasped in a small piece of sandpaper folded so that the rough surface provides traction. The drawing action is continued using progressively smaller holes until the final size is reached. Tiny flaws in the wood are bound to cause some breakage. Strips 4in to 6in long have been found convenient to work with. Elm and apple wood are also suitable for making dowels. Using the procedures outlined above, dowels reduced to the minimum diameter of .0135in have been produced successfully.

With the frames complete, it is time the stem, deadwood and stern post were cut out and assembled with the keel. Again, Plate 5 furnishes patterns for those parts which can be cut out and cemented onto the wood. When the finished pieces are glued together, they should be laid on the master frame plan to be sure that the design is duplicated exactly. The stem will be the same thickness as the keel where they join, and taper thinner to the end. The stern post should match the thickness of the keel at the bottom and taper to a thicker section at the top. The deadwood should be thinner than the keel by the thickness of two 2in planks to scale. With this assembly complete, the rabbet lines can be drawn in on both sides and cut out with a 'V' groove. The knife or skew chisel used for this can be guided by a steel straight edge along the keel, but must be controlled freehand on the curve of the stem. At this stage, the pieces marked IX on the frame details can be glued to the stem with reference to the lines on the drawing that locate them. Photograph 2 shows this assembly.

The last step to be taken in preparation for assembling the hull is to cut out the frame jig. The pattern for this is on Plate 5. Hardboard masonite, $\frac{1}{8}$in thick, was used for the model of *Hannah* which is pictured. In addition, a rectangular box was built of plywood, large enough to hold the masonite jig on parallel rails just below the top and deep enough to allow the assembled hull to be inverted for work on the interior and deck. The box was also a means of storing the model safely on occasion. The same box was used for both the models of *Hannah* and *Halifax* and would be suitable for any future model of similar size. The parallel rails to which the masonite jig could be fastened guarantee a flat, true working surface which happens to be the reference plane on the drawings from which measurements will be made to locate details on the hull. The paper jig pattern is rubber cemented to the masonite and the hole cut out on a jig saw. The pattern is marked for easy reference to locate the frames in their respective positions. The notches should be cut to have a moderately loose fit with the frame extensions. This should be checked at each station. A tight fit would be likely to cause alignment difficulties when the frames are glued into the jig.

It is finally time to start assembling the hull of the model. First, the whole frames will be glued into the notches in the jig. This is done two at a time starting with the two whole frames that are farthest apart. Those two frames have their extensions glued into the corresponding notches in the jig. Then the keel assembly is set into the frame notches and the sides of the frames checked for squareness with the jig surface. This stage can be seen in photograph 3. Once the glue has

The first step in assembling the frames in the jig.

set, this squareness will have been established for the whole assembly; and the keel can be removed. Now two more frames can be glued in place and the keel set back into place while the glue hardens. Each step is of short duration if a quick setting white glue is used, so there is little to be gained by rushing the process with more than two frames at a time. Before the glue sets, the frames can be adjusted slightly when it seems necessary to ensure that the keel will fit easily into the notches. When all of the whole frames have been set into the jig permanently, the keel should fit into the assembly with no evidence of strain. Photograph 4 shows that stage with the keel removed and sitting alongside the assembled frames. The keel can then be set into the frame notches with epoxy glue and a check made to be sure that the stem and stern post are square with the jig surface.

With the keel permanently fastened to the whole frames, assembly of the half frames and cant frames can begin. Positions of those members should be marked off on the stern deadwood. It can be seen that the bow cant frames fit closely together on the stem deadwood. It is advisable to fit and glue them in as matching pairs working from the whole frames toward the bow or stern

as the case may be. The ends that fay against the deadwood may need some modification to improve the fit and alignment. If it is remembered that the parts as drawn are intended to fair up perfectly and care is taken to make these minor adjustment, there is no reason why the ideal condition should not be closely approximated. Photograph 5 shows the bow with the cant frames installed. The next photograph shows the stern cant frames in place plus some patterns and wood pieces cut out for the wing transom and the stern frames. The half frames and cant frames should all be trunneled to the deadwood.

The stern assembly of a model is one of the most difficult features to draw and describe adequately. Perhaps it can be understood best from a study of the photographs 7 and 8. First, the transoms that bridge the gap between the last cant frames and the inner stern post must be fitted and glued in place. They will furnish a surface to which the planks can be fastened. The wing transom is notched as shown on the drawing. Since the hull has a round tuck design, it must curve smoothly into the start of the counter. With the wing transom in place, the stern frames can be cut and fitted to reach from their notches to the reference plane

All the whole frames are first glued into the assembly jig.

4

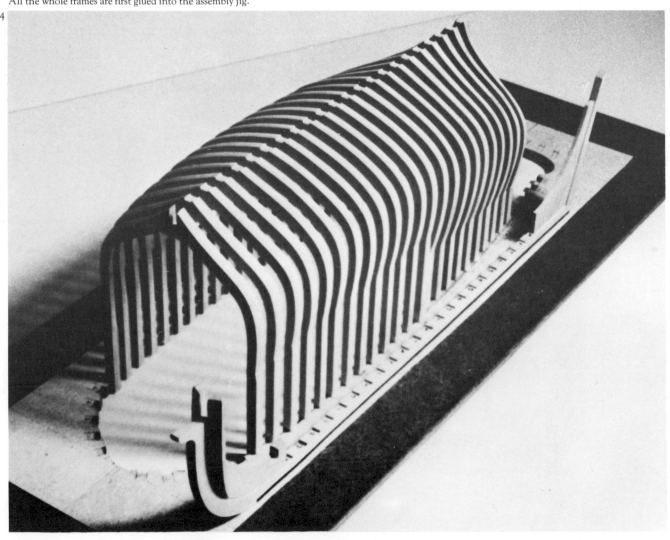

positions marked on the frame jig pattern. Their corners at the top edge of the counter should line up in a pleasing curve. Before the stern frames are glued in place, those corners should be notched out to take the transverse timber which will be fitted next. Another cross piece is notched and fitted to the insides of the stern frames at deck level. It should be cambered to match the deck beam curve and will, in fact, support the ends of the deck planks. On either side, at deck level, a piece is fitted between the last cant frame and the outside stern frame. This timber provides support for a bulwark stanchion which is notched into it and also for the deck structure. All of these features can be seen in photographs 7 and 8.

In order to fair up the stern structure with the lines of the hull, it will be necessary to build up the outer stern frames with filler blocks of wood. Then, when a sandpaper block is swept over the run of frames, the excess material can be rounded off to form a smooth line for planking the hull. The outside framing can be faired up quite easily with sandpaper blocks. Flat blocks are used where the surfaces are convex and rounded blocks in the concave surfaces found at the bow and stern. If all of the preceding work has been done accurately, there should not be much material to remove. Low spots can be located by holding battens against the frames and marked with lead pencil. To preserve the correct hull shape the sanding must be held to a minimum and certainly not continued once the low spots have been

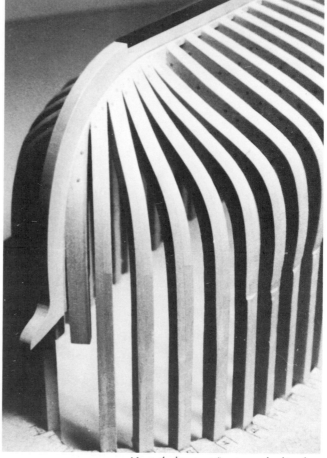

Next, the bow cant frames are glued in place.

Finally, the stern half and cant frames are glued into the jig.

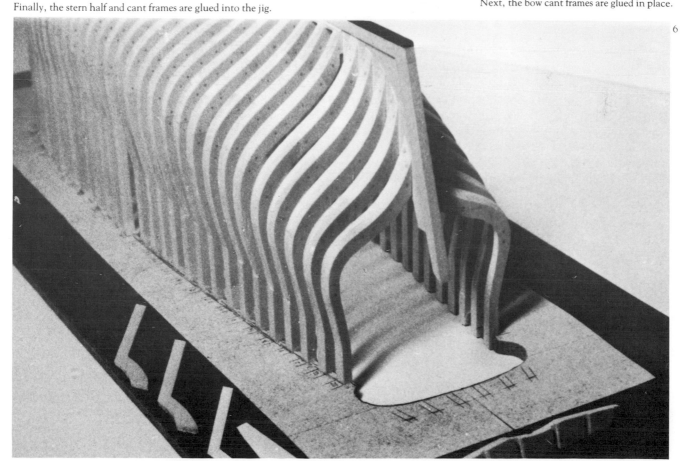

The assembly of the stern.

The stern assembly as completed and faired.

reached. Fairing up the insides of the frames is more difficult to accomplish. The value of designing the frames to fair up inside theoretically will be better appreciated. Inflexible sandpaper blocks are not practical for this work. The best approach is to fold some emery cloth into a pad which is stiff enough to hit the high spots and yet flexible enough to shape itself to the curvature of the hull.

A final addition to the basic framework of the hull is the keelson. The pattern on Plate 5 should be used to make this piece. When the keelson has been fastened in place with epoxy glue on top of the frames and some brass pins driven into holes drilled right through frames and keel, the hull assembly will truly be locked together.

CHAPTER ELEVEN

Finishing Hannah's Hull

The last two chapters have been written in the impersonal mode. Unfortunately, this approach to writing tends to give it an authoritarian sound which is not really intended. Over the years. I have come to have a healthy respect for the knowledge and skills exhibited by other ship modelers. They often have quite a different way of solving a given problem from the one that I happen to favor. It has become apparent to me that equivalent results can be achieved by a variety of methods; or as my dad used to say 'there is more than one way to skin a cat.' Men who have been building plank-on-frame models for years by the usual methods will possibly see little advantage to the procedure that I am trying to promote here. Since I have never built a model their way, I can't honestly say they are wrong. My description and illustrations will have to stand on their own merits. Whatever their influence may be, the reader should not be inhibited from following his own natural inclinations, although they may differ from suggestions made in this text, since they may be more suitable to his way of doing things. In any case, it would perhaps be better to continue this narrative in the first person with the understanding that it simply explains the way I like to work.

With the framing of *Hannah*'s hull complete, the problems of planking can be attacked. As a first step, I marked off the lines of the wales on the frames as well as the sheer lines under the cap rails, the gun ports, the reduction of frame thickness to form bulwark stanchions, and the four extensions of the stanchions which will project as bitts near the bow. Measurements for all these features can be accurately transferred from the sheer view on Plate 2, equating the surface of the frame jig to the reference plane line on the drawing. Before cutting into the frames to make the stanchions and install the sills for the gun ports, I felt it would be wise to fasten on the wales and as much planking as possible to tie the assembly together for strength. The wales form the most distinctive lines on the hull and so were the first planks to be fitted. If this initial step is taken with special care to follow lines correctly marked on the frames, the planking work that follows will fall into place quite easily.

My preference for using natural wood colours rather than paint on my models may not have a universal appeal to model builders, but the technique I used to fit the ebony wales can be of particular value where thick planks are required. Ebony is a dense, hard wood that does not lend itself to the usual forming methods which employ soaking in water, heating, or steaming. I have been advised that soaking in an ammonia solution does the job but have not used that procedure successfully. However difficult, all but the very mildest curves should be preformed in a plank before it is fastened to the framework of the hull. Strains caused by forcing the planks into place are liable to cause them to split at the fastenings, throw the hull out of shape, or result in eventual failure of the joint.

My solution to the problem of the ebony wales or thick planks having sharp curves such as are found at the bow or stern of a hull is to laminate two or more thinner strips together with glue by clamping them in a form. The shape of this mold can be taken from the appropriate waterline section on the plan view of the model drawing. I transfer this shape to a piece of pine and saw it out with some allowance for the thickness of the material to be clamped between the halves of the form. For the wales on *Hannah*'s bow, I used a strip of ebony .040in thick by 1in wide and one of boxwood

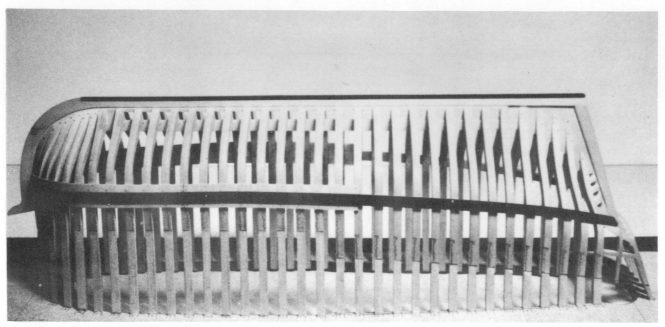

The wales and the first strakes are fastened to the frames. Note the marking for the bulwark stanchions.

with the same dimensions. The wood was soaked in boiling water and then clamped up in the form with ordinary white glue to join the pieces. Wax paper was placed between the surfaces of the form and the laminated wood to prevent what would have been an obvious fiasco. The next day when the clamps were removed, the laminated piece retained its shape by virtue of the glue joint. In the forty years that I have used this method, I have never experienced a failure of the glue joint allowing the laminations to separate.

The section of wale at the stern poses a slightly different problem which can still be tackled by applying the same principle. Here, it is not a sharp curve that causes difficulty so much as the twist in the member. After laying out lines on the opposite sides of a softwood block to develop this twisted plane, I cut the former by hand with a hacksaw which can be guided to follow the skewed shapes. If the laminations tend to slide out the side when clamped up in this former, I fasten a stop to the block which acts as a retainer when pressure is applied. Two more lengths of laminated ebony-boxwood strips were prepared to fit the slight curvature along the side of the hull. An extra advantage to following this system is the fact that all the plank material which can be seen inside the hull is uniformly of boxwood. When complete, the wales consisted of four sections fitted end to end on each side.

The wale strakes at the bow and stern were fitted and fastened in place first. The fitting was accomplished by holding the inch wide laminated piece against the frames with one edge shaped until it matched the line marked on the frames. The inside surface of the piece, of course, was resting flush in contact with the frames for its whole length. Then the width of the wale was marked and cut off. At the bow, the one end of this strake was fitted to the rabbet in the stem and the other end cut off so that it would stop at the middle of a frame. I scraped the inside surface slightly concave and fitted it until it could be held in position on the frames with a minimum of pressure. White glue was touched to the frames, the wale section was set in place, and held by hand for the short length of time it took for the glue to set. With the sections at bow and stern fastened in this manner, it was a simple matter to fill in the middle sections. At this stage, there was danger of breaking individual glue joints between frames and the wales. For that reason, I trunneled the wales to the frames before proceeding with additional planking. Boxwood dowels, .025in in diameter, were set into .026in diameter holes with epoxy glue to give permanence to the assembly.

I made the wales .080in thick, less whatever was lost in fitting and finishing them. The rest of the planks were cut from boxwood and holly sawed .040in thick with the veneer saw. The strakes on the bulwarks which surround the quarterdeck were made from cherry laminated to boxwood so as to show the color of cherry on the outside while retaining the uniform boxwood appearance on the inside. The same form which had moulded the wales at the bow was used to hold boxwood strips that had been soaking in boiling water. When these pieces had been allowed to dry thoroughly in the mold, they held their shape nicely. Another simple and quicker procedure involved the use of a large aluminium teakettle. With water in the kettle brought to a violent boil, the superheated steam issuing from the spout provided a medium for quickly inducing a curve in a strip of boxwood. This shape could be modified readily to suit the requirements. Extra length was needed so that the piece could be held in the fingers without subjecting them to the scalding steam.

When a piece was steamed in this manner, a twist could be produced as required for planks at the stern. This could be checked immediately against the frames themselves and corrected as necessary. At no time was a plank cut to a finished width before this forming was completed. It would have been difficult to predict and control the exact shape beforehand. The individual planks were all fitted along the edge of preformed strips and the width marked and cut in the same fashion as was described for the wales. There are other methods for producing curves in straight pieces of wood which some modelers prefer. Since I have not used them in my work, I will not try to describe them here. One final technique that I have used is to burnish the concave side of a thin piece of wood. Compression of the fibres on that side helps in close fitting by increasing the

The frames are cut out and the sills fitted for the bulwark stanchions. In the foreground is the keyhole saw used for cutting out the frames.

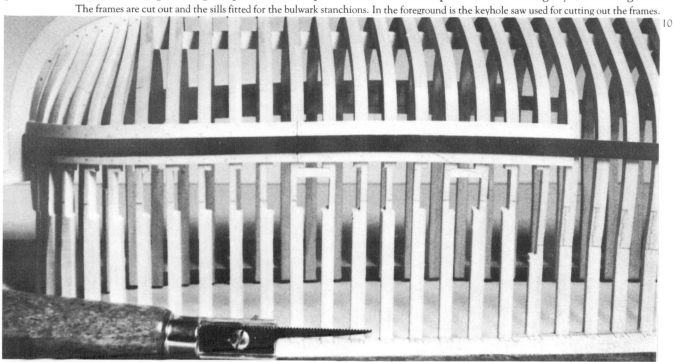

10

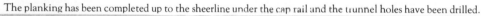
The planking has been completed up to the sheerline under the cap rail and the trunnel holes have been drilled.

11

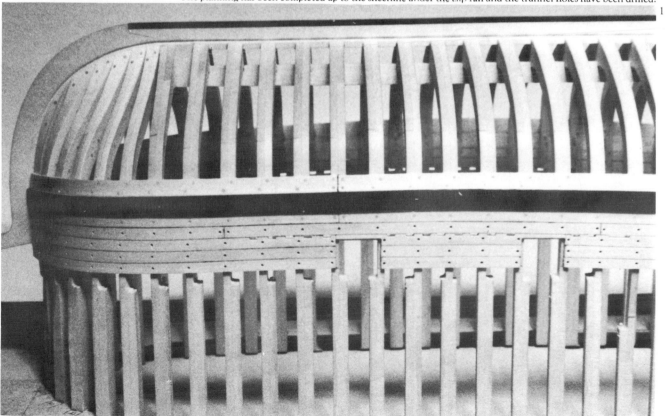

curvature slightly.

An observant reader when comparing the photographs which illustrate this chapter with the plans for *Hannah* will note a significant difference. The rectangular slots which serve as scupper holes to drain the deck of water are located in the lower edge of the third plank above the wale as shown in photographs 11 and 12. When I had completed the hull of my model and was adding deck furniture and fittings, I discovered that the 4 pounder cannon would have to be mounted on special, low-slung carriages in order to center their muzzles in the gun ports. Rather than inflict this handicap on anyone who might want to use the plans in the future, I decided to drop the deck level 6 inches. Thus, the scupper holes should be cut into the bottom edge of the second strake up from the wale. This can best be done before those planks have been glued to the frames.

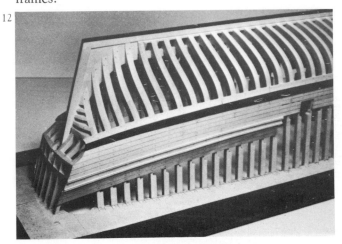

12

The planking completed. Note the trunnel holes.

Before proceeding that far with the planking, it will be necessary to reduce the frames to stanchion thickness from the deck level up and to fit in the gun port sills. Be careful to mark and cut these steps in the frames accurately. They will prove to be useful later when the deck is framed and the deck planks laid. With the wales and one plank below them trunneled to the frames, the structure will prove quite sturdy under this treatment. However, it can be realized that this would be an awkward time to find one of the futtock joints adjacent to a cutaway section. I used a small, fine tooth keyhole saw pictured in photograph 10 to perform this operation. The cut surfaces were trued up and finished with a smooth file. Do not worry about the moulded thickness of the stanchions – that will have to wait until the hull has been cut loose from the frame jig.

With this modification of the frames completed, the planking work can move right along. I divided the space evenly from the wales up to the caprail around the fore deck and the first line of molding which extends from it toward the stern. The shape of the topsides is enhanced when the planks are fitted properly to those lines. I like to run a thin coat of black paint

along the edge and end of each plank before gluing it in place. Japan paint thinned slightly with mineral spirits and picked up on a finger tip works well here. It dries quickly; and if not thinned too much, it will not run into the fibers of a close-grained hardwood like boxwood. When the planks have been trunneled and the surface scraped and sanded smooth, I think the effect is quite attractive.

There are steps of molding interspersed with the planks as can be seen from the model plans and the photographs. They are glued right to the frames and against the adjacent plank. I do not feel it necessary to use trunnels to secure them. The moldings are easy to produce. Using a jewelers saw, I cut a short slot into the edge of a piece of soft sheet metal. The slot width is equal to or just slightly greater than the thickness of the strip of wood that I want to give a molded edge. At the bottom of the slot, I use the saw blade to cut the shape that will be used to form the molding by scraping. Jewelers files are generally too thick to form the delicate shapes that are required. I round the sides of the slot slightly so they do not cut into the strip of wood while the edge is being scraped. That strip should pass freely through the slot.

To use it, I hold the plate down firmly on a flat table surface with the slotted side overhanging the edge. Grasping the lower end of the wood strip. I draw it down through the slot at a small angle with the perpendicular which enables the cutting edge of the former to scrape the wood with the application of a light pressure. If the full length of the piece is to be molded, I turn the plate over and pull on the other end of the strip. I let the wood feel its way into the cutter with several strokes rather than trying to produce the shape in one pass. When the edge has been shaped, the width required to fit against the frames and project beyond the planked surface is marked off on the wood strip and the piece of molding sawed off for application to the model. Photograph 12 shows the after end of the model with all of the planks and moldings that can be fastened to the topsides of the hull while the frames are still joined to the assembly jig.

Photographs 13 and 14 show the stern frames before and after being planked over. What number 13 fails to show is that I filled in between the stern post and the adjacent frames with some small blocks of wood to provide support for the planks on the counter and the rudder hole. Photograph 14 makes evident the scheme that I followed when adding on the covering boards at each end of the counter, the decorative ebony molding strips, the arched shape on the stern, and the planks above it that merge with those on the sides of the hull. Rather than cover up the nicely finished frames, I decided to leave the planks off the lower body of the hull although some of my friends and critics are sure to be concerned about a schooner that obviously could not float.

With the planking completed on the outside of the

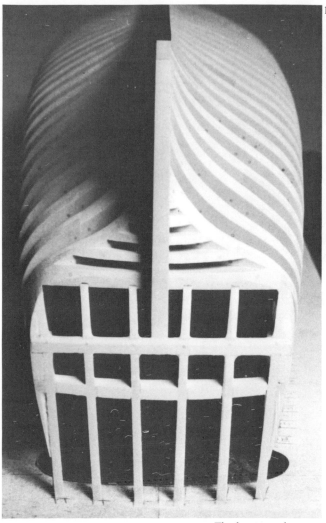

The framing at the stern.

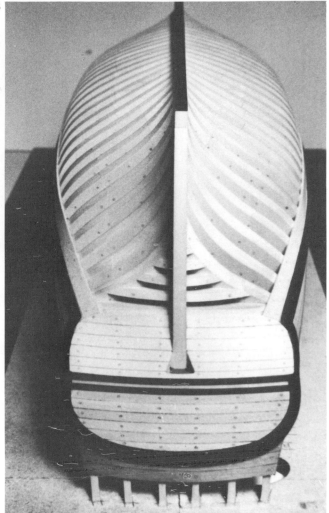

The stern after the planks and mouldings have been added.

hull, I had the choice of cutting the model loose from the assembly jig or simply turning the unit over to continue work on the interior and framing of the decks. In the case of the *Hannah* model, I opted to cut the jig away and work with the hull held separately. While the model is still integral with the jig is a good time to drill holes which will later be used with pedestal mounts to secure it to a permanent base. If a temporary work cradle is desired, it can be designed to utilize those same holes. After selecting suitable locations, I drilled and tapped for machine screws right through the keel, frame, and keelson at two places. The jig mounted hull was placed in a drill press set up at an angle so that the drilled holes would be perpendicular to the waterline. Thus when the model was set on its pedestals, the retaining screws would pass into the holes at right angles to the base and hold the hull in its normal 'floating' position. The size of the tapped holes was determined to fall within the thickness of the keel into which the screws were to be threaded.

When cutting the hull loose, I used the keyhole saw which was pictured earlier to cut through the frame extensions at the sheer line where the planking ends. I cut as close to the plank as possible without cutting

into its edge. A few frames were left intact at either end of the hull while the rest were cut as neatly as possible. Then, as those last few extensions were sawed off, I supported and held the hull in place to avoid breakage. It can be noted from photographs 15 and 16 that the knightheads and four of the stanchions at the bow are cut to extend above the sheer line to serve as bitts. With the hull cut free of the jig, the stanchions can be reduced in moulded thickness down to the deck level with a sharp chisel. Then, the positions of the deck clamps can be marked off on the insides of the frames and those strips of wood fastened in place to support the deck framing.

If they have been laid out and cut accurately, the steps in the frames where the bulwark stanchions start indicate where the tops of the deck beams and ledges should lie along the side of the deck. The beams are the heavy transverse members in the deck framing which reach all the way across. Ledges are smaller in cross-section and support the deck planks for no more than half the width of the deck. I locate the level of the deck clamps along the side so that ledges resting on them will be at the correct height. The bottoms of the heavier beams must be notched to bring them to the

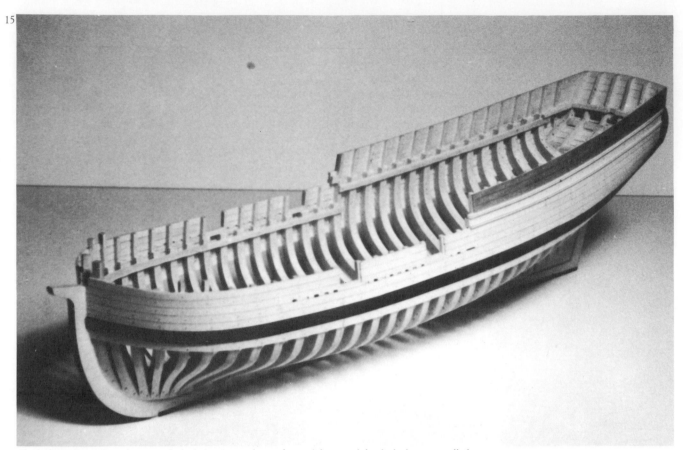

15

The hull, cut loose from the jig, with the bulwark stanchions thinned down and the deck clamps installed.

same level when they are set on the deck clamps. Photograph 15 shows these operations completed and the hull ready for the deck framing.

Before framing the deck, I located the positions along the keelson where the masts should be stepped. This can be determined readily in relation to frame positions from the master frame plan. I drilled ⅛in holes at the two locations to serve in locating the ends of the lower masts later on. The position for the fore mast happens to fall right in the middle of the first whole frame at the bow. The hole drilled there can be seen in photograph 16.

In preparation for framing the deck, I sawed out and finish sanded a supply of beams and ledges calculated to complete the job. (There is a pattern on Plate 2 which shows the shapes of those pieces.) I cut a piece of thin cardboard to the camber shown for use as a template. This template was used to lay out the beam and ledge pieces on boxwood strips that had been sawn to the thickness or 'sided' dimension indicated on the plans. The beam and ledge stock was then cut out on a jig saw. In order to clean up the curved surfaces of those pieces, I made two sand paper blocks shaped to the concave and convex curves of the pattern. These I faced with 100 grit garnet paper. I have found that it is better to use a contact cement for this than a water base glue which has a tendency to warp the pine block slightly out of shape. The sawed beams and ledges are rubbed over these blocks to give them the smooth, uniform curves

16

The windlass brackets as fitted on the deck beam.

which form the camber in the deck.

The first deck beam that I fitted was the one near the bow that interlocks with the sides of the windlass. These members were also pegged into the frame below and became an integral part of the hull structure. Photograph 16 gives a good idea of how they were made. I cut and shaped each one out of a single piece. The hole for the windlass barrel was drilled and then filed to a slightly oval shape in the fore-and-aft direction. Holes were drilled for the two pins used to hold the parts together, and then the piece was cut vertically through the center of the hole with a jewelers saw. The thickness of the sawcut was taken up when the resulting pieces were reassembled with pins, and the hole became round once more. This is probably a good example of a picture being worth a thousand words.

Photograph 17 shows the framing of the fore deck at an early stage. I cut a cardboard template to match the fore-and-aft curvature of the deck at the centerlines as shown on the plans. After fitting a beam in at either end of the deck, those in between were notched to the deck clamps so that they followed the sweep of the template. The carlings fill in between the beams to provide frames for hatch openings as well as support for the ledges. The angular notches I use to fit the pieces together are a model making convention which has proved to be very practical. The samson post which will support the inboard end of the bowsprit should be fitted into the deck framing. If it is pegged into the stem deadwood, it will become a sturdy addition to the structure. Photograph 18 shows the deck framing completed and ready for the planks.

I like to use holly for the deck planks for its color and the contrast with the other woods in a model. To prepare the plank material, I sawed a smooth-sided strip to a thickness equal to the desired width of plank. One side of this strip was given a couple of coats of black paint and then ripped into planks of suitable thickness. I did this with the circular saw attachment on my Unimat. The deck planks for this model of *Hannah* were ⅛in wide and sawn .040in thick. The first plank on each deck level was laid along the centerline in one piece which crossed right over the hatch openings. When planks were added on either side, they fell in line from end to end; and the pieces of the first plank which crossed over the openings could be cut out. The butted ends of plank were coated with black paint to show the joint. On this model, the planks were carried

right up to the openings in the deck framing. They were glued to the framing with white glue and trunneled with the combination of boxwood dowels and epoxy glue used for the planks on the hull.

The nibbing strakes were the fussiest part of planking the deck. This work was complicated by the fact that they had to be fitted around the open bulwark stanchions as well as to the staggered edge of the deck planks. I fitted them to the stanchions first, and then by means of offset measurements plus a certain amount of cut-and-try. A sharp, single edge razor proved to be a very handy tool for this work. Photograph 19 offers a graphic version of the procedures described above.

To complete *Hannah*'s basic hull construction, it was necessary to top off the bulwarks with the cap rails. I cut cardboard templates to match the outside shapes of those rails which had to follow the lines of the bulwarks on the model. Boxwood strips about 1in wide were sawed to the proper thickness. The cap rails for

17

The deck beams with carlings in place.
The deck framing completed.

18

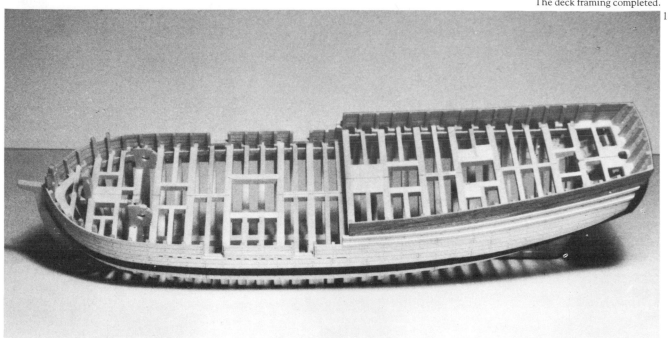

19

Deck planking finished with the nibbing strakes ready for installation.

At the stern, the seat-like cross member was fitted inside the stern frame stanchions, and knees were glued into the corners. Then a taffrail piece was shaped and glued across the stern as shown in photograph 20. The quarterdeck cap rails were half-lapped onto this taffrail. The finishing touch was to carve and glue in place the two scroll pieces that blend with the second molding strip at the break in the deck.

The cap rails are added.

20

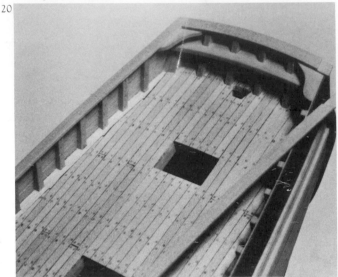

the fore deck bulwarks were made and installed first. They were made in two sections on each side. The piece at the bow was carried around to the middle of the second bitt while the second section continued on to the break in the deck where it merged with the lower molding strip. The outside edge was cut to the cardboard template and shaped to match the molding already in place. Then, the width of the rail was marked off and the piece was sawed out. The sections were notched out to fit around the knightheads and bitts at the bow so they could be glued to the top of the bulwarks.

CHAPTER TWELVE

Hannah's Deck Furniture and Fittings

It has been claimed that the sailing ship is the most beautiful, composite, utilitarian structure ever devised by man. Dedicated ship modelers will second this opinion and oppose those philistines who would deny it. What is it that attracts men to ship modeling? Some will say it is love of the sea while others like myself have a personal interest in historical subjects. But I believe that these are really just secondary motivations. It is the inherent urge to create an object of beauty that stirs the imagination and spurs us on. Ship modeling is just one of a multitude of outlets that can be used to satisfy this very human need. I have long noted a phenomenon in my model work which I am sure most craftsmen will recognize from their own experience. The process of building a model is broken down into a series of projects or steps which form a logical progression from start to finish. I find that at each step the immediate subject assumes an importance to the eye far greater than its significance in the overall scheme. Previous work, no matter how intricate or well done, fades into the background as I study my model. Naturally, this is a form of self-delusion, but it is a delusion that should be fostered. Without it, the model could very well languish on the shelf and never see completion. It makes possible enjoyment of work that can be exacting, which sometimes seems never-ending, and is oft-times nothing but a tedious repetition of detail. Model building should be enjoyed from start to finish. Leave it to family and friends to admire the finished product.

With *Hannah*'s hull complete, the many details that go to dress up the model can be added: there are pads on the bow to strengthen the hawse holes; other pads over the planking protect the bulwark from the anchor flukes where they are swung up to the rail; knees must be cut out and notched into the cap rails in the form of cat heads; their sheaves can be simulated with drilled holes grooved in between, or they can be properly slotted out and fitted with brass sheaves mounted on spindles. (A method of doing this and also for making working blocks will be suggested later in the chapter.) Stanchions for mounting the swivel guns must be made and fastened to the bulwarks. The appearance and positioning of these various fittings can be determined from the photograph and from the details on Plate 1.

I made the windlass barrel in three pieces which were turned on my Unimat. The two long sections on either side were made from boxwood with grooves having the correct diameter to fit the holes in the split side pieces. One section was drilled to admit the dowel turned on the end of the other section. I turned a short length of ebony with a hole for the same dowel and designed so that when the three pieces were assembled, the grooves would be correctly spaced to fit into the frame of the windlass. Before the pieces were glued together, I filed the ratchet teeth into the ebony piece which would work with a pawl mounted on the fore mast. After the three pieces of the windlass barrel had been permanently assembled, I filed the eight-sided shape. The final step was to drill and shape the square holes for the windlass bars. To produce the square holes, I used a large nail that had been filed to a square taper. When this tapered end was pressed into the drilled holes, the square shape was formed. (The disas-

The various parts of the windlass.

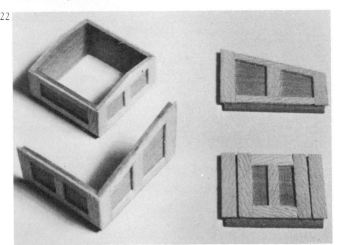

Parts of the deckhouse before completion.

The deck furnishing finished on the foredeck.

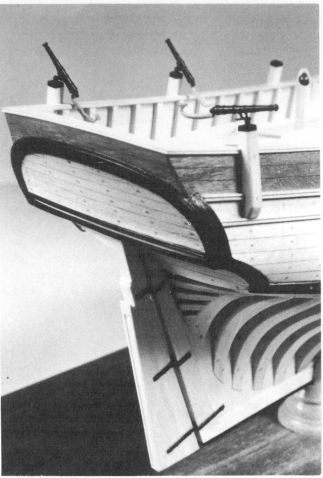

A stern view with the swivel guns mounted.

Fittings on the after deck: ship's bell, swivel guns, etc.

sembled windlass is shown in photograph 21.)

The openings in the deck all required coamings except for the rudder hole. On this model, I made each four-sided coaming from two strips of boxwood glued together so that one edge provided a recess for a grating or a deck house structure. The other edge was made with a wide apron which extended down into the deck opening with the outer piece of wood resting on the deck surface. Rather than assemble these coamings with mitered joints, I half lapped the corners together. First, the two sections of coaming on the fore and aft sides of the opening were fitted and glued in place. Then, the two sections to make the sides, port and starboard, were cut to length and the inside or apron piece was cut back so that it would slip down between the other sides. I had tapered the outside pieces of the coamings so that they were thicker at the deck level and rounded the top corners for appearance.

Making the deck houses and binnacle is a fun project. The method I use is detailed on Plate 1 and pictured in photograph 22. The principle is based on using two layers of veneer. It is not necessary to employ the paneled effect shown for the outside, but a sturdy assembly is produced by gluing the corners together with the two-layered step as shown. I used cherry and sycamore for the color effect. The inside veneer pieces extend down to fit into the coaming recess. Hinge and handle details were made of blackened brass. Strips of thin veneer were built up to form a slide for the small door on the binnacle. Techniques for making hatch gratings to fit into the other coamings will be discussed in a later chapter. Other features such as the combination belfry-bitts, Charley Noble, the rudder with its tiller, pintles and gudgeons, and the pumps are clearly shown in the details of Plate 1 and in the photograph.

The four pounder cannon and the swivel guns are also detailed on Plate 1. I turned the barrels of brass, cross-drilled them, pressed in the trunnions, and chemically blackened the cannon. The design of parts for the swivel guns is shown in detail. The double-ended swivel pin, made of brass, was turned with the long end to be inserted in a hole drilled in the top of a stanchion. A small piece of shim brass, shaped and drilled as shown, was set onto the short end of the pin with its center hole which had been countersunk. The end of the pin was riveted over and lightly soldered to make a secure connection. The 'ears' of the bracket were then formed so that the other two holes could engage the trunnions of the swivel gun. An annealed piece of brass lill pin was formed around the small diameter of the cascable, soldered in place and bent sharply back to form a 'tail' on which to mount the wooden handle. The whole assembly of brass parts was then chemically blackened. There are formulas for making up solutions to be used in this blackening process, but I have no personal experience with them since I have been using commercially available agents. The wooden hand grips were drilled for and permanently fastened onto the pins with epoxy glue.

I have a technique for cutting out shim brass parts when they are needed in quantity which may be of some value to others. I cut three or four pieces of shim stock and mount them sandwich-like on a piece of hard wood ⅛in thick. The pieces are held together with a strong contact cement such as is used to fasten formica to counter tops. After coating the top surface with Dykem Blue, I scribe the design of the piece as many times as necessary to produce the number of pieces needed from the sandwich. Holes are center punched and drilled where indicated. This may cause the shim stock to separate in places, but it can be forced back together with a clamp. The designs are cut out with a jewelers saw. The small cut out pieces can be separated and cleaned up easily.

The anchors for *Hannah* were made of brass with wood stocks. The shanks were turned from brass to diameter large enough to produce the square sections which were filed to shape. One end was turned with a pin which was fitted and soldered into a hole drilled through the middle of the fluke piece. The fluke piece was hammered and filed from a piece of brass rod to the shape shown on Plate 1. In pieces this small, it may not be necessary; but if the hammering and bending should work harden the brass enough to start cracks, the metal should be annealed with a torch during the forming process. After the shank has been soldered to the fluke piece, the palms can be soldered to the flukes. They could be drilled and riveted in place with soft copper wire if desired. I also riveted the wood stock to the shank.

While describing the work involved in making various fittings for *Hannah*, I think it logical to consider some of the tools and materials involved. The jewelers saw is high on the list of tools that I feel are indispensible to my model work, in fact I was familiar with and skilled in the use of a jewelers saw long before becoming involved in model building. However, it is possible that some craftsmen who are not acquainted with this type of saw do not realize what a valuable addition to their tool chests it would make. It is similar in appearance to a coping or fret saw. It differs from them in that the saw blades it holds are much finer and thereby more suitable for delicate model work in both wood and metal. The saw frames can be bought from tool specialty supply houses, hobby stores, or artists' supply stores. Where there is a choice, the deeper frame would be more universally useful. Unfortunately, local stores are not likely to carry many of the wide range of blade sizes that can be obtained from mail order houses. One such source lists 21 sizes ranging from one with 80 teeth per inch with a cross section .007in x .014in to one at the opposite extreme having 12 teeth per inch in a blade cross section of .020in x .085in. The most useful sizes fall near the smaller end of this range. While the very finest blades have a definite use, their steel is quite brittle and they must be used with extreme care and a sensitive touch to avoid excessive breakage.

Most often, I use the jewelers saw while the work piece is held flat over the opening in a wood fork which projects from the edge of my work table. This opening is cut out with a fairly sharp 'V' shape and most of the sawing is done near the apex of the 'V' where the fork provides the most support for the work. As with most cutting operations, it is best to let the tool 'feel' its way into the work. The saw handle should be held securely but with a light grip so that the hand can react to the cutting action. This action cannot be forced, and momentary carelessness which throws the blade out of line with the saw slot will snap it off in a hurry. In fact, breakage is a normal part of the game; so it is well to stock up on sizes of blades that have been found most useful.

There are some economical and readily available sources of material for model work that should be recognized. The copper found in stranded electrial wiring comes in many diameters. When I finally found how useful this wire could be to me, I collected several feet of as many sizes as could be located. After stripping off the insulation, I untwisted the strands, cut them to practical lengths, and bundled them in tape with labels to identify the various wire diameters. This electrical wire is in a soft, annealed state which makes it very workable. It can be hammered flat, will take a sharp bend without breaking, and can be used to rivet parts together. Having a large, well-identified stock of this useful copper wire on hand has proved well worth the small effort it took to collect, prepare, and store it.

Nickle-plated brass lill pins are offered for sale by model supply houses. They fit snug in a .021in diameter hole made by a number 75 drill. These pins can be used in a variety of ways, but I find that they usually require some modification. As manufactured, the brass has become work hardened and brittle so that the pin usually cracks when subjected to a sharp bend. This deficiency can be overcome easily by heating the pin to anneal it. The flame of an ordinary candle will do the job. I use these pins for fastenings such as are needed with the chain plates or for the rudder's pintle and gudgeon straps. They were also used to hold the windlass brackets together on this model of *Hannah*. However, the head of the pin as purchased would be large and unnatural in appearance on a model. I chuck them in my Unimat, file the heads to a more suitable shape, and then use the small file to cut the pin off to length with a sharp point. To offset the pressure of the file, the head of the pin can be supported by a strip of hardwood held in the other hand. With the plating removed from the head of the pin, it can be blackened along with other brass parts or left bright as desired. Larger brass pins which may be found useful on occasion can be purchased in local stores.

Another useful material that can be found for sale in hobby shops and hardware stores is thin brass tubing. The smallest size has a 1/16 outside diameter with a 1/32in hole through it. Each successive size is 1/32in larger than the last. With a wall thickness of 1/64in, the complete range of tubing sizes can be telescoped together. This tubing can be cut off in rings to serve a number of purposes. The smaller diameters make excellent thimbles for use with rigging. Like the lill pins, the brass tubing became hardened in the manufacturing process. It also can be softened by annealing when the usage requires it. To cut rings from a piece of tubing, I chuck it in my Unimat. I score it with a sharp pointed lathe tool at regular intervals which allow for the width of ring desired plus cutoff stock. To actually cut off the rings, I use my jewelers saw fitted with a blade strong enough to take the stress. Brass chips tend to clog the gullets of the saw teeth. I find that the problem can be eliminated by loading the teeth with beeswax at intervals to keep the saw cutting freely. The cut off rings can be caught on a rod which is smaller in diameter than

the hole in the tube and held in a Jacobs chuck mounted on the lathe tailstock. If some such precaution is not taken, the tiny pieces are likely to dance about with gay abandon and become lost.

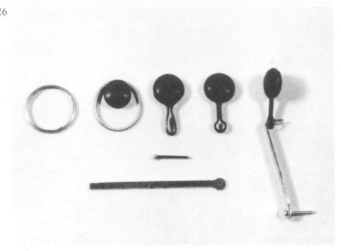

Preparing to mount the deadeyes on their channels.

The strapped deadeyes are fitted to the channel.

The preceding discussion of tools, materials, and techniques has been presented in order to introduce and clarify some of the description that follows. At this stage in building the model of *Hannah*, I had prepared a permanent base and set of pedestals on which to mount the hull for the light finishing operations which were to be followed by masting and rigging of the model. The channels had been made and fastened to the bulwarks in a manner that can be understood from a study of photographs 27 and 28. The individual channel was made and fitted as a single piece. The line and locations of the deadeyes was marked off. Holes for the pins meant to fasten the covering board in place were drilled, and then the covering board strip was cut off with a jewelers saw. The pre-drilled holes made it possible to reassemble the two pieces with a perfect fit. Lill pins

All the deadeyes are fixed in position.

²⁸ drilling the three holes that the model builder can gain the most benefit. I turned these jigs in my Unimat from short pieces of brass bar. There are seven on hand now which cover a range of deadeye diameters from $\frac{1}{16}$in to $\frac{1}{4}$in. Using them makes drilling holes in the deadeyes a simple, rapid operation.

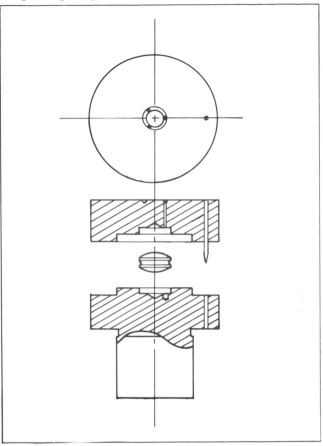

altered as described earlier were made for a tight fit in the covering board while a slightly larger drill was used to open up the holes in the main body of the channel which was then glued and pinned to the bulwark through its stanchions. Supporting knees were glued in below, and the edge was notched out for the deadeye straps where they were to pass through the channel.

Making deadeyes for a model would be a long, tedious process as described by some authors. The methods I use help the work to pass rapidly and produce excellent results. The deadeyes for *Hannah* were made of ebony although I have used walnut or boxwood where the color seemed more suitable. Ebony is a truly excellent material that provides a hard, smooth finish. I make the deadeyes in two steps. The first step is to turn finished blanks on my Unimat. A length of ebony is turned to the diameter of the required deadeye size. The blanks are then shaped and cut off one after the other. The end of the stock in the lathe is rounded with a smooth file to form the face of a deadeye. A groove is scored with a pointed lathe tool to hold the strap or the end of a shroud. A second groove is formed where the deadeye blank is to be cut off. This back side can be chamfered and rounded with a file to improve the shape of the deadeye, and the wood buffed to a smooth finish with fine steel wool. Finally, the blank is cut off by holding the jewelers saw in the second groove while the machine is running. Again, some precaution must be taken to prevent the tiny piece from bounding away into obscurity.

Turning the blanks is pretty much a routine lathe operation. It is in making and using special jigs for

The drawing shows the configuration of those jigs. The bottom half is turned with a short stem which can be set into the 'V' of vise jaws used to confine but not clamp on the jig. With the vise located properly and clamped on the table of a drill press set-up such as can be arranged with a Unimat or a Moto-Tool outfit, the jig can be swiveled from hole to hole without need for realignment. With a shoulder turned on one half of the jig and a corresponding counterbore in the other half, the two pieces are made to have a close but easily assembled fit. Holes for the deadeye blank are drilled and counter-bored to locate it inside the jig. This work is completed in such fashion that the wood blank will hold the halves of the jig slightly apart. Thus, finger pressure on top of the jig can hold the deadeye from shifting while holes are drilled in it. The next step is to chuck the top of the jig in the lathe and turn a groove of suitable diameter to locate the three holes. I find that I can chuck and rechuck round pieces in the universal three jaw chuck on my Unimat without any significant loss of concentricity so that the groove turned on the top of the jig runs true with the hole counter-bored for the deadeye inside.

Before drilling the three holes located in the groove, I drill a hole near the outside diameter of the jig for a locating pin which keeps the halves from turning in relation to each other. This serves two purposes: it reduces the likelihood of having the deadeye shift inside the jig, and it keeps the holes in the upper half lined up with clearance holes in the lower half to guard against drill breakage. After he has used them for a number of models, the model builder will be amply rewarded for the time invested in making these jigs because the job of drilling holes in deadeyes is made so easy.

Photographs 26, 27 and 28 show how I mounted the deadeyes on *Hannah*'s channels. Reference to earlier descriptions of various work methods will supplement the information that can be derived from the pictures. Photograph 26 shows how the deadeyes were strapped with annealed and blackened rings cut from brass tubing. It pictures the chainplates as drilled and sawed in multiples from a sandwich of brass shim stock and the lill pins modified for use in fastening the chainplates to the hull. Photograph 27 shows the channel covering board removed and two of the strapped deadeyes set into their notches. Photograph 28 has the covering board partially assembled and about to be fixed permanently in place on the channel.

To conclude this chapter about fittings for *Hannah*, I would like to offer a description of my method for

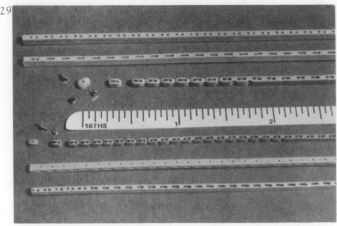

29

The production of working blocks.

making the working blocks that were used. A technique has been published for doing this work which produced the wood shells for the blocks by gluing small segments properly spaced between strips of wood. Here is an example of how model builders can use different approaches to achieve the same end. For several reasons, I preferred to make the blocks from solid wood. Photograph 29 illustrates how that can be done. The smallest blocks that I have made in this fashion are ³⁄₃₂in long.

The first step is to establish the cross section size for the block in question from its sheave size and cut strips

Quartering bow view of the completed model.

30

Finished model of *Hannah*, now in the Navy Memorial Museum, Washington Navy Yard, Washington DC.
Courtesy of the Mariner's Museum, Newport News, Virginia.

of boxwood to those dimensions. I found 5in to be a convenient length of strip to work with. The next step is to locate and drill the holes that frame the ends of the sheave slots. Since I anticipated repetition of this work in the future, I made a device which would center-punch the hole locations in pairs and space them uniformly along the wood strip. Using a thin block of boxwood. I cut a slot to fit the strip closely while allowing it to project beyond the surface. For the single blocks shown, three holes were drilled through the center of the slot and pieces of lill pins pressed into them with modified points projecting into the slot. These tiny 'punches' were spaced so that the first one could be set into the last previous punch mark made. The space to the second pin equalled the space between the slots of the blocks in the strip while the space from the second to the third pin produced the sheave slot. A small hammer is used to punch mark the strip of wood as the jig is moved along it, indexing from one sheave slot to the next by means of the first pin. This ensured accurate, uniform spacing with no need for measurements. Similar jigs were made for double and triple blocks with slots to suit by doubling and tripling the numbers of pins used as punches.

A basic part of the design process was to decide the diameter and thickness of the sheave to be used for a given size of block. The sheave diameter established the spacing of the holes. The thickness determined the

size of holes to drill. After those holes have been drilled, tiny punch marks made with the point of a scriber are located along the side of the strip which will center in the sheave slots after they are cut. Transverse holes are then drilled to fit the size of wire that will be used for spindles to mount the sheaves in the blocks. The next step is to cut the slots with a jewelers saw. I found it best to use a saw blade that was less than half the thickness of the slot material to be cut out. With the blade inserted into the hole at one end of a slot, this makes it possible to take a full cut on each side of the slot for better control of the cutting action. It is also necessary to develop a feel for keeping the saw blade paralled with the drilled holes.

The brass sheaves are turned with a groove for the 'rope' and a hole drilled several thousandths of an inch larger than the diameter of the wire spindle. I cut them off in the lathe with the jewelers saw. The sides were cleaned up to the correct thickness using a smooth file with the sheave set into a drilled recess in a block of wood. The wire to be used for spindles is, of course, the soft copper wire described earlier. The sheaves are set into their slots and the wire inserted through the holes in the side of the strip. This calls for a bit of fishing, but the oversize hole in the sheave helps with this. The wire is cut off and the ends leveled with a file so as to project a few thousandths of an inch beyond the side of the wood strip. With the assembly resting on an anvil, the end of the wire is hammered gently to rivet it in place. Following this, I file the blocks to their rounded shape. Then grooves are incised on the side of the strip with an engraving tool from the wire spindles to the dividing lines between blocks. A final operation before cutting the blocks apart is to drill transverse holes which will form grooves on the ends of the blocks. These holes are located by the engraved grooves midway between blocks in the strip. By this time, the connecting material between blocks will have become quite fragile and, in most cases, can be cut through with a razor blade. When this has been done and any rough edges rounded off, the working blocks will be ready for use on the model.

CHAPTER THIRTEEN

Tools and Equipment

There have been many how-to-do-it books written for the neophyte ship modeler. They are useful to all of us since they include fundamental information about ship design and basic approaches to model building. However, their emphasis lies in encouraging and guiding the beginner in his first attempts at the craft. There are relatively few works oriented to the concerns of skilled craftsmen who have developed an abiding interest in building ship models. I am writing this book with the hope that it will help to fill that void and stimulate even greater development of latent skills. None of us can honestly expect ever to produce the 'perfect' ship model, but it is that search after perfection which holds our interest and promotes continued efforts in that direction. I think that it will be agreed in general that we usually expect the 'next' model to be the best ever.

Some authors, who apparently are chary of frightening off the beginner with the complexities of ship modeling, emphasize the idea that models can be be built on a kitchen table or, as in my case, on a sturdy card table with a minimum outlay for equipment. This is true up to the point were frustration starts to take command. Beauty is in the eye of the beholder, and a first model though built on compromises can look lovely indeed to the beginner. It is also true that the great majority of operations performed in constructing a model are done by hand with simple tools, but there is certain work that demands the use of proper equipment. I am happy to be living in a house with a basement where a workshop with the usual combination of wood working machinery can be maintained. I sympathize with apartment dwellers who lack this advantage. Those people must find some outside source of help for cutting their boards to manageable

sizes and doing other operations that cannot be performed on machinery suitable for use in the limited space available to them. However, I know that many people through necessity have been able to overcome this handicap.

It is the smaller machine equipment which can be set up and used anywhere that should be recognized as necessary and invaluable to the model builder. I shudder every time I read a description of how a cannon barrel can be turned with files from a piece of wood dowel chucked in a hand-operated drill. When I decided in 1960 to resume my earlier interest in building ship models, my first consideration was to obtain a small lathe capable of turning brass. I knew from experience that without it I would be stymied. Fortunately, the Unimat was on the market at that time. After a short period of indecision about the cost involved, I bought one sight unseen on the basis of a magazine advertisement. It is a decision that I have never regretted. The initial cost may seem high; but for the craftsman who anticipates many more years of model building, the expense pro-rated over those years of use becomes insignificant. Of course, parts made on such a machine can be purchased from ship model supply houses; but I believe that sooner or later the serious model builder will want to enjoy the satisfaction of making and controlling the quality of all the parts that go into his creation.

It would be easy to heartily recommend the acquisition of a Unimat or its equivalent and let it go at that. Certainly those men with a machine shop background do not need any advice on how to use this versatile machine. However, I believe that there are model builders lacking in machine tool experience who would benefit from some suggestions on the subject.

32

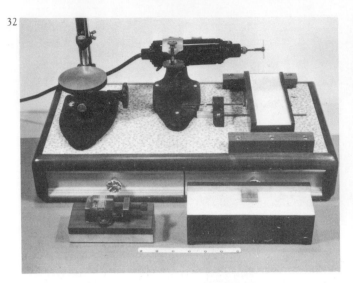

The author's compact portable work center.

with a diameter large enough to resist deflection under the cutting load. This tiny diameter can be turned to any length so long as it does not whip out of line and self-destruct from centrifugal force. Brass bar because of its homogeniety is better than boxwood in this respect. When I want to make multiple copies, I mark the cross feed dial with a pointed, felt tip pen at the two or three settings that need to be repeated each time. If the backlash between the cross feed screw and the carriage is taken up at each setting, the turned diameters will be duplicated. It will be necessary to have a pair of one inch micrometers for measuring all of the diameters. Most of the model work is $\frac{1}{4}$in or less in diameter. The Jacobs chuck is the most convenient means of holding such stock in the live spindle. Quite often, holes need to be drilled as part of the turning operation such as in the muzzle of a cannon. For this reason, I found it practical to buy a second Jacobs chuck which could be mounted on the tailstock when the other one was in use on the spindle.

Actually, I find it hard to class the Unimat as a machine tool in the broader sense. It transmits very little horsepower to the cutting tool; but within its limitation, it is an ideal piece of equipment for producing rapidly and conveniently the many small parts that can be made from easily machined brass, wood or plastic for a model. I have been particularly impressed with the accuracy that can be maintained with this relatively inexpensive machine, and it operates well at the high speeds required for typical small diameter model work.

The Unimat has a wide range of speeds available with two belts driving three triple step pulleys. Still, I very seldom find it necessary to change speeds. A spindle speed of about 2000rpm is suitable for all the small diameter work that predominates, and it is easier on the bearings than higher speeds. There is little need to get technical about cutting speeds when working with wood and easily machined brass. By the same token, the tooling can be kept quite simple. For years, I have used the same lathe tool for external turning; it is ground to a point with a 30° included angle. The end is dubbed with a tiny radius. It has a very small positive rake and cutting edge clearance on both sides so that the tool can be used to cut while traversing in either direction. When the work piece is long and slender, I set the cutting edge perpendicular to the axis of rotation to minimize the forces tending to deflect the piece. This eliminates the force which pushes the work away in the horizontal plane but does not counteract the lifting force of the cutting edge. The best antidote for this is a well-sharpened and honed tool to reduce the cutting force.

The small diameter turnings required in model work do not demand expertise in lathe operation so much as the simple application of a little common sense. For example, the $\frac{1}{64}$in diameter of a belaying pin can be turned easily if it is machined in one pass from stock

33

Slotting the strips to make hatch gratings.

I generally turn pieces that are to wind up with a square or rectangular cross section if they need round pegs on the end or have to be drilled axially. It may seem strange to take a piece of wood that was initially sawn to a square cross-section, hand plane it to an octagon, turn it round, and finally plane or file it to its finished square shape. However when many duplicates are required as with railing stanchions or gun carriage axles, the work can be set up to go rapidly and efficiently. To measure the lengths and locations of various features on duplicate pieces, I mark the edge of a piece of cardboard and hold it up to the workpiece during the turning operation. This is an easy way to locate shoulders or, in the case of cannon, the positions of decorative rings and reinforces along the barrel. The fact that my Unimat headstock can be swiveled to any angle makes it readily adaptable to turning the taper on cannon. After turning the brass bar to the maximum diameter of the cannon, I drill the muzzle and turn it to its finished shape. Then removing the headstock locating pin, I swivel the spindle to the predetermined angle which will produce the correct taper on the barrel of the cannon. The taper is turned to the outside diameter of the rings. Next with the cardboard template held up to locate the various features on the workpiece, the tool is fed in to the barrel, moved along the taper, and withdrawn wherever raised rings are indicated. The headstock is then returned to its normal position and pinned with the spindle parallel to the ways. The end with the cascabel is roughed out with the lathe tool and finished with fine Swiss files. The final step after buffing the piece with fine steel wool is to file the round ball on the end to the point where it is cut loose from the bar stock. Thus, the cannon can be finish turned in a single set-up.

The Unimat is a versatile machine that can be converted from lathe to drill press, milling machine, sander, circular saw, jig saw, or tool grinder. All of these functions are limited in scope by the small amount of available horsepower. I have found the drill press and circular saw accessory set-ups to be the most useful in my work. I never use the saws that are designed with a set in their teeth for cutting wood. The so-called metal saws, with no set, cut my deck planking and other dimension strips accurately and with a smooth finish. A hollow ground blade would be even better for this purpose. The drill press set-up is very useful except that the Jacobs chuck will not hold the smallest number drills. I have remedied this deficiency with the purchase of a small adaptor chuck than can be held in the Jacobs chuck.

An accessory that I use more often than the machine itself is the small machinist's vise that is designed to be mounted on the carriage of the Unimat. In addition to its uses in conjuction with the machine, I have found this vise invaluable for many hand filing, sawing, and carving operations because of its convenient size. Its hardened jaws are safe from damage by saws or files.

The Dremel Manufacturing Company offers small motorized tools that are very useful in ship model work. Their Moto-Shop which is basically a jig saw with accessories is a handy size that can be moved about easily. The Moto-Tool with its accessories can be used as a hand grinder, buffer, sander, or drill. I use it mostly for drilling the many small holes required to build a ship model. At one talk I attended, the speaker emphasized his belief that small diameter drills must be used in a hand operated pin vise to avoid breakage. This does not agree with my experience. Hand drilling in a tedious process which in itself is conducive to drill breakage. I use the pin vise as little as possible and then only if it happens to be a convenience. I was so impre-

ssed with the versatility of the small hand grinder that I built a portable work center to take better advantage of it.

34

A drawer holding accessories and a complete set of number drills.

The work center which is pictured in photographs 32, 33 and 34 serves a number of purposes. In a very small space, it provides a place to store the Moto-Tool and its accessories on a platform which can be moved easily to the most convenient work area. There is a miniature drill press. The adjustable goose neck clamping device holds the tool for off hand use of the various grinding wheels, burrs, sanding discs, and buffing wheels. The drawers provide storage and ready accessibility for the many tools including a complete range of smaller number drills. At the right side is a moveable carriage which can be positioned accurately under a cutter mounted in the Moto-Tool.

The drawing shows a cross-section of the homemade carriage taken through its lead screw. This screw which adjusts the position of the carriage is simply a length of threaded brass rod which was purchased, along with the washers and hexagonal nuts, at a hardware store. I chose a 6-32 thread which moves the carriage 1/32 in with every revolution of the screw. There have been times when I thought that a screw with 40 threads per inch because of its correlation with micrometer measurements would have been a better choice. However, the fractional lead also has its advantages. As can be seen in photograph 33, there is a calibrated dial mounted under the handle which is fastened to the end of the screw. The pointer on the

131

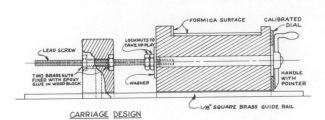

35

a

b

c

d

Cutting hatch grating strips by hand.

handle indicates movement of the carriage by thousandths of an inch on the dial.

The screw threads through two hexagonal nuts mounted in a fixed block that is fastened to the surface of the work center. The nuts are fitted in hexagonal holes cut into the block and cemented in with epoxy glue. The lead screw passes through the carriage with thrust washers on either side and a pair of locknuts to take up play. The bottom of the carriage is slotted in line with the lead screw to fit a ⅛in square brass strip which was fastened to the base as a guide. A pair of 'L'-shaped blocks are closely fitted over projections of the carriage, front and rear, to hold it down on the base. This contraption makes it possible to cut exactly spaced slots in a work piece with a disc saw mounted in the Moto-Tool.

There is one condition to this application that must be observed. I discovered that hand grinders built with bronze sleeve bearings had spindle end play which defeated the accuracy maintained with the carriage movement. It is necessary to use a Moto-Tool with a ball-bearing mounted spindle if the axial position of the saw is to remain fixed in relation to the base while the machine is running. The carriage and its associated parts were made from pattern maker's mahogany surfaced with Formica. The block to be noted in the left foreground of photograph 32 was designed to slide between the raised sides of the carriage with the machinist's vise mounted at a practical height for passing work pieces under the Moto-Tool saw. The second block in the picture provides a smooth surface at the same level with a parallel guide. With this block in place on the carriage, individual work pieces can be passed under the cutter. A simple application for this set-up would be the slotting of side pieces for a ship's ladder. Those ladder sides can be made as a matched pair if cut from a single piece slotted at right angles to the grain.

The first block with the vise mounted on it was designed primarily as an aid to making hatch gratings. I have seen a number of different methods for doing this work presented in journals, but the only approach that I have noted in books on ship modeling suggests cutting grooves for cross strips in the grating with Swiss pattern maker files. Such a procedure would result in gratings of rather coarse proportions suitable only for a large scale model. For some reason, the production of good hatch gratings has remained a mystery to the

132

majority of model builders. I very rarely see true-to-scale built up hatch gratings even on museum models. Actually, it is not a difficult thing to accomplish. I have two ways for cutting strips to suggest.

Most people make the strips for hatch gratings by cutting slots in a solid block and then cutting that block into the required strips. I understand that this is done best with a small hollow ground slotting saw. Still, I would be concerned that the tiny nibs left between slots would be vulnerable to breakage while the strips were being sawn off. My technique involves cutting the strips to size first and clamping them in a vise sandwiched between supporting pieces of Formica. I set blocks of wood in the vise underneath the strips to support them at the proper level while they are being lined up and having the jaws tightened on them. This set-up is shown in several of the photographs. The support afforded by the two pieces of Formica and the unified strength of the wood strips clamped together protects the pieces from breakage while the slots are being cut.

For the model of *Hannah*, I decided to make the grating strips $\frac{1}{32}$in thick. This represents $1\frac{1}{2}$in full size in the $\frac{1}{48}$ scale of the model. Actually, the strips were made .030in thick by $\frac{1}{8}$in wide with a length slightly greater than corresponding dimension of the grating to be produced. It is important that the wood be held to a uniform thickness and the slots cut to the same width plus a small amount for clearance. When the pieces are assembled, it should be possible to fit them together with a minimum of force if breakage is to be avoided. I would suggest boxwood, hard maple, or apple wood as the best materials to use. With the sizes chosen, sixteen strips of wood will be required per inch of grating. I usually add one or two extra pieces to the sandwich as insurance although I seldom have use for them. In an actual ship's grating, only one set of strips was notched out; but for model gratings, I prefer to notch both sets for better strength and uniform spacing. Just the top side of the grating can be seen after it has been set into the hatch coaming.

I number the grating strips in sequence on a common end so that they can be lined up and then assembled in the same order that they were cut. If they were put together haphazardly, small variations in slot spacing could pose a serious problem. Based on the size of strip chosen, two turns of the carriage lead screw moves the work under the saw a distance of $\frac{1}{16}$in to provide the correct slot spacing. Unless the saw cuts the exact width of slot required, it is necessary to make two passes for each slot. With a fixed point on the carriage dial selected for spacing the slots, the additional movement needed on the dial to line up the second cut can be determined. The finished slots should be checked with one of the cross strips of wood before the pieces are removed from the vise.

The second method that I use to cut slots for hatch gratings follows the same rules for holding the wood

A machine set-up for cutting hatch gratings.

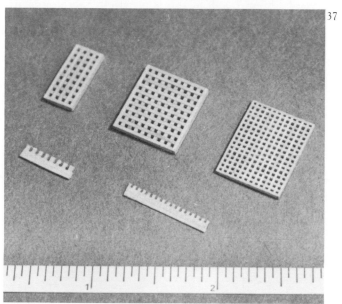

Hatch gratings in two sizes.

strips in the vise. It differs in that a fine tooth hacksaw blade is used to cut slots .020in wide in the strips which have been finished to a .019in thickness. A special jig is used to guide the saw and index the cut from slot to slot. I fasten the vise to a drawing board by screws with its jaws parallel to the edge of the board which serves as a guide for the saw jig. The jig itself is designed around a core composed of five layers of copper strips which were sweated together with soft solder and fastened into the wood frame with epoxy glue. The core was made from sheet copper .020in thick. The first copper strip projects down to engage a slot in the work piece while the saw slot in line with the third strip is spaced .020in away. Thus after each slot has been cut, the jig can be moved so that the indexing strip falls into that slot and the saw blade is lined up for the next cut. Photographs 35a-35d show the various components described above. I use the gratings made to these proportions for models scaled to ⅛in per foot.

After the two sets of strips have been cut by either of the methods described above, I assemble and finish them as illustrated by the photographs 38a-38d. It can be noted in photograph 38a that the pieces have been arranged on the work surface in numerical order. The first strips from each set have been assembled with the marked ends together. I like to line up all the longer strips first as shown in photograph 38b. Then when the shorter strips are set in place as in 38c, there are fewer slots to match up. During this assembly process, I keep a drop of white glue on a handy surface. Using a sharply pointed tool like a scriber, I touch each slot with a bit of glue just before sliding the cross strip into place. Assembling the second set of strips requires special care since the slots must be centered in both directions if the pieces are to slide together without interference. Also, this assembly must be accomplished before the setting glue creates an interference of its own. The completed unit is shown in photograph 38d along with some left over strips.

The rough assembly looks hardly at all like a finished hatch grating. The slots which were cut less than half way through the ⅛in width of the strips leave the uncut edges standing well above the squares of the mating strips. I dress these edges down on both sides by rubbing over a fine grade of garnet paper. This should be done in the direction at right angles to the uncut sides of the strips as indicated by the arrow in photograph 38c. When the surface has been reduced to the level of the slotted squares, the cross strips will support them to protect against breakage while the sanding continues. When the faces of the grating have been finished in this fashion, the edges can be trimmed by sanding in a direction that will support the cut squares against the backs of the strips. The grating will then appear as in photograph 38d. I have continued to reduce the thickness of such gratings to as little as ⅟₃₂in where appearances required it. It is necessary, of course, to avoid sanding the uncut edges of either set of strips completely away. The surfaces could be shaped for a camber if desired with the use of curved blocks such as were used for finishing deck beams.

Photograph 37 shows examples of finished hatch gratings in the two different sizes and produced by the two methods described above. I am in the habit of gluing additional strips around the sides to finish a grating. I give it a coat of flat varnish to protect it and also to help the glue bind the strips together.

38

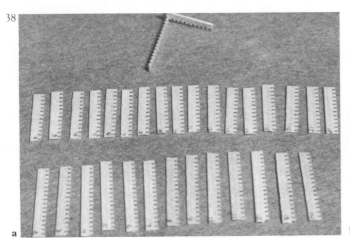

a

The first step in assembling the hatch grating.

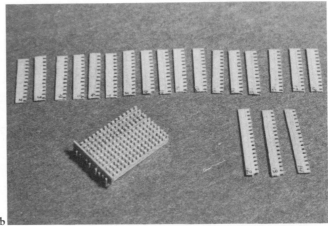

b

The second step.

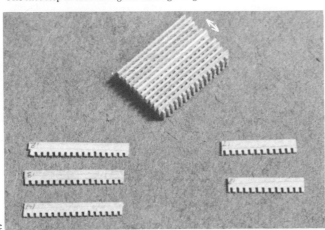

c

The third step; the arrow indicates the direction in which the ends should be rubbed down.

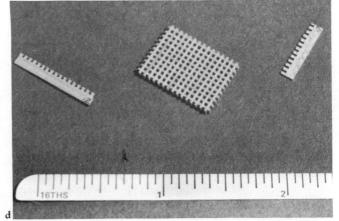

d

The hatch grating dressed down.

134

Framing and Planking Halifax

The model of *Hannah* was chosen to serve as the first example in this book because its simplicity of design makes it suitable for a first attempt at plank-on-frame modeling. There are no complications to distract the attention from the basic concern with framing and then planking the hull. Very few eighteenth century ships can be modeled without consideration being given to quarter galleries, stern windows, head rails, figureheads, and a variety of decorative carvings. *Hannah* also represents the option of reconstructing the appearance of a famous vessel from little more than a general knowledge of contemporary designs and a personal interest in the subject. Although no legitimate claim can be made that the model of *Hannah* bears a close resemblance to its prototype, it is a reasonable approximation and could very well represent any one of the schooners included in George Washington's navy. There is no possibility on the basis of the little positive information that has been passed down to us of recreating one of those vessels with any greater certitude of authenticity.

The model of *Halifax*, which will now be considered, is just slightly larger than the *Hannah* model. There are other similarities. While *Halifax* has somewhat fuller lines than *Hannah*, the two schooners are much alike below the waterline; and they exhibit the same bluff bows at the deck level. The model of *Halifax* has the advantage of authenticity since its design comes from a drawing made with measurements taken off the actual vessel. The Admiralty draught shows the changes made to the original design to fit her out for the Royal Navy as well as her appearance while employed as a packet between Halifax and Boston. I had already built a model of Halifax in 1/96 scale which embodied the original design. Since the information pertaining to her history was concerned almost exclusively with the period of service in the Navy, it was logical to develop this model along those lines. The Admiralty drawing gives details of the below decks arrangements which helps in bringing to life the schooner's story. It seemed a shame not to use this information while designing and building the model.

For some time I had been corresponding with Robert Lightley of Cape Town, South Africa. Bob is an accomplished model builder who had just finished a model of *Endeavour* for the National Maritime Museum about the time I was making plans for this model of *Halifax*. He sent me some photographs of his *Endeavour* which had been constructed with some unusual features. He had cut away the hull on one side to expose the interior. The other side had been set in a 'sea' made from a sheet of plastic. This displayed the ship as she would have appeared while afloat but did not obscure the hull below the waterline. I thought his ideas offered an excellent way to present a model and decided to make full use of them in my *Halifax*.

Whether or not other ship modelers care to complicate their work by following this scheme, they will find that a model of *Halifax* affords a number of challenges to their skill that were not present in *Hannah*'s design. The headrails, figurehead, quarter badges, windows, and various decorative carvings add to the interest and to the difficulty of building the model. It is still a far cry from a frigate or a ship-of-the-line, but serves as a modest step in that direction since many of the complicated problems will be encountered in relatively simple forms.

The system I use to make the frames for a model, assemble them in the jig with the stem-keel-sternpost unit, and then plank the hull, was thoroughly covered in the description for building *Hannah*. *Halifax* was put together in much the same way. Instead of boxwood, I used Swiss pearwood for the frames. The contrasting wood color shows only on the one side where the hull is cut away, but it made an interesting experiment, and I was pleased with the way the pearwood worked. The port side of the hull was completely planked; on the starboard side, I had to decide just where the frames should be cut away to provide the best possible view of the interior without affecting the integrity of the structure or hurting the appearance of the upper deck works on that side. Once that design had been decided on, the hull was planked up to the lines of the area that was to be removed. The one exception to this was the wale which I carried along the full length of the hull. This might be considered wasted effort, but having the wale fastened to them did help to stabilize the frames until it was time to cut out the opening. It also served to establish the run of the planks with some authority.

Holly was used to plank the hull below the wales. Three strakes of boxwood filled in the space up to the channels and their molding strip. Two strakes of walnut furnished color contrast above the channels; and a single, narrow strake of holly finished the planking aft from the break in the deck. The wales and strips of molding were made of ebony.

It will be recalled that *Hannah*'s hull was cut loose from the frame assembly jig as soon as the external planking had been completed. I followed a different procedure with *Halifax*. My thought was to build in as much support as possible before cutting out the opening on the side of the hull and then to construct the cabins and top deck framing to further strengthen the model while it was still held securely in shape on the assembly jig. The frames faired up well enough on the inside so that after a small amount of correction with a pad of emery cloth I was able to locate and fasten the deck clamps in place and then ceil in the frames with strips of boxwood. Then the beams for the lower forecastle deck and the cabin deck were fitted and fixed at their proper level. Measurements made from the jig surface to position these various items equalled the distance as picked off from the reference line on Plate 2 plus the thickness of the masonite jig. Locating holes had been drilled in the keelson for the mast steps. Provision was made to fit pegs on the bottom of the windlass brackets into holes in the frame below and notches in the after end of the forecastle platform. The lower decks were planked and trunneled, and breast hooks were fitted into the bow. All this work was nearly complete when photograph 40 was taken.

It was finally time to cut out the frame sections for the opening in the side of the hull. Using the fine tooth keyhole saw, this was done with care to avoid splintering the cut ends of the frame which were then trimmed with a file and sanded smooth. It seemed a shame to discard the perfectly good section of frame, but the end justified the means. I had decided to retain one complete frame at the forward end of the cabin deck. It provided some insurance against having the hull go out

39

The model of the *Halifax* used in the diorama.

of shape, and it really did not obscure the view. Furthermore, the curve of that frame suggested the actual hull shape. I also left short sections of frame attached to the ends of the deck beams. Two short lengths of planking were trunneled to eight of the frames where they were needed for fastening the deadeye chains. Photograph 41 pictures the model just after the sections of frame had been cut away to expose the interior of the hull.

Before the upper decks could be completely framed in, it was necessary to partition off the cabins and install whatever was intended in the way of furnishings, doors and figures. The stern frames of the counter were planked over in the captain's cabin and a seat added. Certain of the upper deck beams had to be integrated with the arrangement of partitions and were installed at the same time. The tubes for the pumps were fitted but not fastened in permanently. It should be noted that the pumps angle together toward the keelson. This is a perfectly logical condition with the consideration that the bottom end of the pump should extend as far down into the bilge as possible, but it is a detail that could easily be overlooked. To confirm this observation it is only necessary to note that the pumps are shown closer together where they pass through the cabin platform than they are at the upper deck level. Photographs 42a, 42b, 43 show the model at an intermediate stage in this work.

When all of the details that would be inaccessible later on had been installed, the work of completing the upper deck framing was continued. Brackets for the windlass were made and fitted in place as had been done for the model of *Hannah*. A galley stove was made of ebony and set in place under the opening where the Charley Noble was to be mounted. *Halifax* had an unusual arrangement for leading the anchor cables through the hawse holes up to the deck. The hawse holes were located just above the breast hook knee in the bow. I made a shallow, 'U'-shaped trough for each side for the cable to rest on. One end sits on the breast hook in line with the hawse hole while the upper end is let into the side of the main beam just abaft the bitts. Pads with holes for the cables were mounted on the deck surface.

The bits in front of the foremast were fitted through the upper deck down into round holes drilled in the lower forecastle platform. They are utilized to hold the

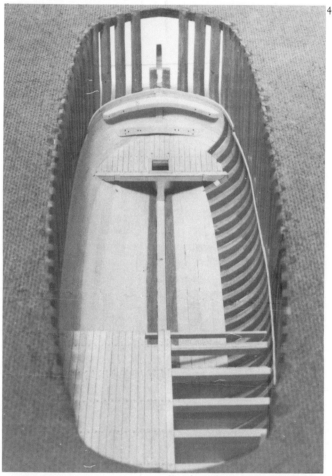

Finishing the interior of the *Halifax*.

The frames of *Halifax* cut away to expose the interior.

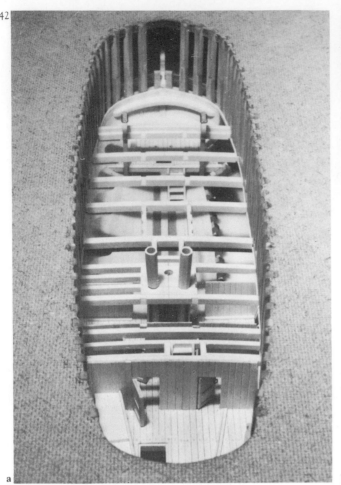

The upper deck of the *Halifax* partially framed.

end of the bowsprit below. I used a different method for making the hatch coamings than was described for the *Hannah* model. Strips of Swiss pearwood were sawed with a step on one edge. This work was done on the Unimat with the use of its circular saw accessory. The strips were cut to length and mounted directly on the deck framing with the inside surface of the coaming flush with the framed opening. The coaming corners were still fitted together with half laps rather than mitered joints.

Photographs 44a and 44b picture the model with as much work as possible completed before cutting it loose from the assembly jig. The decks could not be planked until the frame extensions were cut off and the inside surfaces shaved down to give the bulwarks a reasonable thickness. During the time that work was being carried on before the hull was cut loose, the masonite jig was supported on the rails in the box that had been made for *Hannah*. As was described earlier, this was a convenient way to hold the model steady and protect it from damage. The special work of making the window frames and doing the carvings for the quarter badges and the stern decoration will be dealt with in the next chapter.

The model was cut loose from its frame extensions with the keyhole saw as before. I decided to make a cradle to hold the model securely for the work that was

to follow because the special character of the permanent mounting made it unsuitable for use as a work stand. Holes had been drilled and tapped in the keel for mounting screws, so the cradle was designed to suit them. After sawing and filing the supports to fit the hull, I lined them with felt to protect the planking from damage.

Photograph 45 shows the model in the work cradle with the frames reduced down to the deck framing on the inside to the desired bulwark thickness. This was done quite easily with my carving chisels. I was not concerned here with shaping the extensions of the frames as stanchions like those in *Hannah* since the insides of the bulwarks were to be planked over. I used waterways with a triangular cross section to frame the sides of the two intermediate deck levels. On the forecastle and quarterdeck, the deck planking was carried right up to the bulwark planks. The reddish brown of Swiss pearwood on the bulwarks matched the color of the bitts, the windlass brackets, and the hatch coamings.

On *Hannah*, the deck planks were laid right up to the deck openings before the coamings were installed. In contrast, the planks on *Halifax* had to be fitted around all the deck obstructions. I would say that the choice of which way to work is purely arbitrary since I can see no clear cut advantage to either method. Photograph 46

43

44

a

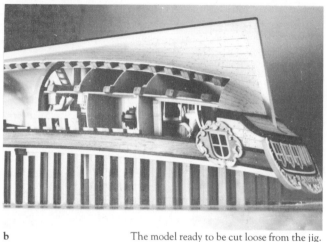

The upper deck of the *Halifax* completely framed.

b

The model ready to be cut loose from the jig.

45

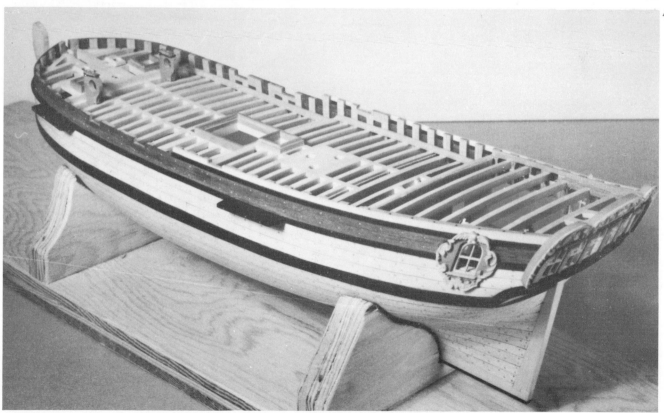

The hull cut loose from the jig and mounted in the work cradle.

gives a good idea of how the deck and bulwarks were planked on the forward end of *Halifax*. It also offers a view of the catheads, the way they are mounted on the forecastle deck, and how they pass through the low bulwarks under the cap rail. A dummy bowsprit has been fitted on top of the stem between the knightheads and lodges under a cross piece notched into the bitts below decks.

Photograph 47 pictures the forward end of *Halifax* again but with the addition of cap rails, bitts, the Charley Noble, and blocks that serve to frame the gun ports. The sections of cap rail are strips of ebony with their outer edges molded. While the bitts and knightheads on *Hannah* were integral parts of the bulwark stanchions that were modified extensions of the frames, all of those features on *Halifax* are separate pieces set into holes drilled in the cap rail. Each piece was turned with a peg as described in the last chapter. The square or rectangular sections were filed from the round.

The final picture in this chapter shows the after decks on *Halifax*. The small openings for the companion-way ladder has yet to be covered by the deck house. The pumps are still unfinished. While they have been fitted to the deck surface, they can still be removed to be completed with the addition of the linkages and pump handles. The delicate hand rail with its stanchions was made of ebony. The stanchions were turned with .060in diameter pegs on the bottom to be set into holes through the cap rail. All such holes along the bulwarks were drilled in a machine set-up since I did not trust myself to hand drill them. I find that even with the greatest care I cannot be sure that the locating holes I drill by hand will be accurate enough as to direction. Misalignment of such prominent features as the rail stanchions would stand out like a sore thumb.

The top ends of the stanchions were turned with pegs .020in in diameter. The bodies of the stanchions were turned to carefully measured lengths with a diameter $1\frac{1}{2}$ times the thickness of the square section. Such a diameter is slightly larger than the diagonal dimension of the square section. The sides of the stanchions were filed while the pieces were held in the small machinist's vise. After the first flat was filed, the piece was turned 90° so that the flat was against the jaw of the vise. Careful use of the file then produced a second flat at 90° to the first one. The procedure was repeated until the stanchion was completed with a slight taper to make it smaller at the top end. As this work progressed, a micrometer was used to check sizes and maintain uniformity. Since the angle of the stanchions with the cap rail varies as the sheer line changes, it was necessary to trim the lower ends of the square sections to eliminate unsightly gaps. The uprights were then glued in place along the bulwarks.

A cardboard template was made to follow the line of the stanchions on both sides with the same curve to ensure symmetry. This template was used to mark the shape of the rail on a thin strip of ebony. The outside

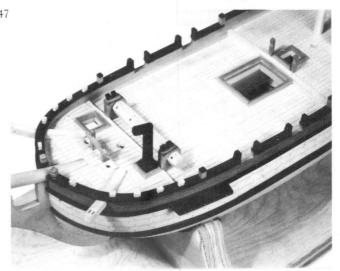

47

The cap rails and miscellaneous fittings added.

46

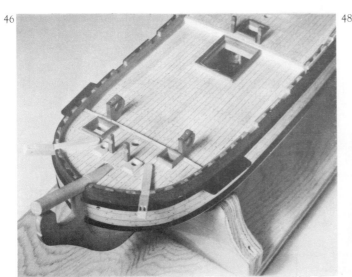

The deck planking as completed.

48

The railing added to the stern section.

shape was cut, its edge was molded, and then the inside shape was sawed to the proper width. The finished strip of railing was held on top of the stanchions against the turned pegs, and the locations of those pegs were transferred to the center of the rail. Holes were drilled through the rail using a drill several thousandths of an inch larger in diameter than the pegs and with some attention to the angles the pegs made with the line of the rail. After it had been determined that the rails could be assembled with the stanchions without undue force which would crack the pegs off, they were glued in place; and the projecting pegs were trimmed off flush. This completed the basic hull structure of *Halifax* in preparation for adding the head rails, fittings, deck house, armament, and the masting and rigging.

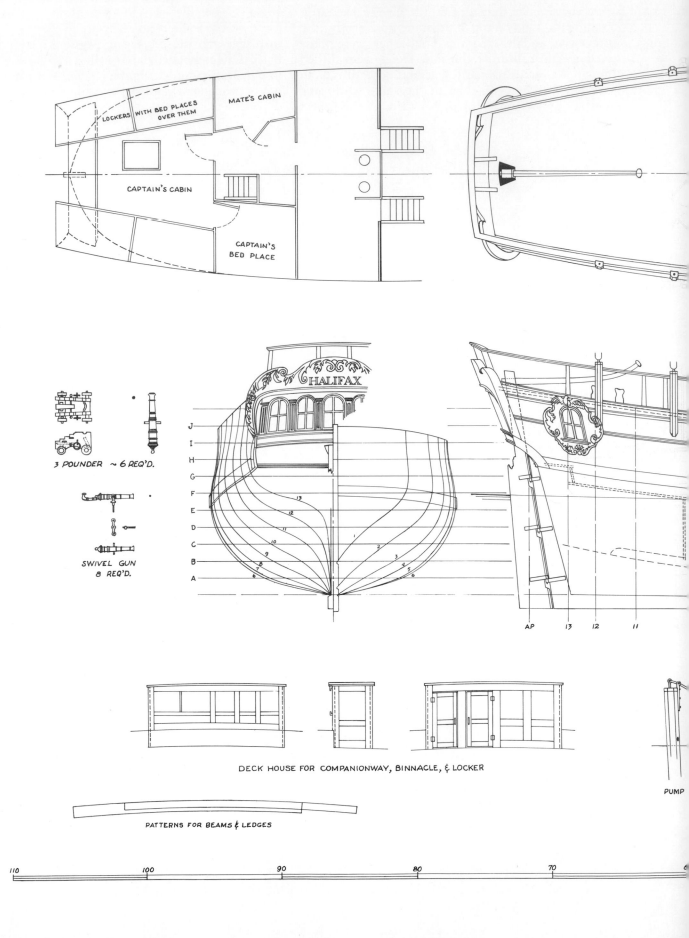

LOCKERS WITH BED PLACES OVER THEM

MATE'S CABIN

CAPTAIN'S CABIN

CAPTAIN'S BED PLACE

3 POUNDER ~ 6 REQ'D.

SWIVEL GUN 8 REQ'D.

HALIFAX

J
I
H
G
F
E
D
C
B
A

AP   13   12   11

DECK HOUSE FOR COMPANIONWAY, BINNACLE, & LOCKER

PUMP

PATTERNS FOR BEAMS & LEDGES

110   100   90   80   70

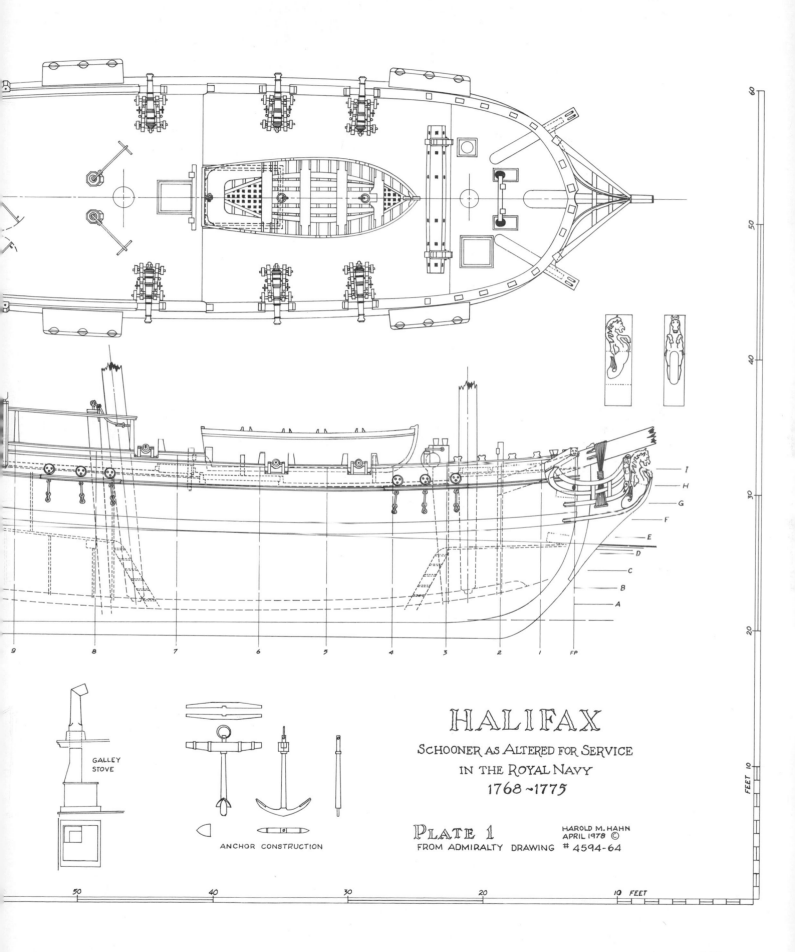

HALIFAX

SCHOONER AS ALTERED FOR SERVICE
IN THE ROYAL NAVY
1768~1775

PLATE 1

HAROLD M. HAHN
APRIL 1978 ©
FROM ADMIRALTY DRAWING # 4594-64

GALLEY
STOVE

ANCHOR CONSTRUCTION

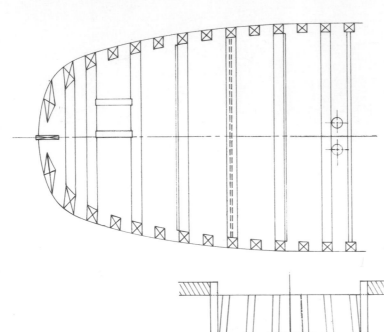

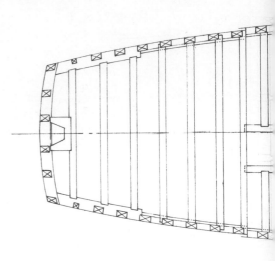

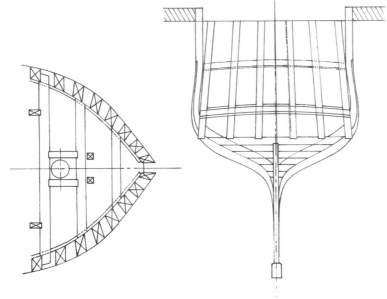

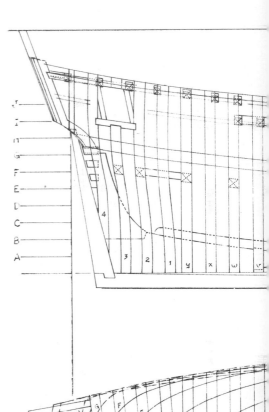

HALIFAX

SCHOONER AS ALTERED FOR SERVICE
IN THE ROYAL NAVY
1768~1775

PLATE 2

HAROLD M. HAHN
FEBRUARY 1977

FROM ADMIRALTY DRAWING # 4594-64

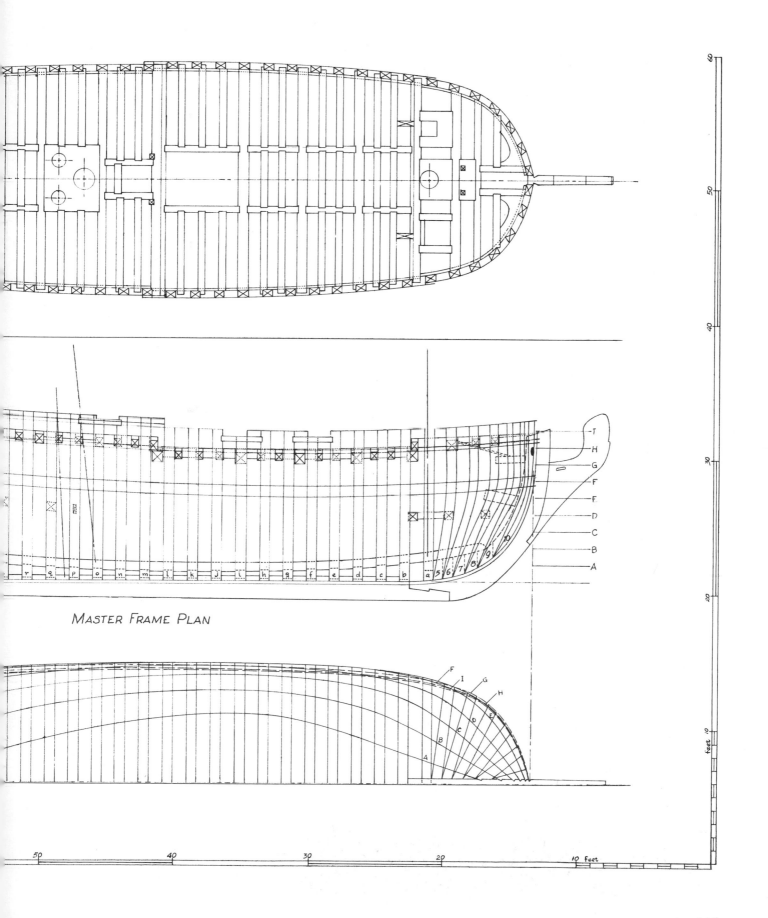

MASTER FRAME PLAN

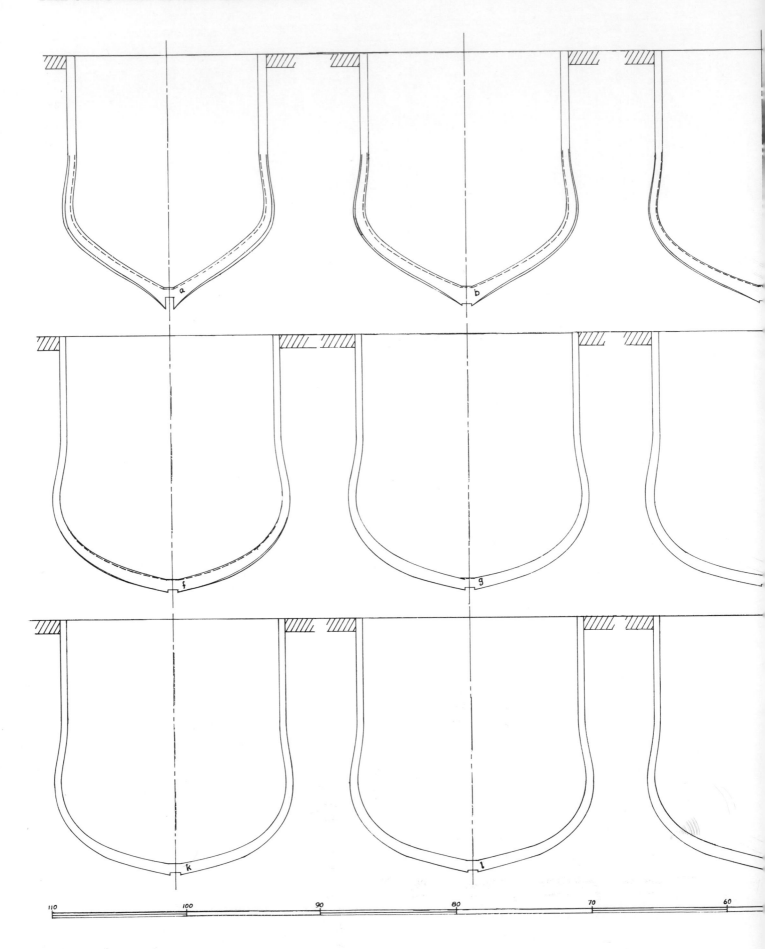

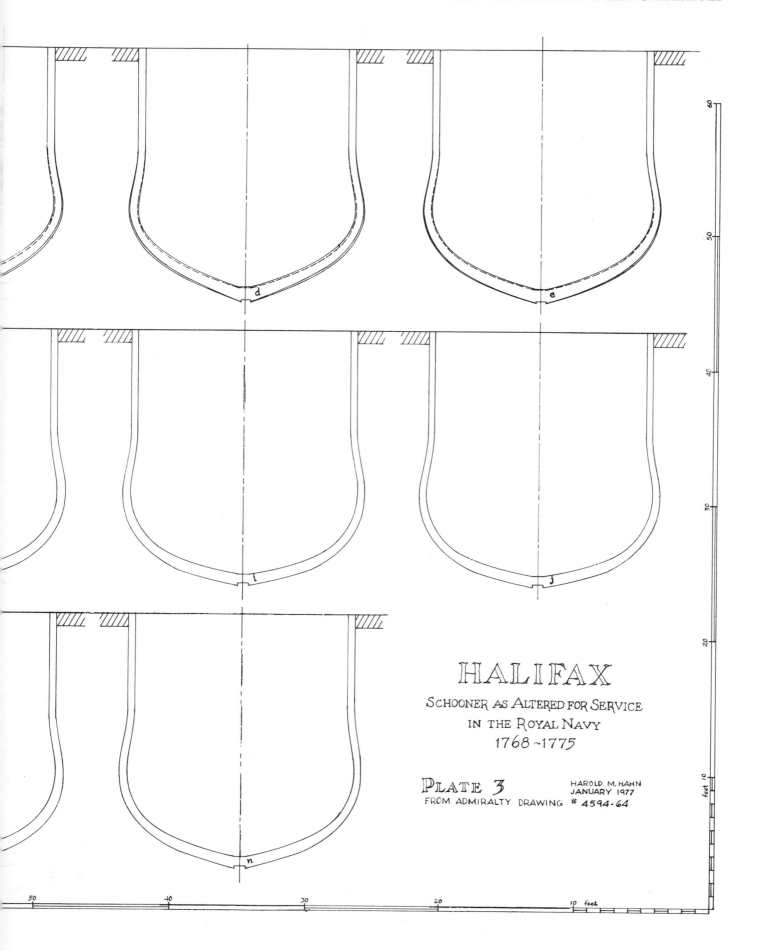

HALIFAX

SCHOONER AS ALTERED FOR SERVICE
IN THE ROYAL NAVY
1768~1775

PLATE 3   HAROLD M. HAHN
JANUARY 1977
FROM ADMIRALTY DRAWING # 4594-64.

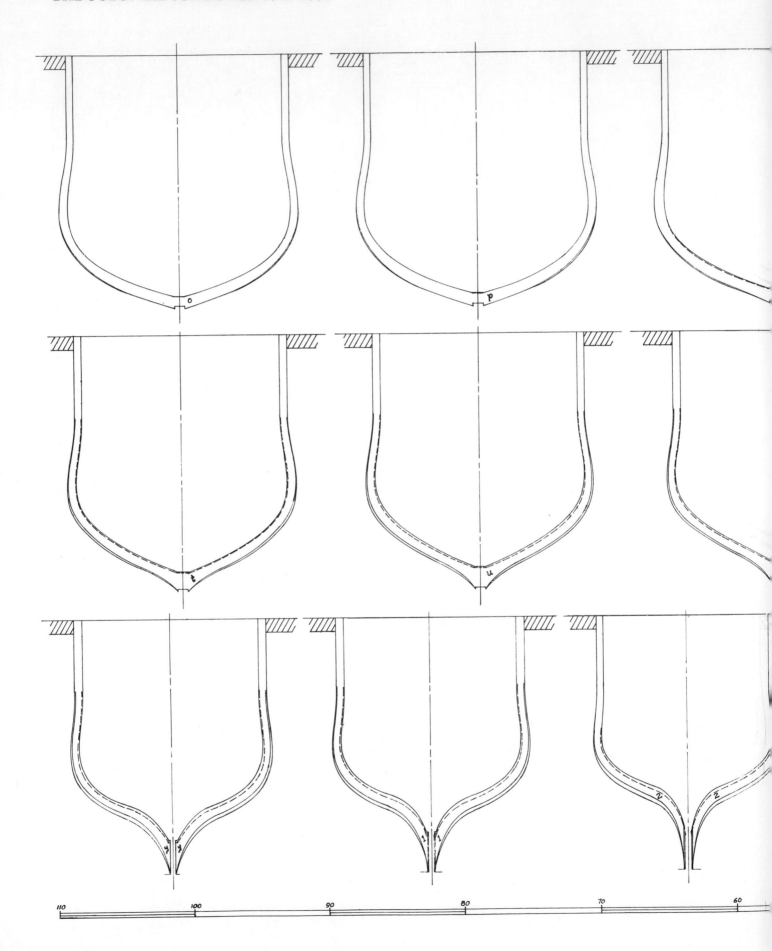

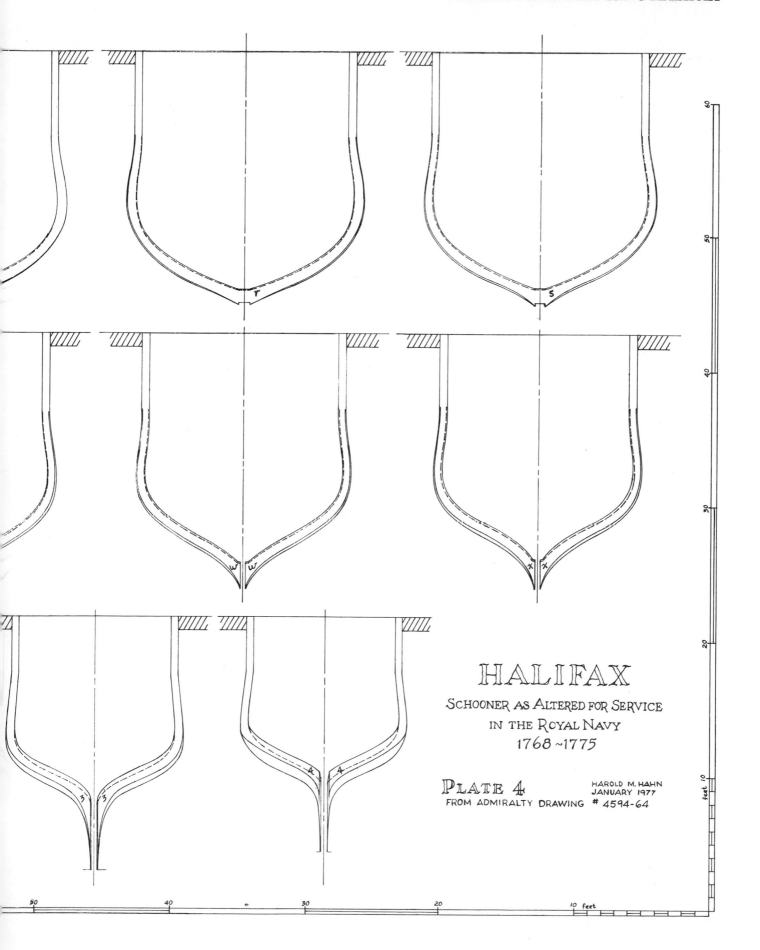

HALIFAX

SCHOONER AS ALTERED FOR SERVICE
IN THE ROYAL NAVY
1768~1775

PLATE 4

HAROLD M. HAHN
JANUARY 1977

FROM ADMIRALTY DRAWING # 4594-64

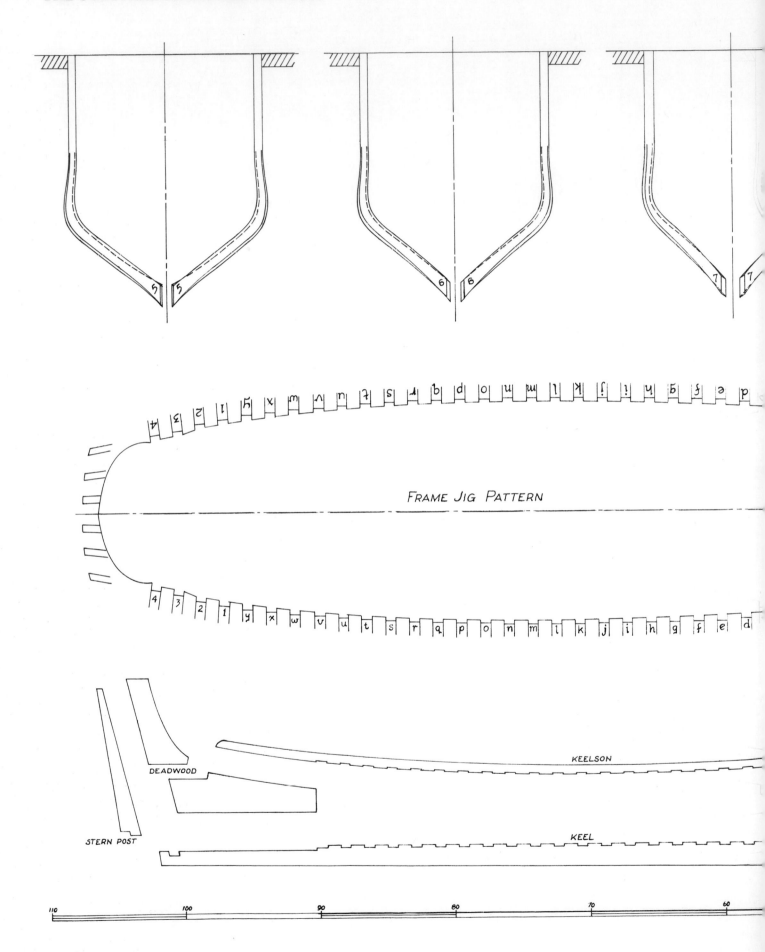

FRAME JIG PATTERN

KEELSON

DEADWOOD

STERN POST

KEEL

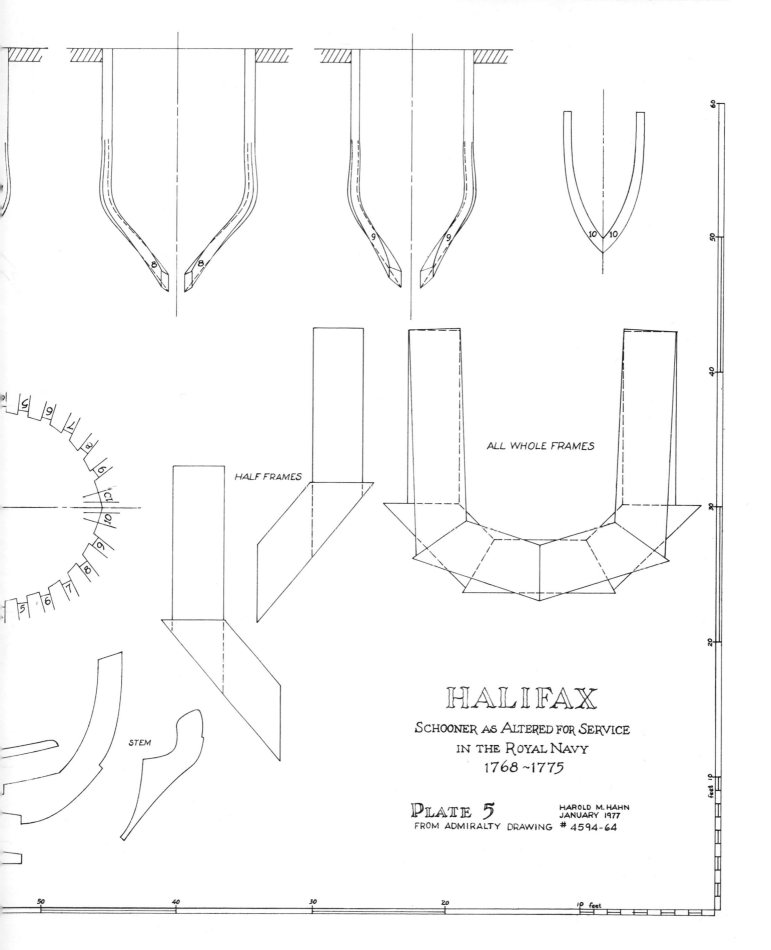

HALF FRAMES

ALL WHOLE FRAMES

STEM

HALIFAX

SCHOONER AS ALTERED FOR SERVICE
IN THE ROYAL NAVY
1768 ~ 1775

PLATE 5

HAROLD M. HAHN
JANUARY 1977

FROM ADMIRALTY DRAWING # 4594-64

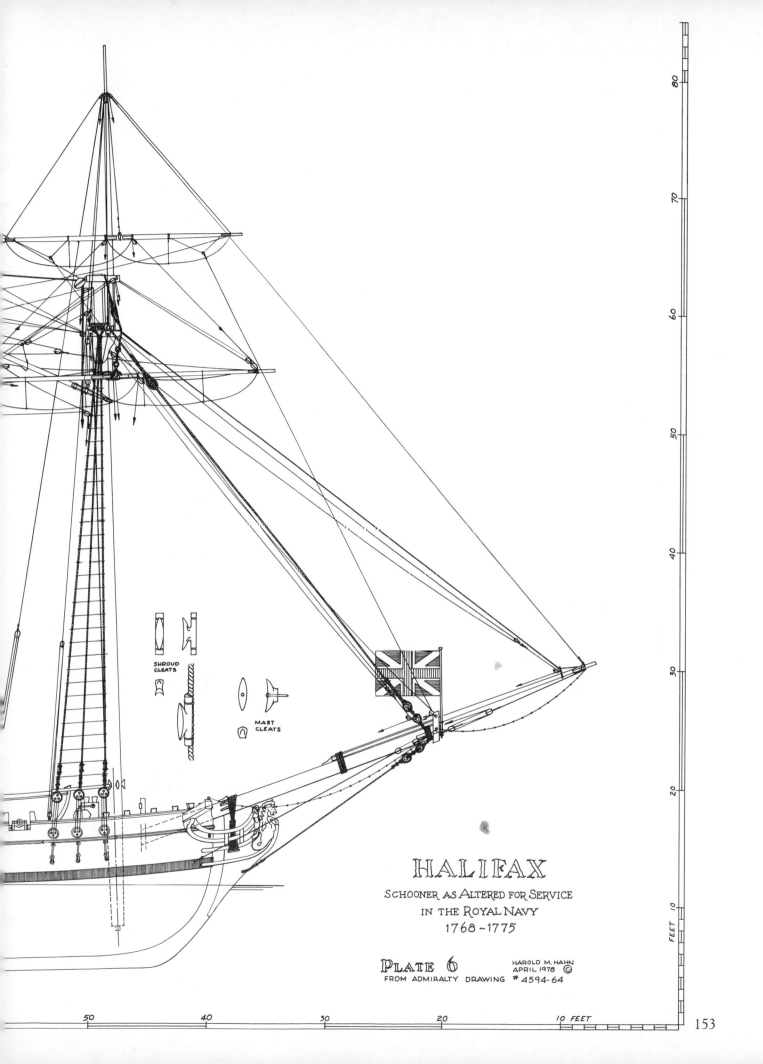

SHROUD
CLEATS

MAST
CLEATS

HALIFAX

SCHOONER AS ALTERED FOR SERVICE
IN THE ROYAL NAVY
1768~1775

PLATE 6

HAROLD M. HAHN
APRIL 1978 ©

FROM ADMIRALTY DRAWING # 4594-64

80

70

60

50

40

30

20

FEET 10

50   40   30   20   10 FEET

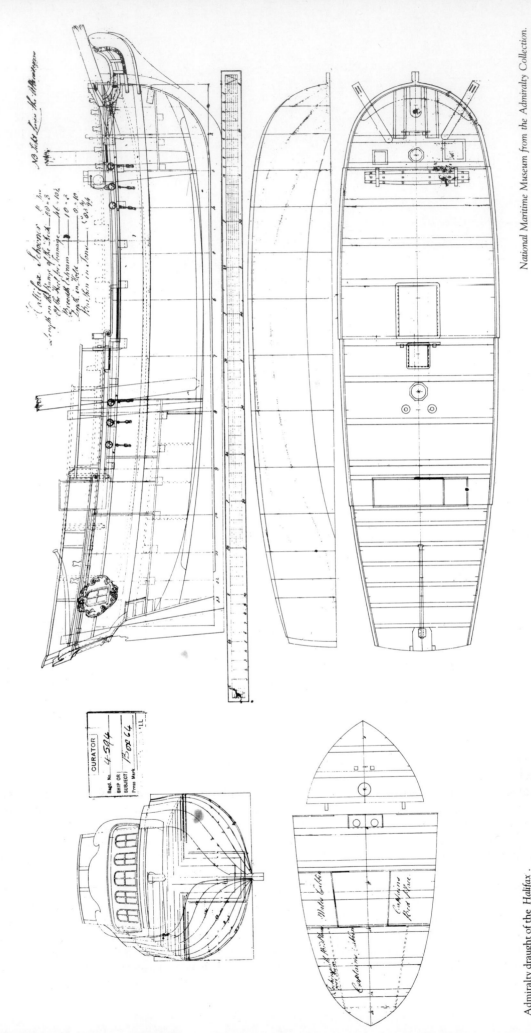

National Maritime Museum from the Admiralty Collection.

Admiralty draught of the *Halifax*.

CHAPTER FIFTEEN

Carving Ship Decoration and Figures

Building ship models from scratch makes it necessary for the craftsman to be a 'Jack of all trades'. He must not only be skilled in all the ways of working with wood, but be able to machine, shape, and join metal parts, understand how to manipulate paint, and handle rigging cordage. If he is to realize full satisfaction from his efforts, it will not be by begging off from the need to master these many demands on his skill and ingenuity because of their diversity. The real satisfaction with improved results comes from a recognition of steady improvement in all departments and the occasional revelation that solves a sticky problem with a better method. Ship modeling is a perpetual challenge to achieve perfection that is unlikely of accomplishment though seemingly within reach. Perhaps this sounds overly dramatic; but if a thoughtful person is to spend hundreds or even thousands of hours out of his life building a model, there has to be something more to the work than placidly sticking parts together.

Among the many 'trades' that must be mastered is the production of miniature carvings for a model. Even a simple model like *Hannah* requires scroll carvings at the break in the sheer line. *Halifax* calls for a variety of carvings which is still modest in comparison with the requirements for most eighteenth century ships. Since the carved details become focal points of interest on a model, it is important that they be well and neatly executed. Miniature carving demands something more than the mechanical skills needed to make most model components. Artistic training is a big help, but I have known first class model builders lacking such a back-

ground who developed their capabilities for this work by determined application. It should be considered as just one more challenge to be met. All the old clichés apply. It is necessary to 'get one's feet wet' and if at first unsuccessful to 'try, try again' since 'faint heart never won the [victory]'.

A primary consideration on the approach to miniature carving is the selection of suitable tools. As with most model work, there will be differences of opinion on the subject: modified dental tools have found favor; some people will want to use motorized steel burrs while others might prefer the sharp Exacto knives. None of this commercially available equipment suits my needs. I am highly prejudiced in favor of the carving tools that I have made which are tailored to fit my feel for the work. The way that I stumbled on a means for making special carving tools was really quite fortuitous.

In 1944 during the Second World War, I was serving in a rear area on New Guinea as machinist in an Army Engineers Heavy Shop Company. Previously, while studying at an art school, I had developed a special interest in print making for which engraving on copper and wood is just one medium of expression. I had been painting watercolor portraits and landscapes for fellow servicemen at modest fees when I discovered a market for engraving vignettes and inscriptions on silver baubles made by hammering out Australian shillings and later on Filipino pesos. I had seen some fellows in my outfit making knives from power hacksaw blades. It occurred to me that I could make an excellent set of engraving burins the same way. This I did with a view not only to current demands but to the future when I hoped to regain civilian status. Almost as an afterthought and with no immediate purpose in mind, I made a set of four small carving chisels. Those chisels lay idle for fifteen years until I finally resurrected my interest in model building and found them ideally suited to the work.

Use of a broken or worn out hacksaw blade for making carving tools transforms a useless piece of scrap steel into a superb aid for the fine craftsman. The steel in those blades is hard and tough for use in the service for which they are designed. A hardness check shows a range of 60 to 65 on the Rockwell 'C' scale. This represents a steel that will provide a keen, long-lasting cutting edge which is a joy to use. Discarded blades can be obtained from local machine shops if they are alerted and sympathetic to your needs. Failing this, new saw blades could be purchased from a machine tool supply house. The tools to be described here were made from saw blades that had been hardened all over. Some are hardened only along the serrated tooth edge. This can be checked out by testing the back of the saw with a file which should not cut a through-hardened piece.

A piece of broken saw blade can be seen in photograph 49. From the roots of the teeth to the back, it measures 1⅛in and is .065in thick. I split the blade down the middle with an abrasive slitting disc. The resulting strips were dressed to a ½in width and the sides smoothed off on the side of a large, off-hand grinding wheel. If you have access to a surface grinder, you could do a more professional-looking job. A marking fluid such as Dykem Layout Blue painted on one side will help in scribing the shape of the proposed tool with its tang on one end and chisel on the other. The tool can then be ground to those contours, and the cutting edge relieved as necessary. Care should be taken to avoid overheating the steel during this grinding operation. The thin cutting edge is especially vulnerable. If it should turn deep blue, some of the valuable characteristics of the initially hard piece of steel will be lost.

My design for carving tools stems from experience with engraving burins. Such tools are designed with a handle to fit the palm of the hand. However, the blades are rather long, and I found them somewhat awkward to handle and control. Firm control is essential since a slip can have disastrous results. Once, I inadvertently broke a couple of inches off the end of a burin. On regrinding and sharpening the broken end, I found that the shorter tool with its cutting edge close to the fingertips was much easier to control. There are carving tools on the market with palm handles, but I fear that their blades are too long to suit me for use in miniature carving.

I am partial to the shape of handle pictured here. The round end has a substantial feel in the palm of the hand while the slender neck allows the fingertips to hold and guide the tool with a minimum of interference. Photograph 49 illustrates the procedure I followed in making the handles. Since they present an awkward shape to work on and there were quite a few to produce, I jigsawed them in pairs leaving a substantial rectangular section in the middle. This block was clamped in a vise while the handles were carved and sanded to shape. The final shape was finished off by using strips of emery cloth much as a shoe shine boy polishes shoes with a rag. Coarse emery cloth rounded off the carved irregularities and then successively finer grades were used to give a smooth finish.

After the finished handle blanks were sawed off, ⅛in holes were drilled for the tangs of the tools. They were then pressed onto a mandrel chucked in my Unimat, and the straight section for the ferrule was turned. After that, the handles were slotted to take the wide section of the tang. Each handle with its brass ferrule was custom made for a particular cutter blade which had already been ground to shape. Close fits were observed; and when the ferrule was finally driven onto the handle with the cutter assembled in it, a solid unit resulted which required no pins or glue to secure it. The handles were made from Honduras Mahogany. I coated the brass with metal lacquer to preserve the polish and finished the wood with a satin finish varnish. Photograph 50 shows the large variety of tools that I made as described above.

The engraver's burin has been mentioned frequently

Making carving tools.

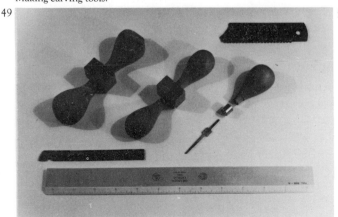

A variety of tools hand-made to suit every purpose.

without comment on the fact that it also can be a useful tool for the ship modeler. One use in particular that I find for it is to cut grooves for strapping blocks and to indicate their sheaves. The burin is not designed to cut like a carving chisel; it acts more like a plow. For this reason, it is not suited to cut across the grain in a piece of wood. Wood engraving, as done commercially in the past and at present in its fine arts context, involves cutting a design on the end grain of a boxwood block. Here, the direction of the wood grain is compatible with the 'plowing' action. The hard, crisp cutting boxwood is an excellent material to use in wood engraving for much the same reasons that the ship modeler values it. The engraving tool can be used to good advantage in ship modeling wherever lines must be scored on the end grain or in the general direction of the grain. It is only across the grain where the plowing action splinters the fibers that a carving tool must be used to incise the line.

Engraving burins can be purchased from artist supply houses that cater to the print maker, or they can be home-made just as the carving tools were. After the blade has been ground to a desired cross section, the sides can be honed to smoothness on an oilstone and polished with emery cloth. When in use, the burin is guided by the thumb and fingers placed firmly on the work surface while motion is imparted with pressure on the handle from the palm of the hand. Control of the pressure and the latitude of movement provides the security needed to avoid damaging slips. This same principle governs my use of the carving tools.

My favorite wood for miniature carvings is, as might be expected, boxwood. In any case, I would restrict the choice to close-grained hard woods. Walnut and mahogany are not suitable for most applications because the open grain would tend to splinter or crack through in small unsupported sections. I would not consider soft woods which lack strength and would not provide clean-cut lines impervious to accidental damage. There are a number of hardwoods that I can recommend from having had actual experience with them. Firethorn, which is favored by August Crabtree, is excellent but is apt to be difficult to acquire. Privet

Carving a figure for the diorama.

51

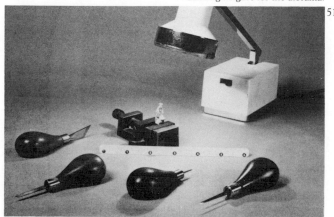

works well when a clear, straight-grained piece can be selected. Apple wood, properly seasoned, is strong and flexible. The pearwood I have used is crisp cutting but somewhat brittle. So long as I have a supply of boxwood on hand, I do not feel a need to look further for material to make miniature carvings.

Photograph 51 includes four of the tools that I use most often. The skew chisel with the cutting edge at a 45° angle is the most versatile tool. The sharp point can be used to cut the finest details. The long edge is handy for slicing away large areas. The wide blade provides a stiffness that gives a solid feel to the cutting action. It only occasionally causes interference that requires use of the more slender chisel also to be seen in the picture. The vise holding the small carving is the one that was supplied with my Unimat. It is an invaluable aid in holding such pieces. I use a pair of pliers to tighten the jaw of the vise so the work piece will not shift under a cut. Good vision is a must, and the high intensity lamp is a big help.

Construction of the quarter badges and the window sash for the *Halifax*.

52

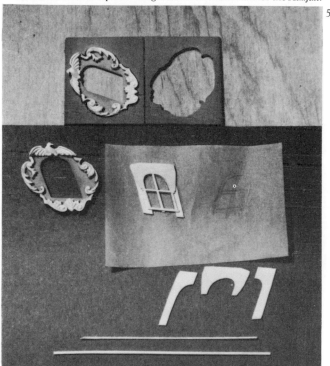

The variety of carvings that is required for the model of *Halifax* is representative of what is called for on most eighteenth century ships. It does make a good introduction to the craft of miniature work since the carvings are modest in design and in quantity. A good place to start is with the quarter badges which are well-defined on the Admiralty draught. Where bas relief carvings on a smooth background are indicated, I like to cut the outlines of the carved details with my jewelers saw and mount them on a wood support with epoxy glue. The carvings can then be developed with the skew chisel. This eliminates the need for the tedious and awkward labor of carving delicate outlines and then lowering the surrounding surface to make a smooth background. In order to provide an attractive color contrast for the quarter badges and also the stern arch boards, I decided to mount cut out pieces of boxwood for the carvings on a foundation of Swiss pearwood.

The first step in making the quarter badges was to cut the background design of Swiss pearwood. Two pieces of the pearwood were rubber cemented together and cut to the outside lines as well as the inside shape of the window openings. I was careful to salvage the outside scrap along with the quarter badge pieces. These cut out pieces were separated easily by inserting a razor blade at the glue line, and the rubber cement was rubbed gently away with the fingertip. The pieces for the boxwood carvings were cut out in two sections – the eagle design made separate from the rest. These duplicate cutouts were made by rubber cementing two pieces of boxwood to a strip of scrap wood which was ⅛in thick. The intricate design was cut with one of the finer saw blades which could be maneuvered in and out of the corners readily. The boxwood cutouts were then cemented to the Swiss pearwood badges with epoxy glue.

The two pieces of pearwood scrap were glued to a wood surface as a right and left hand pair. They were sanded down so that the boxwood to be carved projected well above the surface when the quarter badges were set into their respective recesses. This provided a convenient way to hold the pieces while the carving work was carried out as can be seen in photograph 52. The point of the chisel was used to outline the various curves and scroll shapes which were then chamfered and otherwise modified to enhance the three dimensional forms. The boxwood was shaved away with light cuts to avoid breaking out some of the more delicate sections. When the pieces were sawed out, consideration had been given to the direction of grain that would facilitate carving the details. This was observed to avoid chipping or cracking out pieces by cutting with the grain. This sounds easy enough; but in the case of small, detailed carvings in wood where the grain is not visible, it is sometimes easy to forget or even confuse the direction. Actually when using a very sharp chisel, it is feasible to take light shaving cuts against the grain where convenience is served. With the carving completed, the backs of the quarter badges were shaped with sandpaper blocks until they rested flush against the hull framework. The planks and strips of molding were fitted around them after they had been glued in place permanently.

Although making the window sash is not really a carving operation, this seems like a logical place to describe it. My procedure is illustrated in photograph 52. The rounded shape at the top of all seven windows in *Halifax* makes them something of a problem. My solution was to build them up with two plies of thin boxwood having tverlapped joints to produce a strong

The quarter badges and windows installed on the model.

unit. The outer layer was made narrower to give an appearance of molding to the finished sash. The first step was to draw an exact outline of the window opening on a piece of tracing paper. This was filled in with the window sash framework design. The first layer of boxwood, .020in thick, was glued directly to the design on the paper. White glue was then used to glue the second layer to the first. The pieces that form the curves in the sash were cut to the inside shape with excess material left on the outside. After the glue had set, each unit had its excess material cut away with a fine tooth jewelers saw and was sanded on the edge until it fitted into its particular window opening. The tracing paper on the back side was rubbed away on a piece of sandpaper. The sash was glued into its casement and given a coat of matte varnish to further bind the pieces together. Photograph 53 shows six of the window units permanently installed in the model.

The Admiralty drawing gives a carefully detailed representation of the quarter badge design with its decorative carving. The stern view records an unusual design for framing the windows but offers no suggestion of carved decorations. It seemed reasonable to suppose that there should have been some carvings there to complement those at the quarters, so I designed some that I thought might be appropriate. I made the structure, which arches over the window from side to side, in three pieces joined where it would be least evident.

54

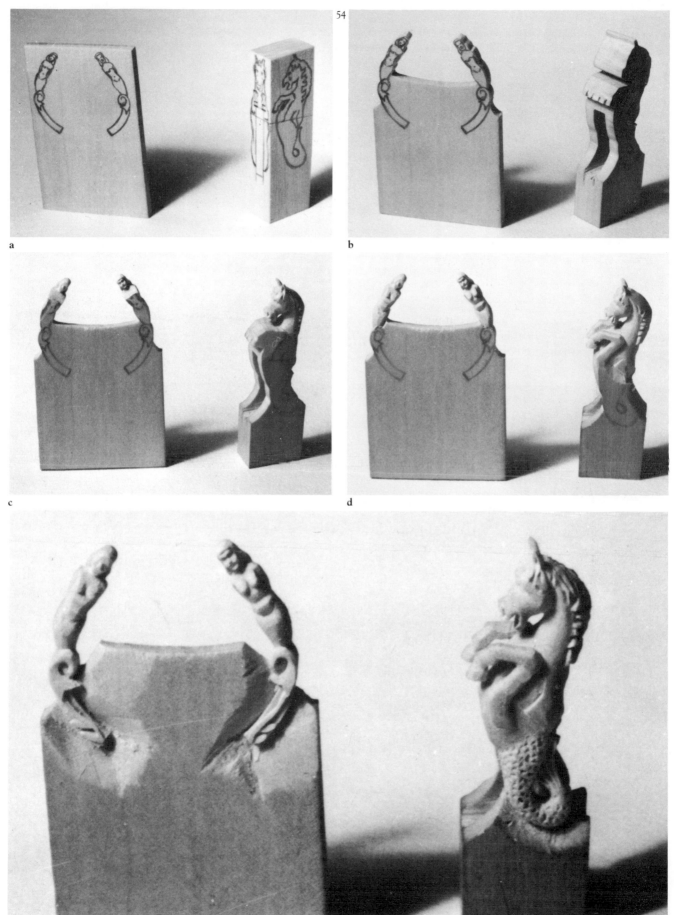

a

b

c

d

e

The process of carving the seahorse and mermaids for the bow of the *Halifax*.

55

a
b

Carvings installed on the bow of the *Halifax* model with cheeks and headrail added.

c

Each section with its carvings was completed before being mounted on the model. The bare structure is shown in photograph 53. Photograph 44a gives an idea of the various structural and decorative parts that I added to complete the stern of my model. The stern frame extensions were cut off at deck level to make way for those additions. A study of the various photographs would be of more value than a verbal description of this work which in any event is just my arbitrary interpretation of the design.

The bow of *Halifax* offers still more interesting problems in miniature carvings. The Admiralty draught shows a mermaid on the extension of the upper head knee. There is also some suggestion of carving along the edges of those knees. It is unfortunate that the draftsman failed to draw in the design of the figurehead. The end of the stem is indicated with a simple conventional shape. With those mermaids located as they are, I find it difficult to believe that there was no figurehead. At first, I was inclined to place a British lion on the stem, but in his book *Ship Carvers of North America*, M V Brewington advised that the lion was going out of style by the middle of the eighteenth century. A human figure would have required some degree of personification that I could not justify on the basis of the schooner's history. It finally occurred to me that a seahorse would fit perfectly into the allotted space and would make an appropriate combination with the mermaids.

As the photographs suggest, I carved the mermaids and the seahorse figurehead at the same time. The head knees with their carved decorations had been fitted to the hull first. This enabled me to lay out the extensions which curve up the side of the stem to include a continuation of the carvings with the mermaid at the end. When there is a right and left hand symmetrical pair of carvings to be executed, I like to do them together. Photographs 54a-e illustrate the step-by-step procedure I followed in carving the pair of mermaids. After the designs were drawn on the piece of boxwood, the shapes were partially cut out with a jewelers saw (54a and b). The forms were then carved with my skew chisel starting with the heads, working down to the tails, and finally the short section that blends with the head knee (54c and d). The final operation was to saw out the carvings where they were still attached to the main block (54c). Photographs 55a-c show how the stem appeared before and after these decorative carvings were added.

Design of a figurehead calls for some careful consideration and layout if it is to fit well on the stem of a model. First, it must be decided exactly how the figure will be fitted in place. This is determined largely by how the shape of the figure can be made to straddle the stem which in turn establishes the precise design of the carving. As can be observed from earlier photographs of the model, I had simply copied the shape of the stem from the original drawing. As a result of designing the figurehead, I was able to cut the end of the stem away to provide a seat for the seahorse carving. The drawing of the seahorse was transferred to the boxwood block and the relative location of the cut away stem marked off. The first operation in carving the figurehead was to cut out the slot in the block. The width had to be held closely to the thickness of the stem where the carving was to be seated. The next step was to saw out the profile of the seahorse. The bottom end was left intact to connect with the block which was designed to be held in the vise.

This seahorse figurehead is a relatively simple piece to use for an initial attempt at figure carving. The head and neck were shaped first. The ears required some special care, but their orientation relative to the grain of the boxwood block affords ample strength. The legs pose the most difficult carving problem. They are arranged so that the hoofs will rest on the end of the stem. The detail carving on either side of the block was done first while the legs still had a solid connection. The space between the legs and the body had to be carved with caution to avoid breaking the delicate parts which then became separated from the body. The rest of the carving was straight forward. When the details had been completed, the shape of the curved tail was gradually cut out on both sides until the figurehead was freed from the holding block. As a result of the careful preliminary planning and accurate cutting of the slot, the little seahorse fitted perfectly in place on the stem of the *Halifax* model.

The photographs of various completed models in this book make it obvious that I am in the habit of carving figures to serve as crewmen on them. I believe that there are some ship modelers who would like to follow this practice. If the craftsman has met with success in carving a figurehead for his model, he certainly could consider creating figures to place on the deck. If he has not had a fine arts training in drawing, he will have to prepare himself with a study of the natural proportions of the human form and give thought to its representation; but it can be done. When Bob Lightley built his model of *Endeavour*, he also carved twelve crew members for her. On seeing the results of his work, officials at the National Maritime Museum commissioned him to carve additional figures to fill out the entire ship's complement. It was only his determination to excel that made this possible since Bob had no formal art training to prepare him for miniature sculpture.

As a suggestion on how to proceed with figure carving for a model, I present here a sequence of pictures to demonstrate my methods (56a-k). The figure was carved for the model of *Hannah* and is mounted next to the binnacle on the quarterdeck. I think of it as possibly representing Colonel Glover's son John who served as an officer on the little schooner. The figure was designed for a height of 1⅜in which in the ¼₄₈ scale is the equivalent of a man 5ft 6in tall. It will be noted

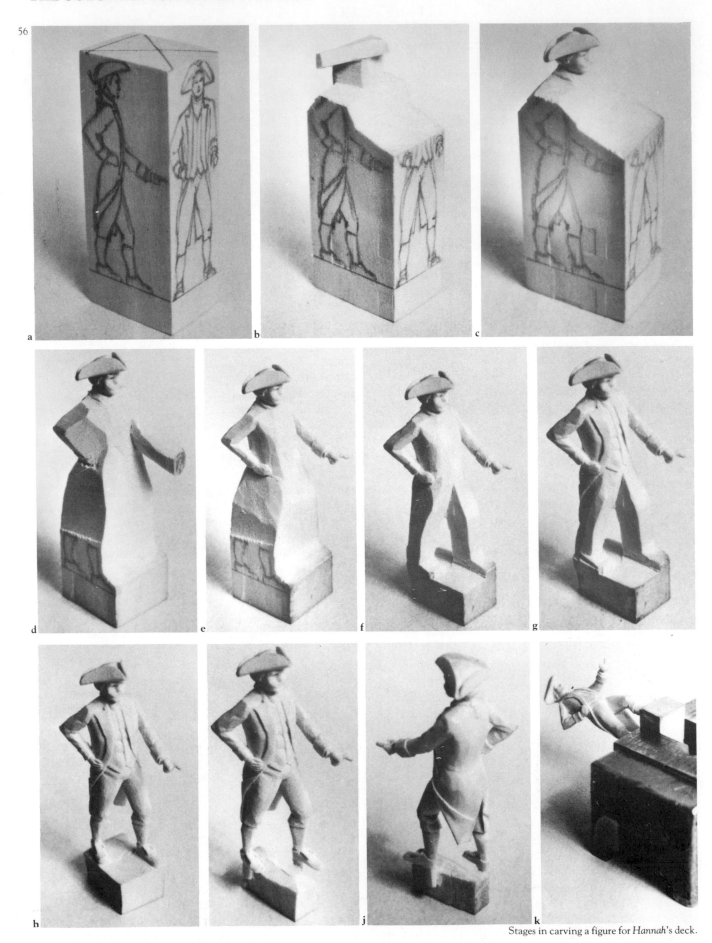

56

Stages in carving a figure for *Hannah's* deck.

that the boxwood block was made extra long to provide material for holding it in the vise and also to make locating pegs on the feet (56a). The image, which had been drawn on paper first, determined the dimensions required for the boxwood block. The drawing was transferred to two sides of the block, and the position of the tricorn hat was located on the top. The first material was cut away with a fine tooth saw to start the work as shown in the photograph 56b; but from that point on carving chisels were used exclusively.

It can be seen that much of the drawing on the block is soon lost (56c). The sculptor must retain a mental image of the figure he is trying to create and have some feeling for how it projects in space. I work methodically from the head to the feet, completing the details as I go. Roughed out shapes necessarily must be left oversize to allow finishing material, but there is danger that the details will not be reduced to proper proportions. This can be checked out by determining and converting actual dimensions to scale. What is an average height, width, and depth for a head ? How long should the nose be ? What is a natural breadth across the shoulders, the legths of arms, legs, and feet ? I could offer a tabulation of those features here, but the craftsman will learn those proportions better by determining them for himself.

With carving of the head completed, the next step is to establish the span across the shoulders and cut away

the excess material. Until this is done, the positions of the arms cannot be developed. One of the challenges in miniature carving lies in shaping a delicate, cross-grained projection without breakage. The extended arm with pointed forefinger is a good example in the case of this figure (55d). The roughed-out arm is substantial enough to support the cuts that must be made to carve the hand. Slicing cuts made by a very sharp chisel with the pressure directed mainly along the arm towards the shoulder of the figure will turn the trick. One obvious rule to follow in carving is to cut chips smaller in section than the piece being worked on. Naturally the weaker section will break first. Still, when very small pieces are being carved, it is surprisingly easy to overlook this precaution. It is best to stay on the safe side by taking many light cuts.

After the arms have been carved, the posture of the body and placement of the legs can be roughed out with stock allowed for clothing details (56e). I finished the torso before moving on to the legs (56f and g). Shaping of the lower legs and ankles must be postponed until the carving is completed on the body and thighs. When the legs have been reduced to size at the ankles, the carving will be much too fragile to sustain any but very light cuts for correcting details (56h). After the feet have been carved, I outline the pegs that will be used to mount the figure and cut the block away beneath the feet until just the sides of the pegs are still

a   b   c   The finished figure after painting.

57

connected to the piece held in the vise (56i-k). I finish the pegs to a predetermined drill size before finally cutting them loose.

A very small brush is required to paint the figure. Paints used will depend on the individual's experience in that direction, but they must be applied in thin coats to avoid obscuring the hard-won details. One paint system that I have employed involves the use of tube Japan pigments in the basic red, yellow, and blue colors mixed on a palette with a white satin enamel to the desired hues. Artists' oil paints could be used. There are also paints prepared for people who paint military minatures. I mount the figure with its pegs in a piece of scrap wood while painting it (57a-c).

Figures on a model give it added interest and dimension that suggests the actual proportions of the prototype. They are certainly not a necessity; but if the ship modeler enjoys the work as I have, the final results can give considerable satisfaction.

CHAPTER SIXTEEN

Finishing and Displaying Halifax

Now that two models have served as illustrations in this book to promote my method for building plank-on-frame models, I wonder how many readers have been convinced of its advantages. I make no reservations in recommending to others the systems that I expect to use in all my future model work. I am aware that there are experienced ship modelers who have solved the various problems in their own way and will see no purpose in changing. This is a perfectly reasonable attitude which I do not question. The people who will benefit most from my suggestions are those who are attempting plank-on-frame models for the first time. If they follow the process that has been presented here, step-by-step and with loving care, I believe that they will be pleasantly surprised by the feeling of easy and accurate control it provides.

The hull of *Halifax* has by now been carried well along toward completion. There are just a few deck furnishings to be added and finished off. The channels, deadeyes, and chains must be installed much the same as they were on *Hannah*. The chains consist of two links added to the deadeye strap. The bottom link, which is pinned to the hull, is made from an annealed ring cut from tubing of suitable diameter. The long, middle link is the only one that requires soldering. I made those links by winding brass wire around a strip of of wood properly shaped to form the link. The wire links were cut through at the rounded end; and after they had been assembled with the strapped deadeye and the third link, the cut ends were solded together.

The soldered joint at the end of the link was inconspicuous whereas one made in the straight section would have been an unsightly lump.

The pump linkage and handle were made as detailed on Plate 1. The tops of the pumps as shown on the Admiralty draught are quite high above the deck. I designed the arm with an 'S' curve to put the handle at a reasonable working level. One of the carved figures on deck can be seen operating the starboard pump. Once again, rings cut from brass tubing were put to good use. This time, they form the top rims to which I fastened the brackets. The parts for the pump linkages were turned, filed, and drilled from brass bar. The finished assemblies were chemically blackened, and a boxwood handle was pressed through the hole in the end of the pump arm.

The deck house which affords space for a companionway, binnacle, and storage locker is a prominent feature on the deck. The ladder down to the cabins is just to the starboard side of the centerline. This much is quite evident on the Admiralty draught, but it is necessary to reconstruct how the rest of the structure may have been utilized. I decided that the space next to the ladder opening on the starboard side must have been used for storage, possibly a weapons locker, and provided a door for that purpose. On the port side, facing the tiller at the stern, I arranged binnacle accomodation for compass and lantern in separate compartments with a sliding door. This left sheltered space on the port side accessible from the companion

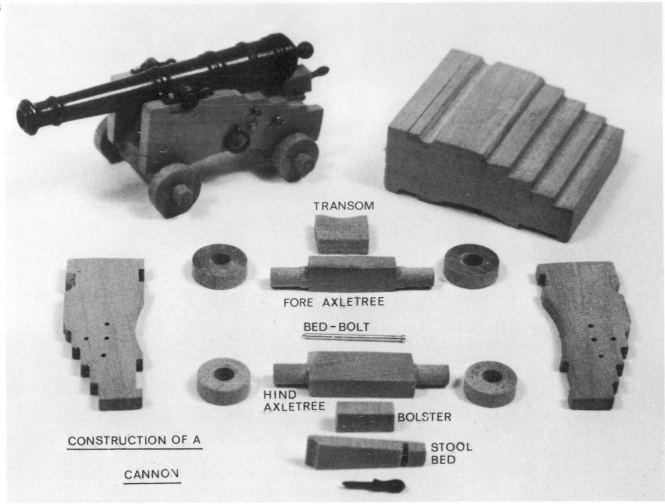

TRANSOM

FORE AXLETREE

BED - BOLT

HIND
AXLETREE

BOLSTER

STOOL
BED

CONSTRUCTION OF A

CANNON

The construction of a cannon and its gun-carriage.

way which could well have been used for additional storage space. I built the deck house with pieces of veneer by the same system described and illustrated for *Hannah*'s structures. The companionway door was left ajar, and the ladder descending to the cabin deck can be seen there and also through the 'broken out' partition on the cut-away side of the model.

The procedure I followed in making swivel guns for *Hannah* can be used to make them for *Halifax*. Perhaps I am at fault in not locating stations for two more swivel guns to bring the total to eight, but I decided to use just the six mounts that are shown on the Admiralty draught. Photograph 58 pictures a cannon similar in design to the ones that I made for both *Halifax* and *Hannah*. Each of the parts that went into the carriages was made in multiples as expeditiously as possible. A long piece of Swiss pearwood was cut off across the grain to make the side brackets. Thus, the finished parts could be cut off with the grain parallel to their length. The cross section of the strip was first cut to the overall height and length of the carriage brackets. Then, with a series of set-ups made on the Unimat circular saw table, I cut the steps on the top, and slotted grooves to locate the trunnions on top and the axletrees on the bottom. The curved arch on the bot-

tom was filed out, as was the semi-circular seat to fit the trunnions which had been positioned with a saw slot.

I have a small miter box made of maple which can be slotted at various angles for use with a small back saw. Right and left hand slots were cut to match the angles of the carriage sides in relation to the cannon barrel. Slices were cut off of the prepared pearwood strip to produce the required number of right and left hand brackets with a few extra for good luck. A uniform thickness was maintained by setting a pin into the bottom of the miter box to act as a stop. Photograph 58 shows what was left of the original strip after the pieces had been cut off. They were all rubbed over a fine grade of garnet paper to smooth out the saw marks. After I had established just where the holes should be located for the bed-bolt, the ringbolt, and the two eye bolts, I made a cardboard template which was used with a scriber to punch mark the pieces. The holes were then drilled in a small drill press setup.

The idea of turning the carriage axletrees was mentioned in Chapter 13. Swiss pearwood dowels were turned to diameters that allowed enough stock to produce the rectangular section that fits the slots in the bottom of the gun carriage brackets. In the first lathe setup for making the axletrees, a finished truck axle was turned on the end of the dowel. Then, with the use of a cardboard template to indicate the lengths, the position of the axle at the other end was grooved and partially turned before the piece was cut off with the jewelers saw to its overall length. When all of the pieces needed had been cut off, they were rechucked and the second end turned to the finished size. Finally, the central section on each of the pieces was filed to its rectangular section designed to fit the slots in the brackets.

The transom fits between the side brackets and is angled back above the fore axletree. A quantity of transom pieces was mass produced to suit the number of gun carriages planned. Brass pins in the same quantity were modified to make bed-bolts. An assembly line was set up to glue the carriage sides, the axletrees, and the transoms together with the bed-bolts pressed through the holes that had been drilled for them. Another piece of pearwood was prepared by filing and slotting in to the longitudinal shape of the stool bed and then cut into separate pieces to make that part. Small blocks of pearwood were used for the bolsters which were glued on top of the hind axletrees. With its groove located on the bed-bolt, the stool bed was glued to the top of the bolster. This provides a sliding surface for the wedge that is used to adjust the elevation of the cannon's muzzle.

I made the eye bolts for the sides of the gun carriage by bending annealed iron wire around the shank of a small drill and twisting the ends together with a pair of needle-nosed pliers. The twisted section was crimped to a uniform shape between flat plier surfaces and cut to length. The eye bolts were then pressed into the holes in the carriage. If there was any evidence of looseness, they were set in with a touch of epoxy glue. The ring bolts were made the same way except that the wire was bent around rings cut from brass tubing. The trucks were turned, drilled, and cut off from a dowel of Swiss pearwood with the jewelers saw. The wedges were made in quantity from another preshaped strip of pearwood and fitted with handles of turned and blackened brass.

My method for turning the cannon and fitting them with trunnions was described in Chapter 13. The caps that hold the trunnions in place were cut off and formed from narrow strips of brass shim stock. A drill shank was useful for bending the pieces to their semicircular shape after which the ends were bent up, trimmed, and drilled to finish the caps. The front end is held down with a modified lill pin while the back end is held in place on top of the carriage bracket with a 'U' shaped piece of wire to simulate the hinge which allows the cap to be swung out of the way when the barrel of the cannon is to be hoisted in or out of the carriage. All these parts form just the basic design for a cannon which could be augmented and refined to make it more complete. In this size, the extra effort seems hardly worthwhile. One more eyebolt which does not show in

the pictures should be located centrally in the back of the hind axletrees for attaching the train tackle.

I installed the cannon on the model with complete sets of tackle. The bottoms of the trucks were touched with epoxy glue before placing them on the deck. The breeching ropes had been reeved through the ring bolts on the sides of the carriages and had their ends fastened to ring bolts that were pressed into holes in the waterways. A good way to keep this rope in place on the cannon is to set it into the throat at the cascabel with a little epoxy glue. Fitting out the cannon on a model with all their tackle adds a great deal to the interest and general appearance.

Perhaps it will seem strange that the small boats made for a plank-on-frame model were not themselves of a similar built-up construction, but I carved them from solid blocks of holly. I think the system I follow in this work may be of value to those who have had trouble carving small boats from the solid. I have seen many such boats on museum models which were poorly done. Too often, the hull was not carved to a shell thin enough to simulate planks fastened to frames. The smallest boats that I have made by the method to be described were 1½in long in 1/96 scale, but I would not hesitate to carve still smaller ones. In addition to the holly used to make the boats for Halifax, I have found poplar to be an excellent, easy working, yet sturdy, mar-resistant wood to use when I planned to paint the boat. The small boat mounted on Hannah's deck was carved from boxwood which is harder to work, but I felt that the unpainted boxwood was suited to the model.

To begin, I cut the block of wood to the exact length, width, and depth of the planked part of the boat's hull. The body plan at the midsection is checked to determine the notch size along the bottom edges that can be cut without coming too close to the finished shape. Then, those notches are cut as can be noted on the block in photograph 59a. Next, the sheer lines of the hull are marked on the side of the block and cut out precisely. The plan view is then drawn on top of the block, cut out, and sanded smooth. The lower block in photograph 59a has reached that stage.

The notches in the bottom make it possible to clamp the irregularly shaped block securely in a vise while the inside is carved out. The shape to be carved is well-defined at the gunwale while the bottom of the block, and the shapes of the stem and of the transom limit the depth of the carving. I carve the transom as an integral part of the hull rather than adding it as a separate piece. I start by cutting away inside the transom using by knife-like skew chisel with a slicing action to avoid putting pressure on the thin section. Gouges were included in the set of carving tools described in the last chapter and are used to hollow out the hull. As the inside is cut out, it should be checked for shape and symmetry with cardboard templates. As the finished size is approached, frequent checks should also be made for thickness along the centerline. The upper work-

59

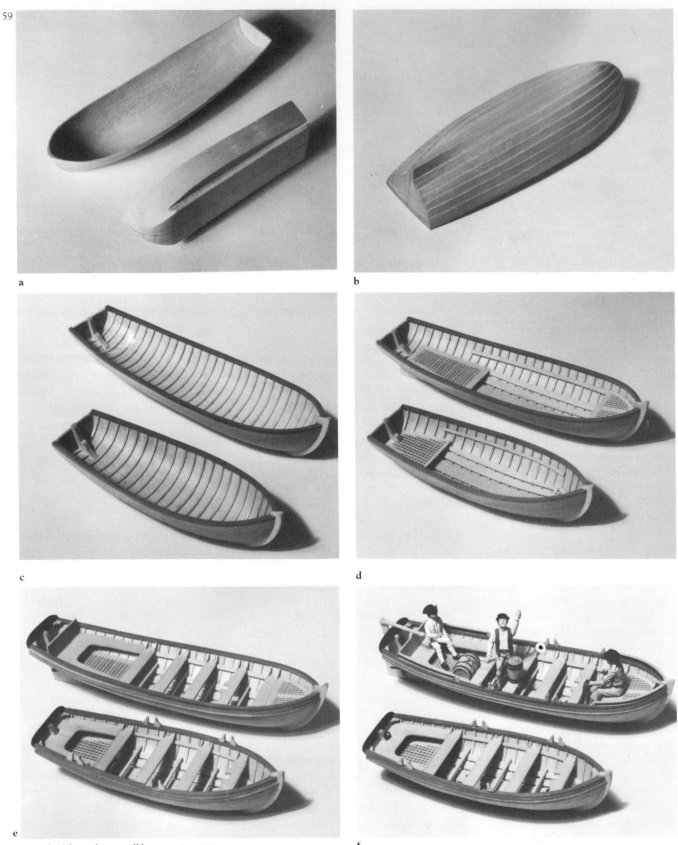

a

b

c

d

e

A method for making small boats.

f

piece in photograph 59a has been hollowed out and then the outside finished to shape.

When the inside has been properly hollowed out, it is relatively easy to finish the outside of the hull. On small pieces, a sandpaper block can be used. On larger models with more material to remove, I use a disc sander. Obviously, care must be taken to avoid sanding the shell too thin; but if the work is done properly, a uniformly translucent hull will result. When I want to give the effect of a clinker built boat, I leave the shell a bit thicker. The lines of the planks are marked on the hull and incised with an engraving burin. The plank surfaces are then carved with a chisel and sanded to an even surface. The small boat treated in this fashion can be seen in photograph 59b.

I like to saw the stem and keel as a single piece. First, a cardboard template is cut to determine the exact shape. The top of the stem is cut to hook over the top of the shell at the bow. After that piece has been glued in place, it is time to form and glue in the frames. If the boat is to be painted, cardboard strips could be used; but I like to use wood. The frames that can be seen in photograph 59c were strips cut from a sheet of boxwood, .020in thick. I soaked the strips in boiling water, wound them around a dowel of about the same size as the hull, and let them dry thoroughly. Sections were then snipped off of the resulting coil to make the frames. I used white glue, positioned the frames and held them in place with my fingers for the short length of time it took for the glue to set. The ends that projected above the sheer line were trimmed off with a razor blade and the top surface trued up with a sand-paper block. The cap rails were sawed out to the shape of the gunwales with sufficient width to cover the ends of the frames. They were glued in place as can be noted on photograph 59c.

Floor boards, gratings and clamps to support the thwarts have been added in photograph 59d. They are all made of boxwood. The gratings had to be sanded quite thin to look right. I have been in the habit of using the matte medium and varnish formulated for acrylic paints to finish the wood in my models. It has been used here to protect the surfaces of the small boats that would be inaccessible after the thwarts were added. This acrylic varnish provides a dull finish to coat the wood. Since it is thinned with water and is not an oilbased medium, there is no need to scrape down to the bare wood before gluing parts to a varnished surface. In fact, the thinned out varnish can be thought of as a weak glue or sizing agent in itself.

There is evidence in photograph 59c of more parts added to the small boats. Parts needed in multiples, such as the knees on the thwarts and the oarlocks, can be mass produced by a simple technique. I selected an inch wide strip of boxwood having a thickness equal to the width required for the particular parts. With the end squared off, I filed it to the shape of the piece. Then, the jewelers saw was used to cut slots spaced to leave the thickness of the part in between. Finally, the shaped parts were sawed off the end of the boxwood strip; and their sides were smoothed by rubbing them lightly over a fine grade of garnet paper. They were set in place with epoxy glue. I made some small strips of ebony to top off the transoms. Square strips of boxwood were glued to the edge of the upper floor boards to serve as foot rests for the oarsmen. The final photograph, 59f

shows the finishing touches added in the form of wash boards, ring bolts, rudder and tiller, and some figures to liven up the scene.

With the model ready for masting and rigging, it was necessary to fit it to a permanent base before going any further. The special design with the starboard side of the hull cut away called for an unusual kind of mounting. I wanted to display the port side with the model sitting in a simulated sea with the finished hull readily visible below the waterline. As ship models are usually exhibited, the overall hull design in evidence makes it difficult to visualize how the ship actually looked in the water. I was pleased with the effect made by mounting the model in this unusual way. From one angle, *Halifax* could be viewed as if afloat, while from another position the complete hull could be seen.

The base was made of $\frac{3}{4}$in plywood surfaced on the top and around the sides with walnut-grained Formica. This was surrounded with solid walnut, molded on the edge and recessed on the top for a plastic cover. A sheet of acrylic plastic, $\frac{1}{4}$in thick, was cut with a length to fit within the confines of the case and its width to extend about $\frac{1}{2}$in beyond the centerline of the model. Within the limits of the yard arms, the base had been planned for the hull to be offset with the cut away side as close as possible to the one side. Room on the other side was allowed for a liberal expanse of 'water'.

I cut a cardboard template and fitted it closely to the hull at the waterline level. This pattern was transferred to the sheet of plastic with allowance fore-and-aft for

The 'sea' is fitted around the stem.

60

the paint was thinned out to give it a translucence for a feeling of depth.

The problem of mounting the plastic 'sea' came next. I had a sheet of pale blue Lucite, ¾in thick, that I the model to fit comfortably into the case. As can be seen from the photographs, the extension beyond the centerline of the hull was made to fit around just the stem, the rudder, and the stern post (60). I cut the shape out on my jig saw, staying well within the line where necessary to allow for a chamfer which needed to be formed for fitting the curvature of the hull. I had to saw a double width of cut to keep the plastic from fusing together behind the blade because of the heat produced. There probably is a better way to handle the problem, but I do this sort of work so seldom that I have not learned the tricks. A second opening was sawn in the plastic to hold the larger of the two small boats. The cutouts were then filed and fitted as closely as possible to the two hulls.

I had prepared a 'sea' like this for my colonial shipyard diorama some years before, and had been pleased with the results. The top surface of the plastic was routed out into wavelets with an egg-shaped steel burr mounted in my Moto-Tool. The pattern of waves was made irregular, but the scooping motion of the burr was maintained in the same direction for consistency. While the results might not be considered a truly realistic representation of water, I think that they do offer a suitable illusion. I painted the top surface with a coat of blue-green acrylic paint thinned out with the matte medium. This produced a moderately shiny fin-

ish without a high gloss. In the area around the model, thought could be used to make suitable supports. Eight pieces about four inches long were turned and polished on my Unimat. A short peg was included on each end. The bottom ends were drilled and tapped for machine screws. After studying the layout, I marked the locations for the turned supports on the base and drilled holes for the screws. The top surface was counterbored to fit the pegs. I clamped the sheet of plastic in position on top of the base and spot drilled the eight holes in the plastic to locate the tops of the supports. Those holes were then drilled out about ⅛in deep to fit the pegs on the tops of the turned pieces. Finally, the supports were fastened into the counterbored holes in the base with screws, and the plastic 'sea' was cemented to the upper pegs with Permabond, a strong, quick-setting glue suitable for plastics.

The model of *Halifax* was set into its openings and the locations for its two pedestal mounts marked. I had turned the pedestals out of ebony with locating pegs on the bottoms and the tops slotted for the keel. Holes were drilled through the base for the machine screws which were to pass through holes drilled in the pedestals and thread into the keel. The top of the base was counterbored for the pegs. The pedestals were fitted so that when the model was secured to the base through them, the hull would be firmly seated in the plastic 'sea' (61). When this work of fitting *Halifax* to its display base had been completed, I returned the model to the work cradle for masting, rigging and miscellaneous other finishing operations.

The starboard view of the *Halifax*, showing the interior of the ship.

61

CHAPTER SEVENTEEN

Masting and Rigging the Schooners

The hull of a ship model can be an object of great beauty just as much as a painting. To me and perhaps to many another ship modeler, the hull construction is the most enjoyable and satisfying part of building a ship model. Still, it cannot be denied that the masting and rigging is what gives true significance to a sailing ship, whether it be prototype or model. This forces a self-confessed landlubber like myself to study and attempt to understand the complexities of shipboard tackle and the management of sails in order to represent them on a model. The basic information is available in the form of tables and text book description that cover standard examples, but the many nuances and special details that apply to a given period are difficult and often impossible to ferret out. Work-a-day knowledge that was second nature to eighteenth century seamen was not considered worth recording and has been irretrievably lost to us. Many modelers like me would prefer to have some acknowledged expert take us in charge and resolve our uncertainties with some reassuring confidence. While this is possible at times, it should be recognized that much of the available advice results from educated guesses and is open to question.

After expressing these cheerful thoughts, I have to face the responsibility of furnishing plans for masting and rigging the models of *Hannah* and *Halifax*. The only contemporary rigging plan for schooners of which I am aware appears in Chapman's *Architectura Navalis Mercatoria*. It pictures a schooner with a single topsail on the fore mast. Otherwise, reconstruction of schooner rigging plans has depended on contemporary paintings, drawings, and engravings. Mast and spar dimensions have been found for a number of vessels which can be used to establish proportionate sizes for schooners where that information is not available. The subject has been investigated and well-presented by E P Morris in his book *The Fore-and-Aft Rig in America* and by Merritt A Edson Jr with his article *The Schooner Rig, A Hypothesis* which appeared in *The American Neptune* in 1965. Investigation of contemporary documents in preparation for this book have uncovered a few specific details which have been mentioned and add to the sum total.

It is unfortunate that details in contemporary pictures cannot be accepted without reservations. There is always the question of artistic license. Paul Revere engraved spritsail yards under the bowsprits of the two schooners in Boston Harbor. Museum models can also be misleading and should not be looked on as being authoritative simply because of their setting. This includes my model of *Hannah* which is now in the Navy Memorial Museum in Washington, DC. The Smithsonian Institute has a model of '*Halifax*' which is rigged incorrectly as a double topsail schooner. The hull of the model was constructed to *Halifax*'s original lines as a packet. Until she was altered by the Royal Navy, she was rigged with pole-headed masts. This has been determined from instructions to the Portsmouth Dockyard that her original masts should be shortened and then fitted with topmasts for topsails. The Smithsonian also has labeled as *Hannah* a model made from the reconstructed plans for *Sir Edward Hawke*. The average museum visitor will be quite unconcerned about these deviations, but they are of critical importance to a serious student of the subject. The poor ship modeler looking for help and guidance will be misled and confused by the contradictions.

There is no sure way to determine how *Hannah* was rigged any more than the hull design could be established. I tried to draw up a reasonable compromise based on the known factors. The strictly fore-and-aft rig which could be handled by a small crew was popular on coasting vessels for the sake of economy. Colonel Glover and Stephen Moylan were concerned with persuading the owners of schooners selected for use in Washington's Navy that they should add sails to improve the performance of their vessels. The owners were protesting at this extra expense which they felt should be borne by the government. To explain the situation to General Washington, Moylan and Glover wrote: 'it is customary for them (local schooners) to have but three sails, Mainsail fore sale, & gib, these are sufficient for the voyages they usually make.' At the time this was written, *Hannah* had been in service for more than a month; and it is likely that experience with her was influencing the agents' policies for fitting out additional schooners.

During the mid-eighteenth century, the topsail schooner was as much standard as the fore-and-aft, pole-masted rig. My decision to give *Hannah* the topsail rig was influenced by two considerations. One was that she was known to have made trading voyages to the West Indies. The other was the fact that she represented an initial experiment under the control of her owner, Colonel Glover. If *Hannah* had carried still more sails, she might have given a better account of herself and not been deposed in favor of 'a vessel of better fame for sailing.' I have drawn a suggested rigging plan for *Hannah* which differs in some details from the model as shown in photographs. The model builder should follow the drawing as being the more correct version.

In contrast to the uncertainties met when rigging *Hannah*, the plan for rigging a Royal Navy schooner like *Halifax* can be developed with more confidence. All the available evidence indicates that a standard procedure was followed with respect to masting and rigging when schooners were fitted out for the navy. There is some information available for the mast and spar dimensions of several schooners. In the case of *Chaleur*, the dimensions were tabulated right on the Admiralty draught of the hull plan. Those measurements can be converted in proportion to the size of a schooner to determine a reasonable sparring plan. However, they should not be regarded as absolute quantities. There is an interesting note on the drawing to the effect that *Chaleur*'s captain believed both the Fore and Main Masts were 2½ feet too long, the Main Boom should be lengthened 5 feet, and the fore mast

was located too far forward. There are other significant questions that cannot be answered with positive assurance. One example relates to the characteristics of the lower square sails that would be called courses on a ship.

The lower yards on the navy schooners were generally identified as cross-jack yards. The usual understanding for that term is of a yard which spreads the foot of a topsail but does not itself carry a sail. It is most commonly found in conjunction with the mizzenmast on a full rigged ship. There does seem to be some consistency in this usage of the term 'cross-jack' to name the lower yard on a schooner. The tabulation for *Chaleur* also lists two dimensions for 'square sail booms' which are slightly greater than the lengths given for the main and fore cross-jack yards. Because of the way in which the tabulation was made up, it is not clear whether one boom should be associated with the fore mast and the other with the main mast. In any case, the terminology has been interpreted as applying to a special type of square sail that furls at deck level on the square sail boom. When in use, the head of the sail would be hoisted to the cross-jack yard. One reconstruction of this design has the middle section at the head of the sail lashed to a jackstaff which along with the corner at either end is raised to the cross-jack while the clues of the sail are bent to the boom below. Some such arrangement as this certainly existed. However, since authentic details of this rig are not available, I begged the issue on my model and simply lashed a boom across the bulwarks ahead of the fore mast to suggest it .

When the question of belaying the running rigging arises, it becomes necessary to decide how and where on the model this should be done. The rigging on a schooner is relatively simple; and since there is no reference to establish belaying points, I am not offering a plan. I used no belaying pins at all. It will be recalled from *Sultana*'s story that while she was still in the Thames estuary preparing for her voyage to North America the carpenter was busy making cleats for both the masts and the shrouds. I made such cleats to serve as belaying points for both schooner models. The cleats were produced in quantity by the method that was described for making small knees in Chapter 16. The bases of the shroud cleats were filed with a concavity to fit the rope to which they first were glued and then lashed for security. The mast cleats were drilled for lill pins. After the pins had been assembled in them, they were glued to the mast with the pins pressed into pre-drilled holes.

The usual method described for making masts and spars is to work them down by hand, first planing a square strip to an octagonal section, and then further reducing the piece to its final round, tapered shape. I prefer to turn them on a lathe. Spruce is commonly recommended as a good, stable wood to use, and in his book, *The Ship Model Builder's Assistant*, Davis speaks against the use of hardwoods. He singles out boxwood in particular as being subject to serious warpage. It is unfortunate if this opinion has had widespread influence. Every model builder should feel free to seek out his own approach to each of the many tasks without prejudice. I have always turned the masts and spars for my models from hardwoods. On *Hannah*, boxwood was used exclusively. *Halifax* has yards and gaffs made of ebony.

Some spars become rather fragile when made correctly to scale. Pinning cleats to yardarms can weaken the slender pieces still more. I am in the habit of turning the cleat (or stop) shape on the spar and then carving away the excess material. Although this procedure may sound complicated, I find it really quite

Halifax seen from the stern.

easy; and it results in a neat, sturdy finished spar. I was able to turn all but the two lower masts and the bowsprit on my Unimat. So long as the rough diameter is less that ¼in allowing the stock to pass through the hole in the headstock spindle, a spar 9in long can be turned by finishing one half the length and then reversing the piece in the machine. I prepare a work piece ½in longer than the finished spar by planing it roughly to a round section which will pass through the spindle. Both ends

are drilled and countersunk for the dead center in the tailstock of the lathe. Then, the piece is rough turned to a uniform diameter over its whole length. The Jacobs chuck is more convenient to use on the head stock than the universal three jaw chuck because the lathe carriage will pass under it and the tool can traverse the exposed length of the workpiece without being reset. Some judgement and caution must be exercised to avoid breakage when turning such spars as the topsail yards which must be reduced to very small diameters. It is helpful that only half the length is being turned at a time to reduce the deflection caused by the cutting load.

On *Hannah*'s cross-jack yard, I tried something out of the ordinary. Steel indicates that it was common for the lower yard arms on merchantmen to have sheaves built into them for the topsail sheets. I turned those sections to a diameter that could be reduced to a square section suitable for the sheave. Slots were cut had brass sheaves installed in the same fashion as was described for making working blocks in Chapter 12. This procedure can be followed wherever the need for sheaves is indicated in the masts or spars.

The bowsprit and lower masts were too large to be turned in my Unimat. This left me with just my wood turning lathe to handle the job. I screwed a round piece of 1in pine to the face plate on that machine. A hole was bored for a tight fit with the end of the boxwood stick that had been prepared to make a mast. The stick had been planed down to reduce the amount of stock removal required to a minimum, and the outer end was drilled to take the point of the dead center. The one end of this stick was glued into the hole in the face plate mounting with the drilled end located by the tailstock center, and the glue was allowed to set. Turning such a long, slender piece without a steady rest calls for careful handling of a very sharp lathe tool. After truing up the workpiece which had already been fairly close to size, I used a strip of coarse emery cloth to further reduce the mast to its finished diameter and taper leaving just enough stock for fine garnet paper and steel wool to clean up the roughness. It was easy enough to turn small diameter pegs at the end where the work was well supported.

I follow a system for making boom and gaff jaws which has served me well. The pair of jaws is made from a single piece. Firstly, flats are filed on opposite sides of the spar where the jaws are to be fitted. Then, a shallow slot is cut across the end to connect the flats. A piece of wood as thick as the required jaws which also fits into the slot is sawed out to fit onto the end of the spar. Except for the hollow that fits around the mast, the shape of the pair of jaws is drawn on the workpiece and cut out. This piece is then glued and pinned in place on the spar. After being thus firmly attached, the inside surface of the jaws can be cut out and fitted to the mast. For a final touch, the assembly should be finished off with simulated iron bands. Rather than use

Detail showing the ship's boat alongside.

strips of brass or the narrow black adhesive tape that can be purchased, I like to make use of the tan, glue-backed tape that comes in rolls. I paint this tape with acrylic color thinned with the matte medium and then use a steel straight edge and a razor to cut strips of the desired width. These strips are moistened and wrapped around the spars where bands are indicated. The finished piece is then given a coat of acrylic varnish for protection.

The problem of making wood parrel beads baffled me for quite some time before I arrived at a technique for producing them. In the meantime, I had resorted to using glass beads, and was not happy with the compromise since I have a compulsion to make all the parts that go into a model. It seemed as though it ought to be easy to turn boxwood or ebony to the diameter of the bead, drill a hole, and then shape and cut off my beads. However, when I tried this, the fragile pieces of wood broke up as they were being cut off. No matter how carefully the workpiece was turned, drilled, and shaped, it became evident that one side was left intact after the other had been cut through while the lathe was running. As this final connection was cut, the forces involved would smash the tiny bead. The solution that finally came to me was to insert a pin or piece of wire into the drilled hole while the beads were being formed and cut off with a sharp edged file. The pin gave

them the needed support and also served to keep the pieces from disappearing after they had been cut loose. No more than three or four beads can be produced at a setting because it is almost impossible to prevent the small diameter drill from wandering off center in a deep hole. However, it does not take long to turn up all the beads needed for a model.

On top of the hounds at the mast doublings, I fitted short trestletrees that were just long enough to box in the lower mast and the foot of the topmast. Two crosstrees were fitted across them just fore and aft of the squared off lower mast to spread the topmast shrouds. These shrouds set up on themselves through thimbles which were held down through holes in the crosstrees with ropes lashed to the lower shrouds. The mainstay which is fastened just under the cap on the mainmast leads through a large block fastened to the back of the foremast cap and then down to a tackle beside the foremast at deck level that belays to a mast cleat. The main topmast stay is treated in similar fashion. On *Hannah*, the main topmast can be braced with simple backstays lashed through thimbles to eye bolts in the deck. Those topmasts which carry topsails should be restrained with running backstays as indicated on the rigging plan.

I have included a jib stay leading from the foremast doubling which is subject to question. It appears that the jib sail on these schooners was usually set flying, independent of a stay. The cross-jack yards are held up by slings that pass over the caps, and held to the masts by single or double trusses which lead to tackle below belaying on mast cleats. There are other methods for securing those yards which could be considered.

I suspect that when I feel 'all thumbs' while rigging a ship model it is typical of what most model builders experience. After a time, one does start to feel more comfortable with this finicky work; but there is always that wish for a third hand to keep things under control. Devising suitable 'third hands' becomes an important part of the game. I have found self-closing tweezers to be an invaluable aid. Setting up the shrouds with their deadeyes is one of the awkward tasks that seems to frustrate ship modelers. Apparently, some even go to the extreme of using castings that incorporate as a unit the pair of deadeyes with their connecting lanyard. I find that with the help of self-closing tweezers the job becomes fairly easy.

After the shroud rope has been wrapped around the groove in the deadeye, I clamp the doubled end in the tweezer so that it is held securely with the jaws close to the deadeye. A seizing is made between the tweezers and the deadeye. Then, the shroud can be repositioned in the jaws so that the other seizings can be made and the rope trimmed. Next, the shroud is passed around the masthead; and the first deadeye is set up with a

lanyard to its corresponding deadeye in the channel. The other end of the double length of shroud rope is wrapped around a second deadeye, clamped in the tweezers, and seized with a single turn of thread tied in a square knot. For convenience, the handle of the tweezers should be held in a portable vise during these operations. If necessary, the vise can be set on blocks to position it. The second deadeye and its shroud are moved from the tweezers to their position over the channel to check the spacing with the lower deadeye. The length of the shroud is adjusted by slipping the loose end of the rope through the seizing, cinching up on the deadeye, and rechecking until the relationship is correct. The shroud is then returned to the tweezer jaws, the seizings completed, and the process concluded by setting up the second pair of deadeyes with its lanyard.

The self-closing tweezers can be used in a similar manner for fastening blocks into the ends of pendants or thimbles where they are required. When working high on the model where it is no longer convenient to hold the tweezers in a vise, it is usually possible to prop the handle against the mast doubling or platform while the jaws dangle from the rope in a handy working position. I make my seizings by tying overhand knots alternately on opposite sides and finish with a square knot, using a touch of glue to ensure that the cut ends will not come loose. Since I do not consider myself an

The hold.
64

175

65

The stern of the *Halifax*, showing the Captain's cabin.

expert on rigging techniques it is probably just as well that I do not dwell too long on a subject which has been treated in detail by others who are better qualified.

The flags for *Hannah* and *Halifax* were made from aluminium, .005in thick. The metal was scoured with sandpaper to provide some 'tooth' to hold the paint. The design was brushed on with acrylic paint well thinned out by the matte medium. Several coats were used to build up the required opacity. Alternate coats brushed on at right angles gave the impression of a woven material. The one edge had holes drilled at intervals through which thread could be passed and tied for lashing the flag to its pole or halliard. After being painted, the aluminium flags were formed to give the impression of a flag flapping in the breeze. Acrylic paint is very flexible, so there is no danger of cracking it when the surface is bent or even creased. A flag made in this manner may not appeal to those who prefer the use of cloth, but I feel that the appearance is consonant with the stylized use of natural wood colors in my model.

This text on model building is not intended to be a comprehensive exposition of the subject except as it pertains to the special technique for building a plank-on-frame model. The purpose has been to present drawings, a photographic record, and a description of the methods I used to build two models. The intent was not to give the impression that all the work should be done exactly as described. It is part of the joy and satisfaction in creative work that every craftsman should have his own personal approach to solving problems. Some of the ideas proffered here will be found useful, some may simply confirm a practice already in use, while others will be rejected for better methods. In any event, I hope that these efforts will prove entertaining and of some value to other ship modelers.